THE FUTURE OF THE GLOBAL ORDER

The Six Paradigm Changes That Will Define 2050

Vincent Petit
Schneider Electric, Hong Kong

World Scientific

NEW JERSEY • LONDON • SINGAPORE • BEIJING • SHANGHAI • HONG KONG • TAIPEI • CHENNAI • TOKYO

Published by

World Scientific Publishing Europe Ltd.

57 Shelton Street, Covent Garden, London WC2H 9HE

Head office: 5 Toh Tuck Link, Singapore 596224

USA office: 27 Warren Street, Suite 401-402, Hackensack, NJ 07601

Library of Congress Cataloging-in-Publication Data
Names: Petit, Vincent, author.
Title: The future of the global order : the six paradigm changes that will define 2050 / Vincent Petit, Schneider Electric, Hong Kong.
Description: Hackensack : World Scientific, 2021. | Includes bibliographical references and index.
Identifiers: LCCN 2020027888 | ISBN 9781786349095 (hardcover) | ISBN 9781786349101 (ebook) | ISBN 9781786349118 (ebook other)
Subjects: LCSH: Sustainable development. | Economic development--Environmental aspects. | Equality. | Social policy.
Classification: LCC HD75.6 .P488 2021 | DDC 330.9001/12--dc23
LC record available at https://lccn.loc.gov/2020027888

British Library Cataloguing-in-Publication Data
A catalogue record for this book is available from the British Library.

For any available supplementary material, please visit
https://www.worldscientific.com/worldscibooks/10.1142/Q0266#t=suppl

Desk Editors: Britta Ramaraj/Michael Beale/Shi Ying Koe

Typeset by Stallion Press
Email: enquiries@stallionpress.com

THE FUTURE
OF THE
GLOBAL ORDER
The Six Paradigm Changes That Will Define 2050

Chapter 1

Change 1 — Three Billion People Reaching Middle Class by 2050

The last 30 years have seen major developments in China, which has relieved 600 million people from poverty. China is set to become the largest global economy in the world in the coming decade, surpassing the United States in terms of Gross Domestic Product (GDP). In China, this economic renaissance comes after two centuries of decline, often considered a humiliation as it was one of the first economic powers in the early 1800s. Notwithstanding these aspects specific to China, which we will return to, it is critical to note that the last decades have cemented the image of a new economic world developing at an accelerated pace, which would soon equal Western living standards. Indeed, the situation in many new economies has considerably improved over the last two decades, but without reaching the globally acclaimed performance of China. Most of the work lies ahead and there is no guarantee that the picture of a "global village" of people living under similar standards will eventually materialize, at least not by 2050. This is a major and critical challenge, which is increasingly aggravated by the rise in global population and larger than ever imbalances across populations and regions.

The Inevitable Reality of Demographics

The global demographic transition is a driving phenomenon of our time. Any demographic transition starts with a drop in mortality — particularly infant mortality — thanks to better sanitary conditions, health services, and access to medicine. This leads to a massive increase in population. As the economic development yields progressively better living conditions and higher education levels, a second transition occurs toward a different family model with fewer children, leading to a drop in natality. The demographic transition then ends, with the population stabilizing. This demographic transition evolves from a model with a high number of children per family and a high mortality rate to a model with fewer children per family and a low mortality rate. In the meantime, the population has expanded dramatically. This transition first happened in Europe and North America at the end of the nineteenth century before progressing to all regions globally.

This transition, when viewed in a global context, has led to a considerable increase in the world's population. It reached around seven billion people in the beginning of the twenty-first century, compared to only 2.5 billion people in 1950 (Planetoscope, 2016).

While world population had stagnated for centuries, it has multiplied three times in less than a century — a unique event in history. This rapid transformation has weighed heavily on the way the world has been shaped and not only from an economic standpoint. The demographic transition first had an impact on migration and cultural evolutions, pushing large contingents of young people away from their birthplaces to more promising areas. In a sense, the industrial revolution would not have been realized without the demographic transition, with millions of people leaving the country to join cities and new-built factories — though some would say that the demographic transition occurred precisely because of the industrial revolution. It could then be argued that this massive contingent of young people had an impact on the evolution of political systems. The twentieth century has simultaneously certainly been one of the most idealistic and brutal centuries of our common history, particularly in Europe, which was decimated by two wars before embracing multilateralism, which ideal culminated in the creation of the United Nations and that of the European Union.

The demographic transition happened in Europe in the mid- to late nineteenth century and stabilized in the second part of the twentieth century. In other regions of the world, it started a few decades ago. The 1950s could be defined as a starting point for most of the countries in Asia. While the demographic transition in Europe (and North America) led to 700 million additional people, Asia is expected to yield four billion additional people by 2050 (from 1950 levels). However, the transition in Africa has been lagging by a few decades compared to Asia, which is expected to continue until the second part of the twenty-first century, leading to three billion additional people by the end of this period.

World population is expected to increase to 8.5 billion people by 2035 (Roser *et al.*, 2017) and between 9 and 10 billion people by 2050 (Planetoscope, 2016). The expectation is that it will then stabilize around 10 billion people, although some forecasts expect a rise of up to 11–12 billion people by 2100 (Roser *et al.*, 2017). These projections could be debated, although demographic forecasts have proven to be traditionally more accurate than other disciplines (Camdessus, 2017).

Focusing on the coming decades, most of the world's population increase would come from Africa (+1.2 billion) and India (+500 million). Other countries in Asia and the Middle East are also expected to increase significantly but less proportionally. China's population is expected to stabilize and even slightly decrease. In total, the world's population is predicted to increase by more than two billion people by 2050, from today's levels. Until 2100, the population is expected to stabilize in most regions of the world and potentially decline (notably in China), with the exception of Africa, which would add another two billion people by the end of the century (Figure 1.1).

The peak of growth of population was reached in the 1970s (2.1 percent growth per year) and is today expected to drop down from 1.2 percent per year to 0.6 percent by 2035 and 0.1 percent by the end of the century. Yet, the decades to come will see a large increase of the population in Africa, as well as a significant slowdown in Asia, following a similar pattern to Western economies. This will bear enormous consequences in terms of the evolution of the world order. For many centuries, the Western world has been the center of gravity of the global economy. As new economies in Asia mature, this center of gravity has clearly moved East at the beginning of the twenty-first century. This has coincided with the decline of the role of Europe, as well as a shift in North American geopolitical priorities under the Obama administration and continued by that of President Trump. Geopolitics in the South China Sea and the Pacific are set to be the big topic of the first half of the twenty-first century, with over 50 percent of the world's population living in Asia (from India to China), the historical role of

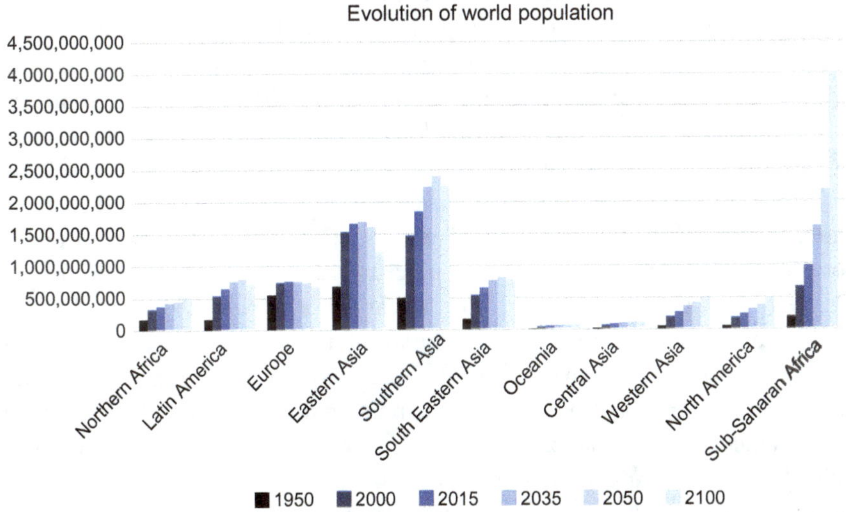

Figure 1.1 Evolution of world population per region (Planetoscope, 2016; Roser *et al.*, 2017)

the United States in the Pacific (notably from a military standpoint), and the considerable resources in Latin America and Australia at the frontiers of the ocean. We will come back to these points in more detail later.

Looking ahead further, the center of gravity will, however, shift from Asia to Africa as the continent starts its transformation. This profound shift will not likely materialize until the middle of the twenty-first century.

An Aging World

The world population is also getting older, and demographic shifts are as impressive here as those of global population evolution. Global life expectancy, which barely reached 50 years in the early 1900s, has started to rise since 1950, firstly in mature economies followed by newer economies. It reached 68 years in 2015, with most regions above 70 years (and close to 80 years in mature economies), except Africa where the average life expectancy is 59 years. This situation will keep improving till 2050, where global life expectancy is expected to reach 76 years, with Africa catching up at 71 years, and most other economies reaching 80 years (He *et al.*, 2016).

A second cause of the global population aging is the drop in fertility rates, which comes alongside economic development and urbanization. Fertility rates are declining everywhere and are expected to reach levels lower than 2.0 (rate of stabilization in the population) in all regions except Africa by 2050, where the rate is close to 3.0 (He *et al.*, 2016). The consequence will be a significantly aging world population. The world today counts 960 million people aged over 60 years, a figure which is expected to more than double at 2 billion by 2050 — a jump from 12.7 percent of the global population to 21.3 percent by 2050.

Most of the growth of people above 60 years should be concentrated in Asia (China and India notably), accounting for over 50 percent of the total growth, but all regions will experience a significant increase in the share of their population above 60 years. Two regions stand out with the largest expected increase: Eastern Asia (China and Japan) and Latin America. There, the share of people above 60 years is expected to reach 25 percent in Latin America and 36 percent in Eastern Asia, the largest jump from current levels globally (Figure 1.2).

This dramatic evolution of the population age distribution will weigh significantly in local and global affairs. The need to develop a robust social and pension system that can partially complement traditional family bonds (which tend to weaken with urbanization) will be of the utmost importance in every place of the world, and particularly acute in China. The notion of solidarity across generations will certainly become a major topic in most regions of the world as the need to support older generations will grow in importance. Then, the overall dynamics of capitalism will likely evolve. A greater share of the

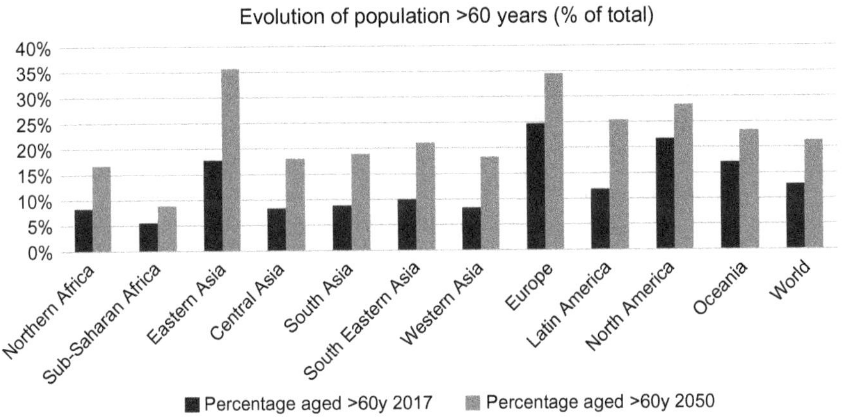

Figure 1.2 Aging population 2017–2050 (United Nations/Population, 2017)

population owning capital — the elderly — will likely foster more conservatism and a rather capital-focused (rather than work-focused) mindset. This could lead to a further rise of inequalities, something we will come back to in the economic landscape review. Yet, it will all depend on the current wealth distribution landscape across regions; if inequalities are already high, then the economic system could likely be steered in another direction. Finally, the aging population and its corollary (stabilization then decline in world population) will have a major impact on global economic development, with low to negative growth rates, more fundamentally changing the economy than any other factor. By 2050, with the exception of Africa, it could be possible to see negative GDP growth rates. At the very least, it can be asserted almost certainly that current world GDP rates at 3.5 percent per annum will no longer be the norm.

Urbanization and the Capital Cliff

A third element that comes into play is the growing level of urbanization, particularly within new economies.

In 1950, 29 percent of the world population was living in urban areas. The ratio today is 50 percent and is expected to reach 67 percent or 2.7 billion people by 2050 (United Nations, 2014). Most of this growth in urban areas would come from new economies, while the actual volume of people living in rural areas would slightly decline. This indicates that most of the additional population growth will actually occur in cities. Yet projections to 2050 expect the urbanization ratio to remain lower than that of mature economies, particularly in India and Africa, despite significant improvement and development to infrastructure. With mature economies' urbanization ranging from around 80 to

90 percent, the ratio of India and Africa is expected to close around 50 percent by 2050, compared to around 30 percent today (United Nations, 2014). If urbanization can be qualified as a definite long-term trend, which is inevitable in one sense, the pace of its change remains an open question. Fast economic development of new economies could accelerate this pace of change while, on the contrary, limited prospects, local economic integration issues, or conflicts could slow down its development. Forecasts from the United Nations, however, expect it to be the fastest of all time — a transition which will create significant opportunities and issues.

In absolute terms, following the United Nations 2014s data, growth by 2050 is expected to be around 2.7 billion people, with close to one billion additional urban dwellers in Africa, 500 million in non-OECD (Organisation for Economic Co-operation and Development) Asia and 400 million in India, with these three regions accounting for two-thirds of the total urban growth. Growth would top 300 percent in Africa and 200 percent in India and Asia. Obviously, such significant changes in the urban landscape, particularly in Africa and India, will create critical inclusion and development issues (Figure 1.3).

Urbanization can come from the natural growth of urban dwellers in the population. In such cases, the economic development of cities with large urban areas already present is the main indicator. Another source of urbanization is the actual migration of rural populations toward cities — those who move to cities in search of opportunities for better living standards. Figure 1.4 illustrates a projection of the share of urban population increase between natural growth and rural migration. It is based on the assumption that population growth is similar

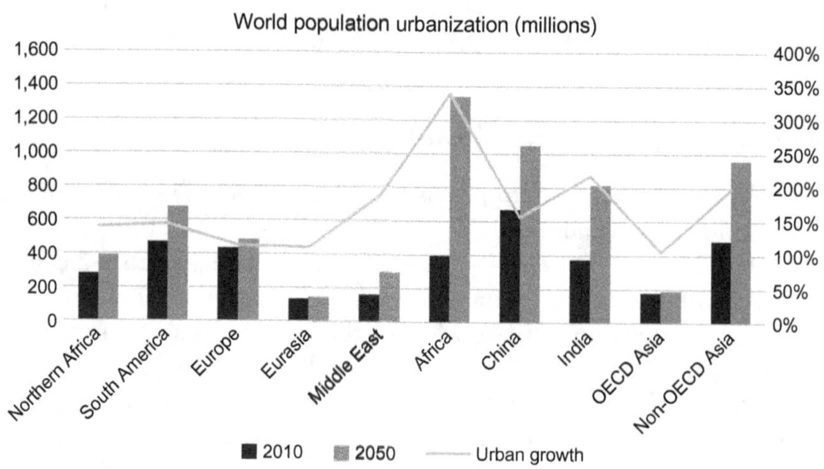

Figure 1.3 Urbanization of the world's population (United Nations, 2014)

Foreword

This book builds on the form of scenario planning pioneered by Kees van der Heijden in his ground-breaking book *Scenarios: The Art of Strategic Conversation.* Indeed, *The Future of the Global Order* can be read as a welcome invitation to 'raise one's game' in the conversations concerning what 'future' might arise.

The most interesting finding this book offers, in my view, is that it proposes that it will not be in Asia, nor in the Americas, that the key roles or decisions of the future might be defined — but in Europe. It is this conclusion, I believe, which makes this book stand out.

The argument the author produces to this — in the literal sense, extraordinary — conclusion, invites readers to extend the usual 'technology X economics X political X societal' centred analyses (which so many professionals and pundits often offer) to also include 'X culture and X values' into one's equations when reading what futures might come to pass.

If a librarian were to hesitate on what part of the library might be the best home for this book, she might consider locating it in a sadly lonely section of the library: the one dealing with Europe's strategic role in the world, but from a cultural and values stance (and not a military, nor legal, nor commercial, nor political, nor security stance). Or it may occupy a position within the 'anthropology of globalisation' section where one might also find books written by anthropologists, and anthropologically literate scholars, such as Graeber's *Debt: The First 5000 Years,* or Frankopan's *The New Silk Roads.* This is because this book proposes that it is cultures and their values which shape, and are shaped, by globalisation — not just economies, societies, power, and technologies.

Yet, unlike many other writers one might find in this section of the library, the author of this book is not a scholar but a professional strategist employed by a world-class firm whose businesses are playing a leading role in the transition from the fossil economy to post-fossil, more sustainable, alternatives. This is his third book and one that moves his work beyond the energy focus of his prior publications.

Vincent Petit is what the late Donald Schön would call a 'reflective practitioner'. Reflection can occur ***in*** practice, and ***on*** practice, and this book is fed by the first type of reflection, nurturing the second type. How do I know this? I know it because I have had the privilege of having had Vincent as a student; and because I have worked with him and his colleagues on their reflection-in-practice.

As reflection-on-practice, the book does not offer guidelines on how to improve one's own practice: this is not a self-help book. Instead, what the book offers is an informed way to reflect on how the world already is, and might be, unfolding. This method of informed reflection has an impact on readers and those they converse with when discussing the topics at hand.

The book assesses a well-curated set of facts and trends concerning how six conditions — demographics, global supremacy contests, scarcity of resources, climate change, economy, and digital transformations — might play out. It interconnects these as joined-up systems presented within four different scenarios.

Manifesting the myriad possible combinations of these elements comprising each of the six conditions in just four scenarios makes it easier to appreciate how such combinations might arise as realities. These possible unfolding realities are those which individuals, teams, organisations, and inter-organisational (including inter-governmental) entities would be well advised to contemplate; and to rehearse in terms of how they might engage with them safely and fruitfully.

Worth noting is that while the manuscript was written before the COVID-19 pandemic changed the world, the arguments this book puts forth appear to remain valid with the pandemic in full swing. This suggests that the analysis the author offers to readers of this volume may withstand the test of time for several years.

Professor Rafael Ramirez
Saïd Business School & Green-Templeton College,
University of Oxford
May 2020

Contents

List of Figures

concentration, the status of financial globalization and its role in the overall economy, as well as the critical issue of debts. Finally, the sixth and last paradigm change looks at digitization. Presented as the major economic booster of the twenty-first century, this chapter reviews the key economic, geopolitical, and societal implications beyond the immediate transformative element of technologies in our everyday lives.

From this detailed account of realities and uncertainties, interconnected within an overarching system map of dependencies, the second part of the book and its final chapter builds four scenarios on how these paradigm changes could unfold, and the resulting transformations to world order. If the world is at a crossroads, scenario planning helps weigh the opportunities ahead and is a well-known discipline for most businesses dealing with complex environments. Energy companies, for instance, have long been mastering this practice having faced extraordinarily complex contexts that required a different approach to conventional forecasting. Scenario planning helps to develop plausible futures that not only enrich the development of strategy but guide the best course of action.

The future scenarios presented in this book intend to illuminate how the key questions developed in the earlier chapters could unfold to create plausible, yet different combinations, of a future order. Based on the indisputable evidence presented, the scenarios illustrate that many of these critical uncertainties, if not adverted, could lead the world into significant transformations of its geopolitical, economic, and social contexts, while reinforcing each other in positive or negative loops. Without being reduced to dystopian perspectives, the changes at stake are massive and, for some of them, unknown in world history. These scenarios also suggest different courses on how nations around the world would react — a key emerging question. In an attempt to protect themselves and prevail, will geopolitical powerhouses follow the old paradigm of Henry John Temple, or will they invent a new way to cooperate and solve these issues that are global by nature? One of the critical outcomes of this study, possibly counterintuitive for some, is the critical role that seems to emerge for a revitalized European Union in global affairs, a region that — as the study shows — is at the epicenter of many of the global issues at hand.

These scenarios do not, however, pretend to be predictions. Rather, they inform possible futures and intend to provide a healthy and factual basis for discussion. It is an exercise that should help us to better understand what matters and what does not while taking some distance from the day-to-day overload of information.

This book intends to provide a unique perspective on the bonds that exist between countries and how they have historically developed, while shedding light on how they could evolve in the coming decades through a critical review of facts and figures, and extensive use of scenario planning. This book is dedicated to all those who want to spend time understanding the mechanics of our world and form an independent opinion about the big choices and decisions that our generation has to face. I can only hope that its conclusions eventually trigger debate. A well-informed conversation is likely what the world needs the most, now more than ever.

Hong Kong,
October 2019

compared, and challenged in detail. Creating a comprehensive repository of objective facts and figures on the main issues at hand in today's world was one of the primary reasons for writing this book.

Secondly, the methodology also differs from other titles. Instead of following a narrative or building up an argument, this book explores six major paradigm changes. Each area is analyzed through several major topics, each with their own set of realities and uncertainties. Overall, we review several of these across all chapters. These topics are then connected with one another in a complex network of dependencies. A system map is charted as the analysis progresses, highlighting how each dependency fits within the overall landscape. From this map, a set of scenarios reaching 2050 is elaborated upon, which builds this objective review.

This systematic approach helps the reader, as he or she progresses through the chapters, to better understand why nations behave as they do, their rationale, and, more importantly, how they could behave in the future, as the set of constraints pressing on them evolves.

We believe these six major paradigm changes to be a rather exhaustive examination of what is currently at play. The first chapter reviews the critical topic of new economies and their likely development in the coming decades. With a rising but aging population, and a truly globalized world, pressure intensifies to accelerate the pace of development. Three billion people on Earth could join the middle classes by 2050, but equally could not. The implications of success or failure could have massive consequences to the world order. The second chapter then explores the complex landscape of security relationships and possible evolutions going forward. For decades now, the world has lived with critical imbalances in terms of military power. Could this paradigm evolve going forward? If so, how? The third paradigm change is concerned with resources. Both raw materials and energy resources have significant impacts on geopolitics because of the dependencies they create between nations. As economic growth intensifies and demand reaches new heights these dependencies are exacerbated, but innovation has the potential to transform the landscape, as it has done many times in the past. Climate change is the fourth paradigm change that this book reviews. Though a generally accepted reality of our time, the pace and extent of change remains a major uncertainty, with impacts that could have terrible consequences on certain parts of the world. The way it is likely to unfold differs significantly from one region to another, leading to the possibility of further critical imbalances between nations that could exacerbate conflicts. As such, global food and water issues are analyzed in detail. The fifth chapter analyzes the current economic landscape, in a broad sense, and its possible evolutions going forward. It looks at the dynamics of economic growth, wealth creation and

Why This Book Is Important

Henry John Temple, two-time British Prime Minister in the mid-nineteenth century, once said, "We have no eternal allies, and we have no perpetual enemies. Our interests are eternal and perpetual, and those interests it is our duty to follow." There is no better definition of what geopolitics stands for — a grueling, cold-blooded game where each state is advocating for its best interests. These motivations, sometimes difficult to understand and predict, are mostly the product of a rational analysis of situations and vested interests. To a large extent, they define a state's program of activity when it comes to foreign relations.

These interests are also often poorly explained to a state's populace, if they are explained at all. Secrecy around intentions and discussions behind closed doors are the norm. While public opinion is often regarded as a way to influence these negotiations in one way or another, it is not given any meaningful weight beyond this. Public opinion is a raw material of the complex and secret foreign diplomacy process.

The complex exercise that mixes historical stances and reputation affects security matters in all domains — including military, resources, environmental change — in the form of exchanges and dependencies, global economic leadership (trade, capital, currency, etc.), and relationships. All these parameters are interconnected with one another and can be complex to handle and disentangle. This is probably why public communications are light-years away from reality.

In this book, we provide a perspective on the key paradigm changes that will shape the future world order. We explore key realities and major uncertainties in detail and build scenarios on their possible unfolding by 2050. In short, this book looks at revealing the game plan of today's Temple and his fellow players in a landscape on the verge of significant transformations.

This book differs from others in two ways. Firstly, it is detail-orientated and based on real-life data. One of the major flaws in similar books has been the lack of quantitative information. The following chapters offer a unique set of data, which helps to frame current realities and uncertainties in a thoughtful and rational way. No assertion has been made that is not evidenced by accurate figures. Historic trends, current states of play, and published forecasts are reviewed,

List of Countries and Regions

Non-OECD (Organisation for Economic Co-operation and Development) Asia (including Eastern Asia, South-Eastern Asia, and Southern Asia)
Armenia, Azerbaijan, Bhutan, Brunei, Cambodia, China, Fiji, Georgia, India, Indonesia, Kazakhstan, Kiribati, Kyrgyzstan, Laos, Malaysia, Maldives, Marshall Islands, Micronesia, Mongolia, Myanmar, Nauru, Nepal, Pakistan, Palau, Papua New Guinea, Philippines, Samoa, Singapore, Solomon Islands, Sri Lanka, Taiwan, Tajikistan, Thailand, Timor-Leste, Tonga, Turkmenistan, Tuvalu, Uzbekistan, Vanuatu, Vietnam

OECD ASIA
Australia, Japan, Korea, New Zealand

MIDDLE EAST (included in Western Asia)
Bahrain, Iran, Iraq, Jordan, Kuwait, Lebanon, Oman, Palestine (West Bank and Gaza Strip), Qatar, Saudi Arabia, Syria, Turkey, United Arab Emirates, Yemen

AFRICA
Algeria, Angola, Benin, Botswana, Burkina Faso, Burundi, Cameroon, Cape Verde, Central African Republic, Chad, Comoros, Democratic Republic of the Congo, Republic of the Congo, Djibouti, Egypt, Equatorial Guinea, Eswatini, Eritrea, Ethiopia, Gabon, Gambia, Ghana, Guinea, Guinea-Bissau, Ivory Coast, Kenya, Lesotho, Liberia, Libya, Madagascar, Malawi, Mali, Mauritania, Mauritius, Morocco, Mozambique, Namibia, Niger, Nigeria, Rwanda, São Tomé and Príncipe, Senegal, Seychelles, Sierra Leone, Somalia, South Africa, South Sudan, Sudan, Tanzania, Togo, Tunisia, Uganda, Zambia, Zimbabwe

EURASIA
Afghanistan, Armenia, Azerbaijan, Belarus, Georgia, Kazakhstan, Kyrgyzstan, Mongolia, Republic of Moldova, Russian Federation, Tajikistan, Turkmenistan, Ukraine, Uzbekistan

EUROPE

Albania, Andorra, Austria, Belarus, Belgium, Bosnia and Herzegovina, Bulgaria, Croatia, Cyprus, Czech Republic, Denmark, Estonia, Finland, France, Germany, Greece, Hungary, Ireland, Iceland, Italy, Kosovo, Latvia, Liechtenstein, Lithuania, Luxembourg, North Macedonia, Malta, Monaco, Montenegro, Netherlands, Norway, Poland, Portugal, Romania, San Marino, Serbia, Slovakia, Slovenia, Spain, Sweden, Switzerland, United Kingdom, Vatican City

NORTH AMERICA

Canada, United States

SOUTH AMERICA (also referred to as LATIN AMERICA)

Anguilla, Aruba, Argentina, Antigua and Barbuda, Bahamas, Barbados, Belize, Bermuda, Bolivia, Brazil, British Virgin Islands, Chile, Colombia, Costa Rica, Cuba, Curaçao, Caribbean Netherlands, Cayman Islands, Dominica, Dominican Republic, Ecuador, El Salvador, Grenada, Guadeloupe, Guatemala, Guyana, Haiti, Honduras, Jamaica, Mexico, Montserrat, Nicaragua, Panama, Paraguay, Peru, Puerto Rico, Saint Kitts and Nevis, Saint Lucia, Sint Maarten (Netherlands), Saint Martin (France), Saint Vincent and the Grenadines, Trinidad and Tobago, Turks and Caicos Islands, Uruguay, Venezuela, Virgin Islands (U.S.)

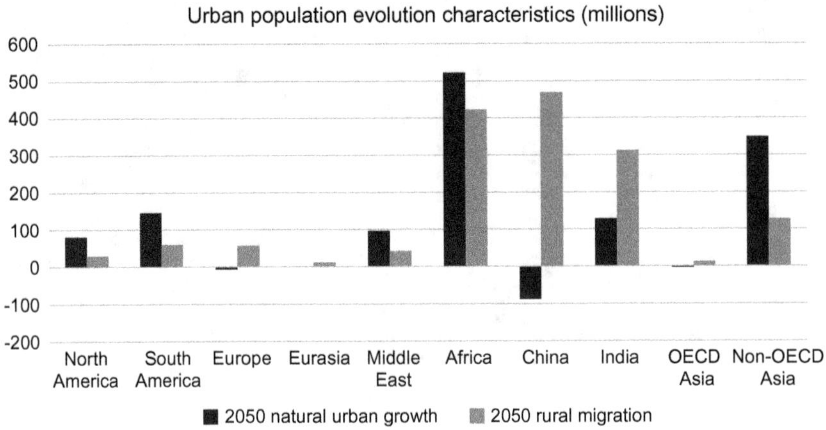

Figure 1.4 Urban population evolution characteristics (Author's evaluation based on data from United Nations, 2014)

in urban and rural areas for a given country. Although an estimation, it yields a rather conservative figure on rural migration as the natural growth of the population in cities is likely expected to be lower than that of rural areas in new economies. With these factors taken into account, the graph shows that China, Africa, India, and Asia will face a significant increase of rural migration in cities, leading to an increased pressure on existing infrastructure.

This accelerated urbanization will also happen in several different ways for existing cities. Those that have more than one million dwellers are expected to account for 60 percent of the total growth, an increase compared to the last two decades. Large cities with more than five million inhabitants would be the fastest expanding urban areas, with a projected growth of 60 percent in the coming decade for cities with more than 10 million people (up to 2030) and 45 percent for cities between 5 and 10 million dwellers. Yet, large cities would only account for one-third of the total growth, with mid-sized cities representing the bulk of the growth (United Nations, 2014). The trend is clear while, historically, the growth of urban populations has happened in small dwellings near rural areas, today's urbanization tends to converge toward bigger cities.

This transition would, therefore, lead to a significant increase in the number of large cities. There could be over 500 new cities with a population above 0.3 million inhabitants by 2030, mainly in Asia (288) and Africa (141). Thirteen cities are predicted to reach 10 million people and above, and 20 new cities will have a population ranging between 5 and 10 million people (Figure 1.5).

A report from the United Nations in 2016 estimated that cities account for 80 percent of the worldwide GDP (Jin *et al.*, 2010). New cities will thus fuel the GDP growth and, to a large extent, enable it to extend further. While

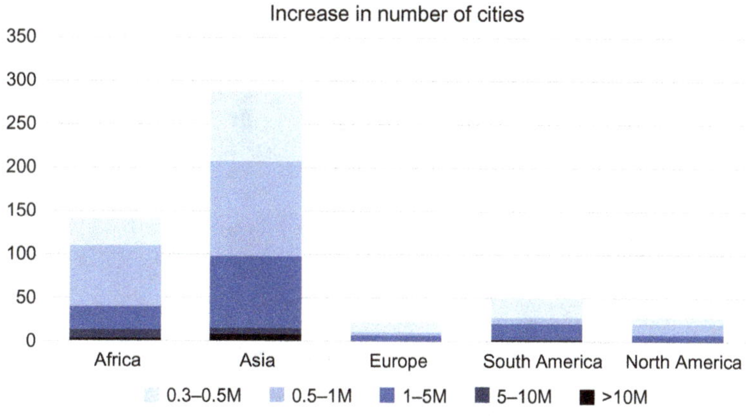

Figure 1.5 Increase in number of cities (United Nations, 2014)

70 percent of cities' GDP was produced in mature economy cities in 2007, these cities will only represent 26 percent of the growth by 2025 according to Dobbs *et al.* (2011). Cities in new economies are expected to be the true engine of economic growth in the coming decade. These reports coincide well with this evidence, assuming a fast acceleration of urbanization in new economies (particularly in Africa and India), as there will be a greater concentration in mid to large cities. Once again, different perspectives on economic development could bend these projections in one direction or another. It is reasonable, however, to assume that urbanization will accelerate, especially as the world's population keeps expanding.

The key question, then, is whether this urban transition will mean development for all and be truly inclusive, or not. This is one of the main uncertainties that our world will face in the coming decades. This is especially true for regions such as Africa, India, and China, where urban populations will come, to a large extent, from rural migration.

The World Economic Forum (2016) ran a global survey on urban services and unveiled a series of problems that apply to cities. The picture differs between mature and new economies. New economies face a variety of significant issues, with some of the most pressing including urban planning, infrastructures (including mobility, sanitation, electricity, ICT [Information and Communication Technologies], etc.), social inequalities, and environment (quality of air and living). As the size of cities expands dramatically, so does the size of its issues. In mature economies, the major challenge relates to environment, although it is far less of an issue than in new economies due to their low expected growth in the coming decades.

Today, cities represent 70 percent of worldwide carbon emissions (United Nations Human Settlement Programme, 2016), thus there is an inherent challenge to decarbonize cities. This is an integral issue as it affects quality of life in a variety of ways. As cities are the first victims of environmental challenges, they are particularly vulnerable to extreme weather events, such as tropical cyclones, heavy rains and floods, or extreme heat. They are the primary living places impacted by agricultural catastrophes from drought or deregulated climate conditions. Infrastructures in cities are also vulnerable to these extreme weather events, such as floods, saltwater intrusion, water quality, and even land subsidence. The estimated costs, resulting from risk to infrastructures, are expected to be multiplied by more than 10 by 2070. The populations in cities are also extremely sensitive to extreme climate changes — like heatwaves — especially aging populations (United Nations Human Settlement Programme, 2011). Last but not least, cities are also exposed to air pollution. The World Health Organization (2016) compiled the various levels of air pollution (particle matter or PM) in various cities around the world. This study has shown significant discrepancies, with new economies being much more exposed to air quality issues in their cities than mature economies. Annually, less than 20 percent of cities in North America show mean PM levels above standard air quality guidelines. This ratio is higher in OECD Asia and Europe, around 40 percent and 60 percent, respectively. New economies largely overshoot these figures, with all countries ranging generally above 90 percent.

These metrics will all be on an upward trend in new economies, meaning environmental issues in new economies' cities are becoming increasingly prevalent (Figure 1.6).

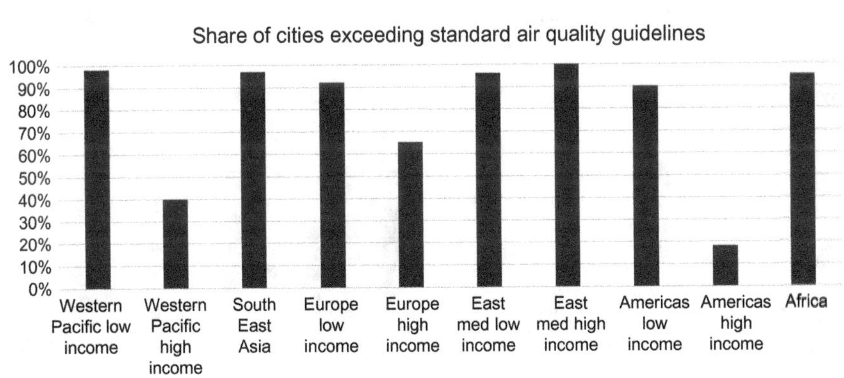

Figure 1.6 Share of cities exceeding standard air quality guidelines (WHO, 2016)

Urban infrastructure is the next challenge. The consequences of poor urban planning lead to significant discrepancies in access to basic services and infrastructures, such as sanitation, electricity, clean cooking facilities, and so on. According to UNICEF and WHO (2015), almost a quarter of the urban population in new economies does not have access to proper sanitation today. This ratio gets even higher in regions like India or Africa, reaching 60 percent in Sub-Saharan Africa. There are still 2.6 billion people in the world who lack adequate access to sanitation (KPMG, 2014). Electricity access is generally well developed, yet there are regions where this access remains insufficient. There are around 170 million urban dwellers without access to electricity, with Africa representing two-thirds of this figure. This factor also prevents access to clean cooking facilities. There are more than 460 million people living in cities who do not have access to clean cooking facilities, relying on solid fossil fuels or biomass. These cities are mainly located in Africa and Asia (Daly and Walton, 2017; Figure 1.7).

All of this poses the issue of inclusion within cities. In 2010, 980 million people lacked decent housing. By 2030, this number is expected to rise by another 600 million (United Nations Human Settlement Programme, 2016). The ratio of people living in slums varies across regions (World Bank, 2013). Overall, the last 20 years have seen a reduction of this number (down from 39 percent to 30 percent in 15 years) that has been more pronounced in South and Eastern Asia. In Africa (excluding North Africa) and the rest of Asia, the ratio has only slightly diminished, and even increased in Western Asia. The ratio has remained the highest in Sub-Saharan Africa — one of the most dynamic regions in terms of population growth in the coming decades (Figure 1.8).

Since the urban population expanded by around 50 percent in the last 20 years, the absolute number of urban dwellers living in slums actually increased

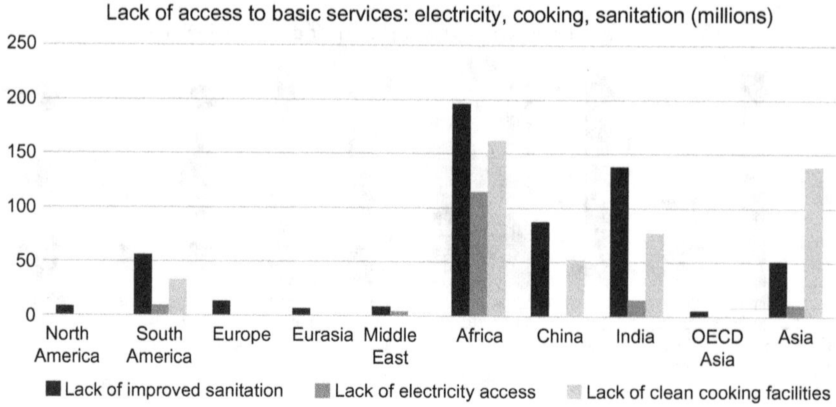

Figure 1.7 Lack of access to basic services in cities (Daly and Walton, 2017; United Nations, 2014; UNICEF and WHO, 2015)

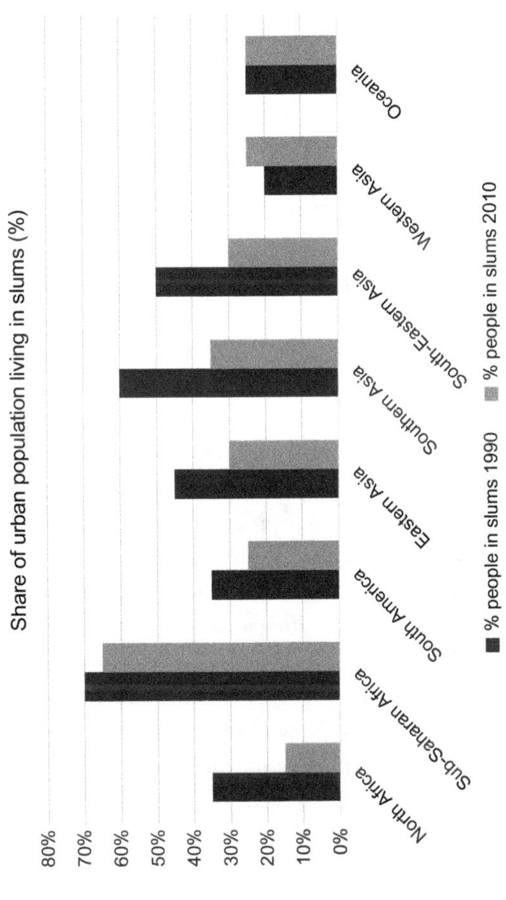

Figure 1.8 Percentage of urban population living in slums (World Bank, 2013)

by an average of 28 percent, or roughly 880 million people. Migration to cities is not always a synonym of increased wealth for urban dwellers (lack of decent housing, proper transportation infrastructures, and access to jobs), and an acceleration of migration could increase the number of those living in urban slums.

Challenges associated to the development of cities in new economies are immense and the social stakes equally large. Will the massive expected urban development keep its promise of access to the middle class, or condition millions of people into a new form of poverty? In response to this question, Jin *et al.* estimate that there is a 30–40 percent shortfall today on the total capital required to develop the necessary infrastructures (2010). The development of cities, at least in certain new economies, could be put at risk.

For the last three decades, public investment in infrastructure has globally declined in almost all economies. In mature economies, it fell to around 3 percent of GDP in 2012, compared to 5 percent in the 1960s. In new economies, it is around 6 percent of GDP, compared to a high of 8 percent in the 1980s. It is only in low-income economies (notably countries of Africa) that these investments have kept increasing, estimated at around 8 percent of GDP in 2012, although this corresponds to a very small figure in the total value of investment compared to new and mature economies (Bhattacharya *et al.*, 2016).

In 2014, the volume of infrastructure spending reached US$3.4 trillion globally, with mature economies representing 62 percent of the total investments and new economies representing the rest (with China alone representing 24 percent of total investments; Bielenberg *et al.*, 2016; New Climate Economy, 2016).

Several studies have estimated that an investment of US$90 trillion in infrastructure would be required between 2015 and 2030 to achieve a scenario of global economic development and urbanization while simultaneously adhering to international guidelines on climate change. This would correspond to an average yearly investment of US$6 trillion or a 75 percent increase compared to the previous decade (Bielenberg *et al.*, 2016; New Climate Economy, 2016). The majority of the increase would come from new economies, representing 50 percent of the total investment required, or growth of nearly 2.5 times in total value. The urban migration runs in parallel with a sharp rise of required investments. According to Bielenberg *et al.* (2016) and Bhattacharya *et al.* (2016), a significant gap in investment could materialize in new economies at up to 50 percent, compared to the 30–40 percent gap identified by Jin *et al.* (2010). This confirms that the acceleration of urbanization is likely to yield an increased number of slums (Figure 1.9).

This massive gap, if not resolved, would hamper the rate of urbanization. It is what is often referred to as the "capital cliff."

One of the key questions that arise is whether or not these regions will have the financial ability to fuel the development of infrastructure. Infrastructure

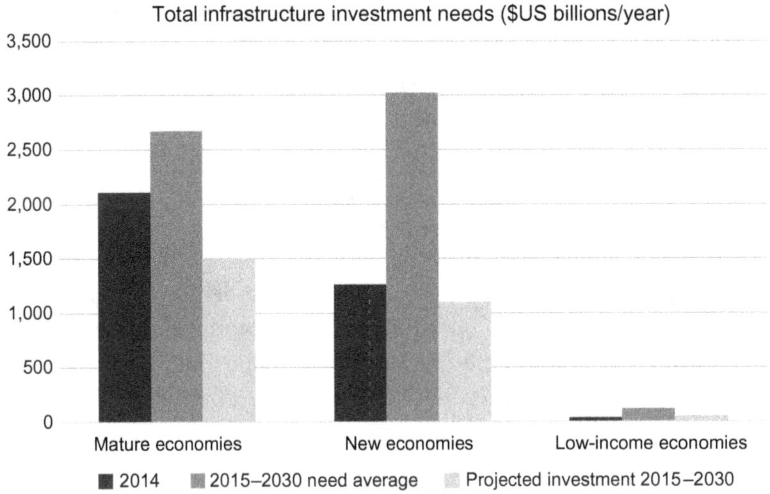

Figure 1.9 Total infrastructure investment needs (Bhattacharya *et al.*, 2016; Bielenberg *et al.*, 2016; New Climate Economy, 2016)

financing is realized through a multitude of channels. Typically, the private sector represents above 60 percent of total investments in mature economies, but it is lower than 40 percent in new economies. The public sector represents the remaining share (Bhattacharya *et al.*, 2016; Energy Transitions Commission, 2017; New Climate Economy, 2016). A number of financial institutions (national development banks, multilateral development banks, and official development assistance) also contribute, though below 10 percent of total investment, yet their importance should not be underestimated. For example, the National Development Bank of China plays a major role here, providing half of the total national development banks' investments, giving an idea of the growing weight of China in global economic development affairs. Public sector investments are highly dependent on global economic conditions and political stability. They can be increased, but not to the extent of the massive requirements previously described.

The key question, then, revolves around the private sector engagement, particularly in new economies. The volume of private investments in new economies' infrastructures is five times lower today than that in mature economies (Bhattacharya *et al.*, 2016). This is where the sustainable development of cities will be decided, or not. It is important to put into perspective the amount of global investment required (US$90 trillion) with the total volume of assets under management (US$100 trillion; New Climate Economy, 2016). Private investment is theoretically available — and we will see later that a greater share of private wealth could be funneled toward infrastructure — yet the securitization of financing remains an open and pending issue to materialize these much-needed developments. Favorable investment policies, transparent and bankable project pipelines, stable and transparent legal frameworks will play a critical role to make it happen, and this is one of the major uncertainties when it comes to the pace of urbanization.

Political Integration or Balkanization?

One of the major questions that also affect this topic is whether political and economic integration will be achieved in the coming decades, in part or in full, within individual countries, regions, and as part of interregional trade exchanges within the global economy. One can say that a major roadblock to the development of these new economies — hence the rise of three billion people to the middle class in the coming decades — is the level of integration of these countries into coherent markets, legal frameworks, and politically stable entities that would create the conditions for accelerated development and foreign investments. The problem is the challenges to this integration have been in existence for a long time and one can question whether they can be resolved in the coming decades. This is, again, a central uncertainty.

In order to understand the contemporary situation in certain economies, looking at historical contexts is beneficial. Let's start with the Middle East. The Mediterranean Sea has long been held as the cradle of Western civilization. More than 2,000 years ago, the Roman Empire was at its peak and dominated a large part of Western Europe, the Middle East, and North Africa.

As a region, the Middle East has had a long history of exchanges and conflicts. For hundreds of years, the region was dominated by two forces: the Ottoman Empire — which also ruled a significant part of South-Eastern Europe and several North African countries — and Persia, which later became Iran. While the borders of Persia remained stable over the centuries, the western part of the Middle East has undergone tremendous evolution. The First World War put an end to the Ottoman Empire's dominance over the region, and after the Second World War the Kingdom of Saudi Arabia emerged as a new regional power. Israel was also created in 1948, a source of discord among many countries in the region and permanent conflicts since (Fisher, 2015). There is significant instability in the region since the period, which can be explained through two main factors. First, there are many different ethnic groups in the Middle East. Major ones are the Arabs in the South (Saudi Arabia peninsula up to Syria and Iraq in the North); Turks in Turkey; Persians in Iran; and Kurds, spreading over Turkey, Syria, Iraq, and Iran. These groups are situated in several countries, particularly in the North of the region, creating ties between minorities. Religion is a second factor contributing to divisions. While Islam is the dominant religion in the region, a historical conflict has opposed the Sunni, predominant in countries in the North of the region, and the Shia, the dominant religion of Iran. Though some large Shia minorities also exist through the Persian Gulf (Iraq, Bahrain, and Qatar), and in Lebanon and Syria. These pockets of different religions and ethnicities led to significant instabilities that, over the years, yielded a series of conflicts among countries. Additionally, the creation of the state of Israel in 1948 remains contentious, as the country has not yet managed to achieve a peaceful process with its neighbors nearly seven decades after its formation, particularly with Palestine on its borders. Finally, the imperialism of a number of western powerhouses over the long history of the Middle East significantly aggravated historical conflicts by creating artificial borders and playing minorities against others in what was long referred to as the "Great Game" (Frankopan, 2017). These conflicts eventually yielded terrorism, a plague which not only affects countries within the region but the rest of the world, particularly Europe, Russia, and the United States.

There is a significant historical interaction between the Middle East, Europe, and North Africa, and the aforementioned inherent factors are critical ones that continue to affect relations between these regions. This situation is also likely to be aggravated in the coming decades by the simple factor of regional demographics. While the current population of Europe is around 740 million people, forecasts to 2050 expect a slight decline (by around 25 million) and, more importantly, massive aging of the population. The number of people above 65 could reach 35 percent of the total European population by 2050. Concurrently, the population in the Middle East and North Africa is around 480 million and is forecasted to reach 750 million by 2050. Migration could thus accelerate and become a defining factor of interregional relationships, even more so than it is today (Smil, 2008). The peaceful integration of these countries and their economies is, therefore, critical to boost development and living standards in the region.

If we then look to the east, India and Central Asia have remained largely separated from the global economy, at least in recent history. When reflecting on India's history, Rosenberg (2017) notes that the country has long been subject to invasions from foreign powers, including Alexander the Great's troops, the Persians, the Mughals and, finally, the British. He also finds it remarkable that these foreign powers always ended up being assimilated into the Indian culture rather than truly influencing it. Marshall (2001) estimates that the geography of the subcontinent is too large and diverse for any common rule, leading to a specific decentralized organization. For over seven decades, India has been an independent country and the largest democracy in the world. It is, however, prey to many internal challenges, despite reforms at the end of the twentieth century that launched a progressive acceleration of its economic development.

For the immediate future, however, India will remain focused on battling some of these internal issues to ensure significant economic and social development of its population. On the outside, a large part of the country's foreign affairs has been dominated by the long-lasting tension with its neighbor Pakistan. Pakistan gained independence in 1947 — the same time as the independence of India — through the partition of the subcontinent. As tensions between Hindus and the Muslim minority were heightened, this move gave the latter group a separate Muslim state. There were four wars between India and Pakistan in the twentieth century, with the situation at the borders remaining a latent conflict, most notably in Kashmir. One of the reasons for this is the access to the water from the Indus, but also because Kashmir represents a door to Afghanistan and Central Asia from India's perspective. The relationship between India and Central Asia is potentially one of India's foreign policy cornerstones in the coming decades, but it will certainly require a peace process with Pakistan to complete.

Another region critical to the future of India's development is the Middle East. Close to 40 percent of the Saudi population would be immigrants and Indians would represent the largest community. It is currently estimated that there are roughly four million Indians in Saudi Arabia and two million in the United Arab Emirates. A large number of religious minorities in India tend to emigrate, particularly Muslims (Connor, 2017; Ghosal, 2017). Significant ties already exist between the two regions in terms of trade. For example, India depends on the Middle East for 70 percent of its oil consumption on imports from the region, leading to strategic dependencies. Once India has resolved its inner challenges, it is expected to become one of the major economic powerhouses of the world (Smil, 2008) and dominate trade in the Indian Ocean. This will create bridges with South-Eastern Asia and the Middle East, as well as heading west — if the conflict with Pakistan resolves — toward Central Asia. It can also be expected that India will challenge China's economic stronghold in South-Eastern Asia.

Finally, Sub-Saharan Africa shows a complex landscape. Africa is a huge continent with some areas in forced isolation given the Sahara in the north and large rivers that do not connect — a geographical factor that has historically prevented economic integration between regions despite the continent dominated by large empires in its past (Rosenberg, 2017). The Sub-Saharan region has also been historically plagued by malaria, with South Africa being the only country in the region not to suffer from it anywhere near as dramatically as others.

Most of the current borders between states were the result of the Scramble for Africa (1881–1914) by imperialist policies from the West, and the decolonization that followed, and have left countries divided between regions and people in an imperfect mosaic of complex relationships, which undermined the economic development of most of these countries. Rosenberg (2017) also mentions that these countries were an important theatre of conflict between the Soviet Union and the West during the Cold War, which further exacerbated the tensions within African countries and between them. The result of this complex and difficult history is a lack of social stability and economic integration and development, making Africa one of the poorest regions of the world.

Yet, this is also the last region that will enjoy population growth. By 2050, over 50 percent of the worldwide population growth will come from Africa, which will see a growth of 1.3 billion additional people — or a doubling of its current population. By the end of the century, Africa will be one of the last regions of the planet not to experience a decline in population, a factor that may help maintain or drive economic growth. Thus, the integration of Africa in the new global order is a critical topic. Based on the modeled predictions, we could say that if Asia is at the center of gravity in today's world affairs, Africa will take its place by 2050. The question of Africa's economic development — largely underestimated today — is critical for the stability of tomorrow's world. It is disappointing not to see this theme take center stage more often as, beyond the critical instabilities within the region, Africa's development could impact other regions, particularly Europe, with whom Africa has long and close historic relations.

These integration issues have been evident for centuries and the process of integration is long, complex, and paved with many roadblocks. However, it is critical to pursue the means to establish a necessary foundation on which further economic and social development can be built. After all, it took centuries for Western Europe to develop the region, which resulted in two world wars that then decimated the continent. Development was also a long process in China, with many periods of decline and fragmentation. One cannot expect this transformation to be achieved in a couple of decades, but the lack of global attention to this process, in a period where several critical issues are arising in this region, add to the challenges faced by those countries and could destabilize them, with ripple effects on other regions of the world.

Accelerated Migrations?

With the massive challenges faced by the aforementioned regions and countries, migration could accelerate if the necessary conditions of further development for a larger population are not met.

The United Nations (2019) has analyzed and estimated current migration flows and projected changes between now and the end of the century. The study shows that migration toward mature economies started to accelerate in the 1990s with larger migrations from Asia (Southern and South-Eastern Asia), while those from other regions, like Africa and Latin America, had started as early as the 1970s. What is critical to understand is the significant imbalance that exists between new economies and mature economies with regards to migration. If the volume of migration today represents less than 1 percent of the population living in new economies (1 percent in Latin America, 0.9 percent for Africa, 0.7 percent in Asia), it does translate into a significant ratio — and impact — for mature economies (3.3 percent for Europe, 6.5 percent in North America). This difference in ratios is what is most important. As migrations intensify toward mature economies, they present a deep risk to destabilizing the social and economic landscape of these regions.

The United Nations also estimated that these flows will stabilize toward the end of the century. This is based on the belief that economic development and reduced inequalities across regions would limit migrations from "poor" to "rich" economies. This evaluation could be questioned. Challenges that apply to new economies with regards to social and economic development, urbanization, and climate change (as we will see later) could yield long-term divides and inequalities across these regions, fostering further migrations.

The bottom line of this is that migrations will certainly weigh heavily in global geopolitics in the twenty-first century, with significant impact on mature economies. It could amplify the divide between regions and potentially lead to social unrest.

Key Interaction Points: The System Map

The key uncertainties, previously described, are now projected onto a system map, which represents the way they interconnect with one another. At this stage, only the uncertainties of the first chapter are projected and the system map will progress as other uncertainties are explored throughout the following chapters.

Five key uncertainties have been reviewed: the inevitability of demographics and aging; the extended urbanization, and the capital cliff that emerges from it; the political integration (or not) of new economies; and resulting migrations.

Urbanization and the capital cliff will depend on demographic transition, meaning people will leave rural areas toward cities, and on the level of political stability of new economies. The extent to which this urbanization will prove successful for global economic development will define the number of future migrations (Figure 1.10).

Figure 1.10 System map

Summary

In 1950, global population barely reached 2.5 billion people. By 2050, it is likely to hit a 9–10 billion mark. Most of the growth between now and then will come from Africa and India. After 2050, the only remaining place with population growth will be Africa, which would add another two billion people to the world's population by the end of the century. At the same time, the population in most countries will age significantly. Today, 12.7 percent of the global population is aged 60 years or more. This figure should reach 21.3 percent by 2050, the equivalent to an additional one billion people (double the current level), and 50 percent of this growth — or 500 million people — will be in China and Japan. Forecasts can be challenged, yet demographics are often proven true, and the considerable trends at play are difficult to ignore.

The evolution of the global population landscape will have a significant impact on relationships between regions. Population growth is an indisputable factor for economic growth. India and, more importantly, Africa will eventually be the last global resorts for economic growth, particularly after 2050. They will also be the regions with the highest shares of young people. Everywhere else, the population will be older, and this will influence significantly a region's dynamism, world views, capital and economic structures, as well as social expectations. It is very likely that we will see migrations accelerate because of such imbalances, as well as different economic models to emerge. For instance, what would a world with negative GDP growth look like?

At the same time this demographic transition is predicted to peak, urbanization will continue to accelerate. Again, forecasts show that there should be an additional 2.7 billion urban dwellers by 2050. The bulk of this growth will be concentrated in Africa, China, and India. Rural migrations will play a critical role, with a massive number of people joining cities to seek home, work, and a different way of living. Yet many challenges lie ahead. First, a significant capital cliff (up to 50 percent of total needs in the coming decade) in terms of infrastructure development could prevent inclusive development and integration of millions of people into the modern economy. Then, the overall lack of economic integration and political instability in many of the concerned regions could also prevent modernization. This is particularly true of Africa, the Middle East, and Central Asia, as well as India to a lesser extent. Most of these regions directly connect to Europe, and the region is often their first commercial partner. This development, therefore, represents a challenge that Europe is likely first to face.

In a nutshell, the rise of population in new economies and the aging of population in mature economies will exacerbate the historical divide between

the aforementioned regions, fostering exchanges, migrations, and potential conflicts of various kinds. Will three billion people migrating to cities by 2050 join the middle class, or will they be sentenced to another form of economic disadvantage, far from the globally integrated economy? This is a major uncertainty with true global implications to other geographies and is likely one of the greatest challenges of our time.

References

Bhattacharya, A., Meltzer, J., Oppenheim, J., Qureshi, Z. and Stern, N. (2016). *Delivering on Sustainable Infrastructure for Better Development and Better Climate.* Washington, DC: Brookings Institute. Available from: https://www.brookings.edu/wp-content/uploads/2016/12/global_122316_delivering-on-sustainable-infrastructure.pdf [Accessed: May 2018].

Bielenberg, M., Kerlin, M., Oppenheim, J. and Roberts, M. (2016). *Financing Change: How to Mobilize Private Sector Financing for Sustainable Infrastructure.* McKinsey & Company. Available from: https://www.mckinsey.com/industries/capital-projects-and-infrastructure/our-insights/next-generation-of-infrastructure [Accessed: September 2018].

Camdessus, M. (2017). *Vers le Monde de 2050.* Paris: Fayard.

Connor, P. (2017). "India is a top source and destination for world's migrants," *Pew Research Center*, 3 March. Available from: http://www.pewresearch.org/fact-tank/2017/03/03/india-is-a-top-source-and-destination-for-worlds-migrants [Accessed: September 2018].

Daly, H. and Walton, M. (2017). *Energy Access Outlook 2017 — From Poverty to Prosperity.* © OECD/International Energy Agency. ©OECD/IEA publishing. All rights reserved. License: www.iea.org/t&c, as modified by V. Petit. Available from: https://www.iea.org/reports/world-energy-outlook-2017. [Accessed: September 2018].

Dobbs, R., Smit, S., Remes, J., Manyika, J., Roxburgh, C. and Restrepo, A. (2011). *Urban World Mapping the Economic Power of Cities.* McKinsey & Company. Available from: http://www.mckinsey.com/global-themes/urbanization/urban-world-mapping-the-economic-power-of-cities [Accessed: September 2018].

Energy Transitions Commission. (2017). *Better Energy, Greater Prosperity* [Press release]. 27 April. Available from: http://www.energy-transitions.org/better-energy-greater-prosperity [Accessed: January 2018].

Fisher, M. (2015). "40 Maps that Explain the Middle East," *Vox*, 26 March. Available from: https://www.vox.com/a/maps-explain-the-middle-east [Accessed: January 2019].

Frankopan, P. (2017). *The Silk Roads: A New History of the World.* New York: Vintage Books.

Ghosal, S. (2017). "How Saudi Arabia's 'Family Tax' Is Forcing Indians to Return Home," *Huffington Post*, 21 June. Available from: https://www.huffingtonpost.in/2017/06/21/how-saudi-arabias-family-tax-is-forcing-indians-to-return-hom_a_22494498/?ec_carp=2819915949931742186. [Accessed: January 2019].

He, W., Goodkind, D. and Kowal, P. (2016). *An Aging World: 2015.* United States of America: United States Census Bureau. Available from: https://www.census.gov/content/dam/Census/library/publications/2016/demo/p95-16-1.pdf [Accessed: March 2019].

Jin, D., Michael, D., Foo, P., Guevara, J., Peña, I., Tratz, A. and Verma, S. (2010). *Winning in Emerging-Market cities — A Guide to the World's Largest Growth Opportunity.* Boston: The Boston Consulting Group. Available from: https://www.bcg.com/documents/file60078.pdf [Accessed: March 2019].

KPMG. (2014). *Future State 2030.* Available from: https://home.kpmg.com/xx/en/home/insights/2015/03/future-state-2030.html [Accessed: March 2019].

Marshall, T. (2001). *Prisoners of Geography: Ten Maps That Tell You Everything You Need to Know About Global Politics.* London: Elliott & Thompson.

New Climate Economy. (2016). *The Sustainable Infrastructure Imperative.* New Climate Economy. Available from: http://newclimateeconomy.report [Accessed: March 2019].

Planetoscope. (2016). *Croissance de la population mondiale (naissances-décès).* Available from: http://www.planetoscope.com/natalite/5-.html [Accessed: March 2019].

Rosenberg, M. (2017). *Strategy and Geopolitics: Understanding Global Complexity in a Turbulent World.* Bingley: Emerald Publishing Limited.

Roser, M., Ritchie, H. and Ortiz-Ospina, E. (2017). *World Population Growth.* Our World in Data. Available from: https://ourworldindata.org/world-population-growth [Accessed: March 2019].

Smil, V. (2008). *Global Catastrophes and Trends: The Next Fifty Years.* Massachusetts: MIT Press.

UNICEF and WHO. (2015). *Progress on Sanitation and Drinking Water: 2015 Update and MDG Assessment.* United States of America: UNICEF and World Health Organization. Available from: https://www.unicef.org/publications/index_82419.html [Accessed: March 2019].

United Nations. (2014). *World Urbanization Prospects.* New York: United Nations. Available from: https://population.un.org/wup/Publications/Files/WUP2014-Report.pdf [Accessed: January 2019].

United Nations. (2017). *World Population Ageing.* New York: United Nations. Available from: https://www.un.org/en/development/desa/population/publications/pdf/ageing/WPA2017_Report.pdf [Accessed: December 2017].

United Nations. (2019). *World Population Prospects*. New York: United Nations. Available from: https://population.un.org/wpp/Download/Standard/Migration/ [Accessed: March 2020].

United Nations Human Settlement Programme. (2011). *Cities and Climate Change: Global Report on Human Settlements 2011*. New York: UN-Habitat. Available from: https://unhabitat.org/books/cities-and-climate-change-global-report-on-human-settlements-2011/ [Accessed: February 2019].

United Nations Human Settlement Programme. (2016). *World Cities Report 2016: Urbanization and Development — Emerging Futures*. New York: UN-Habitat. Available from: https://unhabitat.org/urban-knowledge/publications/ [Accessed: February 2019].

The World Bank. (2013). *Rural-Urban Dynamics and the Millennium Development Goals*. Available from: https://openknowledge.worldbank.org/bitstream/10986/13330/1/9780821398067.pdf [Accessed: May 2019].

World Economic Forum. (2016). *Inspiring Future Cities & Urban Services Shaping the Future of Urban Development & Services Initiative*. Available from: http://www3.weforum.org/docs/WEF_Urban-Services.pdf [Accessed: February 2019].

World Health Organization. (2016). *WHO's Urban Ambient Air Pollution Database — Update 2016*. Available from: http://www.who.int/phe/health_topics/outdoorair/databases/AAP_database_summary_results_2016_v02.pdf?ua=1 [Accessed: February 2019].

CHAPTER 2

Change 2 — Global Supremacy Competition

World history is full of conflicts and wars. As children, we often learn the history of our countries following the milestones of major events that reshaped the environment of our ancestors. For seven decades, the world has lived in a relative period of peace, as the dust of World War II has faded away. The number of conflicts in the world has also reduced significantly over the past 20 years, prompting some to argue that mankind has finally entered a period of sustainable peace and prosperity, although it is key to recognize that several conflicts are still ongoing in many regions (Afghanistan, Syria, etc.). Some have even imagined that the role of nations would eventually be surpassed by global institutions that would orchestrate world exchanges for the benefit of all. This vision has yet to materialize and one could say that, at the time of writing this book, the world is certainly not heading in that direction. Western democracies, which have at one point in time decreed that their regime would be the ultimate state of government, are crippled by rising populisms and face intensified global competition, up to a point where other nations seem further away from converging. Global institutions are deeply weakened, and many around the world have criticized them as being instruments of imperialism (Stiglitz, 2002). The future of strategic relations is thus more uncertain than ever.

Global Supremacy: Is the Position of the United States Sustainable?

The last century has seen the rise of the United States as the supreme global power, notably when the Union of Soviet Socialist Republics (USSR) collapsed in the early 1990s. For the last 30 years, the United States has dominated world geopolitical exchanges, and it seemed that this situation would never be challenged. But there is one critical question to answer: is the position of the United States sustainable? Here we will define global leadership as the ability to project military power to defend one's interests and enforce its policy. There are many other criteria to leadership, such as soft power (including language, culture, and innovation) and global financing capabilities.

National security is one of the main missions of states and has been at the heart of foreign diplomacy for centuries. As Clausewitz states, "war is the continuation of [foreign] policy with other means" (Holmes, 2014). A good proxy to assess military power is budgets that are devoted exclusively to it. The 2017 global military budgets topped almost US$1,700 billion (Cebul, 2018; World Bank, 2018). The US budget tops 35 percent of the worldwide budget (around US$600 billion per year) and remains, by far, the largest in the world. It is worth noting that the budgets in Asia are also extremely high. China, for instance, spends around US$200 billion per year and is the second highest globally. The overall spending of the Asia Pacific zone, including North America, concentrates 70 percent of total global spending. The European Union, in comparison, represents half of the budget from North America, despite a similar Gross Domestic Product (GDP) level. This expenditure shows the limited investment of the European Union on its defense and several of its countries (excluding France and the United Kingdom) have relied on an alliance with the United States through the North Atlantic Treaty Organization (NATO) for their own defense, as part of a historic stance against Russia. The budget of the Russian Federation collapsed since the end of the Soviet Union in 1991, and today it only represents a fraction of the total European Union defense budget. This is a significant change of strategic balance that could reshape bilateral relations between the United States and Europe, though the capacity of the Russian military is certainly not to be underestimated.

The history of military budgets can be examined from data at the World Bank (2018). However, some countries' data is not available prior to 1990, in particular that of the Russian Federation, therefore every record prior to that date should be examined in a wider historical context. The overall picture, however, is that budgets are on the rise in every region since the 1990s. It is worth noting the significant increase of the military budget in North America (post 9/11) and in China over the last two decades. To a lower extent, the sharp rise of military budgets in the Middle East also indicates the regional risk increase, for instance, Saudi Arabia's budget topped US$70 billion in 2017, close to half of that of the region (Figure 2.1).

Military power can take various forms. Nuclear deterrence is the last level of defense, through the promise of retaliation and possibly mutually assured destruction (MAD) — a threat that would kill millions of individuals in one strike. The theory of nuclear deterrence emerged after World War II, in order to turn large powers into sanctuaries against conventional attacks. The opposition between the Western bloc and the Soviet Union in the Cold War was, in part, the result of fierce competition between these powers for geopolitical domination,

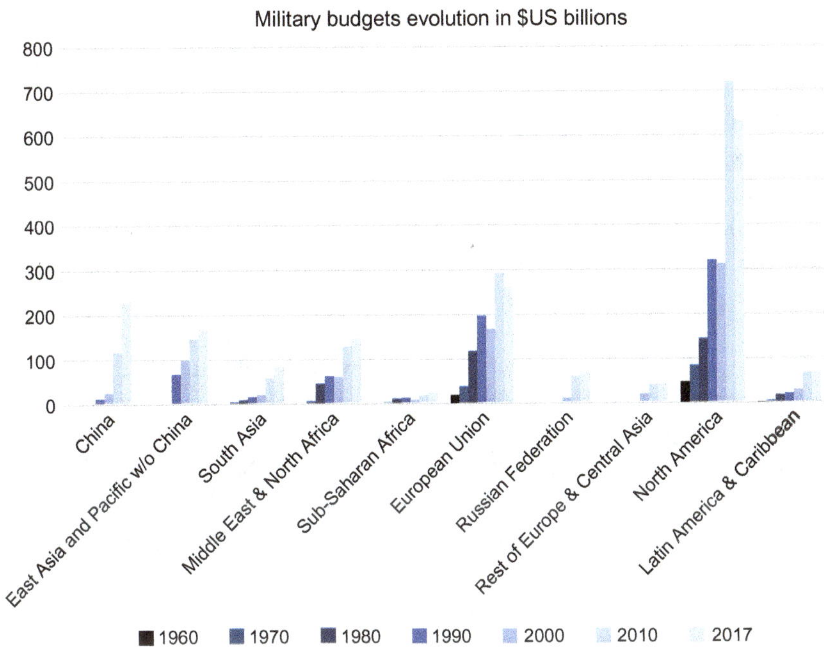

Figure 2.1 Military budgets evolution (Cebul, 2018; World Bank, 2018)

with the prospect of a third worldwide conflict was closer than ever. Yet, the threat of MAD of the entire world prevented this from ever materializing.

In 2019, the Arms Control Association estimated that the number of nuclear warheads worldwide was approximately 14,000 — with 90 percent belonging to Russia and the United States — with 5,000 awaiting dismantlement. This volume, while still high, has significantly reduced since the Cold War. At its peak, the United States had over 30,000 warheads stockpiled or strategically deployed. While there is only a handful of countries today with nuclear deterrence capabilities, the Russian Federation and the United States dominate the landscape. Outside of these countries, China, France, India, Israel, North Korea, Pakistan, and the United Kingdom also possess nuclear arms, but at a mere 10 percent of the world's total, though only China, France, Russia, United Kingdom, and the United States are officially recognized as possessing nuclear weapons by the Nuclear Non-Proliferation Treaty (1968).

The dominant posture of the United States is specific. The doctrine of the country has been that of extended deterrence, or the ability to offer protection to various regions through its strong nuclear arsenal, against the Soviet Union or its allies. For decades, the three main regions of extended deterrence have been Europe, Asia Pacific, and the Middle East. Despite the collapse of the Soviet Union, this balance of forces and the very concept of extended deterrence have slowly evolved. One ongoing debate between Western European countries is whether or not to consider Russia a threat (in light of its significantly larger conventional military power advantage), while Eastern European countries consider NATO nuclear protection shall remain. In the Asia Pacific, the United States has withdrawn some of its capabilities in the 1990s, creating concern from its close allies — something which is becoming even more acute with the rise of Chinese military power. In the Middle East, current concern mainly revolves around the capability of countries like Iran and Syria to acquire nuclear capabilities, which would trigger an arms race in the region (Bush *et al.*, 2010). Beyond these strategic issues, the long-standing conflict between India and Pakistan remains a significant risk for the region, as they both hold nuclear capabilities.

The massive threat that nuclear deterrence poses to global world order has fostered denuclearization programs, notably through the Nuclear Non-Proliferation Treaty (1968) and the Comprehensive Nuclear-Test-Ban Treaty (1996). But in early 2019, President Trump decided to withdraw the United States from the Intermediate-Range Nuclear Forces Treaty (1987) meaning nuclear deterrence is expected to remain a key instrument of power globally (Borger, 2019). The evolution of the US policy, notably in the Asia Pacific, is yet to be seen.

Beyond nuclear deterrence, the ability to demonstrate armed forces globally is a key instrument of global leadership. A good proxy of strength is to evaluate the number of military troops active abroad. The United States has around 587 bases overseas in over 42 countries and 114 bases in US overseas territories in virtually every continent of the world, including Latin America, Africa and the Middle East, Asia and Europe. France has around 11 overseas bases, mainly in Africa, alongside its territories in Guyana and the Pacific. The United Kingdom has 16, including bases in Africa, Canada, and Central Asia. Russia has nine bases, with many concentrated in former Soviet Union countries. Other countries have comparatively lower number of overseas bases mainly in neighboring countries (Jacobs, 2017; SaxManSteve, 2017). The capability of these countries to have a significant global presence is complemented by large naval capabilities, which we will later review in greater detail. However, they follow a similar pattern to that of military projection capabilities, with the United States largely dominating other countries.

Similar to its nuclear and naval powers, the United States also has the highest share of military forces deployed worldwide (15 percent in 2016), followed by Turkey (13 percent), France, and the United Kingdom (9 percent). PricewaterhouseCoopers (2017) considers both the United States and Russia as "global power projectors," with both a significant global security posture and a high percentage of military spend in their budget. One could argue that despite its high share of military spend (as a percentage of GDP) Russia does not play within the same league as the United States anymore, if it ever did. Finally, today China is an emerging force with an essentially regional focus. Most other European countries remain "coalition partners," capable to project forces but as support to other armed forces, with the exception of France and the United Kingdom. The rest of the world has a mostly domestic or regional defense posture. There are, therefore, only a handful of countries that have capabilities to project forces globally, thanks to overseas bases and military structures. This situation is not expected to evolve significantly, except from the rise of China as a military power, with a clear regional focus in the Pacific.

The final element of military leadership is the ability to create extensive damage through cyberwarfare. The rise of the digital economy is creating vulnerabilities in many elements of different countries' infrastructures, particularly as they become more connected. The ability for a country to shut down military systems, power grids, and various state-sensitive applications is a clear threat to national security. A recent example of the damages that cyberwarfare can cause was that of the Stuxnet worm, reportedly developed by the United States and Israel to stop the Iranian nuclear program. Today, 30 countries in the world have engaged in cyberwarfare, both from an offensive and defensive standpoint. Russia, China, Iran, and North Korea are currently reported to be among the most active countries engaging in cyberwarfare, but the United States has clearly taken the lead. The US Cyber Command has approximately 6,000 people employees and, in 2017, President Trump upgraded it to the status of Unified Combatant Command, a similar level to the US Pacific Command, a clear indication of the country's commitment to taking cyberwarfare seriously (Ranger, 2018). The ability for countries, in particular mature economies, to protect their state operations from cyberattacks, as well as the potential to inflict heavy damage to their adversaries, is growing in importance.

From this brief outlook of global military capabilities, we can draw that the United States enjoys a unique situation, as it is largely dominating all other countries on all key aspects of warfare. While the European Union is divided, China has arisen in the last decade as a significant military power. Yet the country remains decades away from reaching a capacity close to that of the United States, and nothing indicates that it could ever reach it, especially considering the ability to project armed forces globally, and capacity to sustain permanent bases abroad.

The question, then, is whether the United States will keep its commitment to its military and maintain it as a powerful instrument of leadership, both in terms of size and efficiency, or not. There are critical ties that exist between North America and Europe given the long and complex history between the two continents, and more recently the engagement of the United States into both world wars that started in Europe. The creation of NATO in 1949 further reinforced the military relationships between the regions, united once more to face the threat of the Soviet Union. NATO has retained its alliance even after the collapse of the Soviet Union, despite some arguing that it has lost its purpose.

On the other hand, there has long been a tradition for isolationism in the United States, which opposes its international relationships. Why would America continue to undertake the responsibility of this leadership when so much needs to be done to achieve the American dream in its own borders? Marshall (2001) notes that the country is almost invulnerable from a geographic standpoint, due to its land acquisition and consolidated control from the Atlantic to the Pacific, down to the vast plains and deserts in Texas, New Mexico, Arizona, and California on the south border. The landmass is also impressive, with around 9.8 million square kilometers — approximately that of the entire European continent — for over 300 million people.

The Monroe Doctrine of 1823 — named after the then-President James Monroe — opposed European colonialism in North and South America and, for the first time, established North American leadership over South American affairs (Rosenberg, 2017). This led to an increase in ties with the South American people. As a result of this, Smil (2008) argues that the deep relations between the Americas have translated into continuous migration flows from South American countries toward the United States, a factor that has many contemporary unprecedented circumstances, which will durably change the political landscape and political orientations of the United States in the long run. Marshall (2001) notes that Mexico is, by its geography, essentially a vast corridor between the two subcontinents and that, despite the efforts from Brazil to create a regional economic powerhouse, migrations continue and will accelerate as gaps in living standards are strained across the region. Flores (2017) has estimated that the population of Hispanic origin in the United States reached 58 million in 2016 (18 percent of total), while it only accounted for 9.6 million (5 percent) in 1970.

The United States, therefore, faces a choice between what could be referred to as "Atlanticism," or the willingness to take charge of world affairs, and "Isolationism," with a stronger inner focus. Demographics — notably the increase in the Hispanic population — are progressively transforming the political landscape, with fewer people sharing European roots and interests. "Nationalism" is also an alternative in between these two poles, which could see the United States have an increased involvement in world affairs in an attempt to maintain global supremacy at all costs. Time will tell whether the United States will reduce its global posture in the decades to come, ceding ground to new powerhouses, like China, to take a larger role in world affairs or, on the contrary, resist and reinforce its level of engagement. Nothing to date indicates that the

United States has any intention to reduce its posture in world affairs. In addition, the weight of bureaucracy should not be underestimated, making it difficult for any administration to actually trigger reform or change the course of action. However, the reluctance of its people to intervene in foreign and distant conflicts could progressively transform the political landscape of the United States, but that would certainly be a long-term transition.

The Great Pacific Ocean Confrontation

One of the key regions where a new geopolitical order could begin is the Pacific, though there are several factors behind this potential emergence. On the one hand, the borders of the Ocean host more than half of the world's population, meaning that this region could also be a place of great rivalry for access to growingly scarce resources. While a large bulk of resources reside in Latin America and Australia, the bottom of the Ocean has remained virtually unexplored and could represent a formidable new race in the coming decades, with a complex landscape of exclusive maritime zones, out of which the United States, France, Japan, Australia, and China will play a critical role. The Pacific Ocean is also the place where China is emerging as a dominant global power, confronting the United States.

Today, 40 percent of the region's commerce consists of trade with China, making it highly integrated from an economic standpoint, as will be seen later. The bulk of global maritime trade — roughly 60 percent — passes through Asia, with 30 percent of global shipping traveling through the Strait of Malacca (China Power, 2018). As a result, sea politics are growing in importance, alongside their complexity.

China's interest in maritime power has therefore been renewed, though historically the country has focused solely on its western borders. Marshall (2001) explained that the North China plain forms the heart of the country, the place where the Han dynasty emerged, and is the favored region of China (Economy, 2018). This region has long been considered as the originator of Chinese civilization. It is from that region that the Han dynasty expanded its control over vast plains, deserts, and mountains, to control a territory where it did not fear invasions. Yet, integration into the wider country has remained an issue. Marshall explains that considerable inequalities continue to exist between regions of China, making the governance of the country very complex. The history that followed is the result of a large series of transformations and shifts. Rosenberg (2017) mentions that much of China's foundation is lost to history — the first recorded date is in 259 BC when Qin Shi Huang reunited the country — and describes the country's history as a permanent balance between periods of strong centralized powers followed by periods of collapse and decentralization. This meant that China had not developed a maritime power for centuries, as it was focused predominantly on inland issues. An exception to this is a brief period in the early 1400s with the seven voyages of Admiral Cheng Ho, leading to a period of migrations of Chinese people to countries in the South China Sea.

Today, however, maritime power is critical to secure globally integrated economies as self-reliance is no longer an option. It is widely acknowledged that China has represented the first economic power of the world, at least until the beginning of the nineteenth century. Some, in China and abroad, see the current period of economic development as a "return" rather than a "rise," having already propelled China to second place in terms of global GDP (Smil, 2008). Therefore, confrontation with other maritime powers of the region seems inevitable.

In this equation, the South China Sea is a "choke point" for East Asian economies, particularly China. Further north, the East China Sea has also been an area of intense rivalry between China, Korea, Japan, and Russia. Many conflicts occurred between those nations and there is significant mistrust between their intentions and conflicts about sovereignty over certain maritime areas.

The control over these maritime routes and exclusive economic zones is of the utmost importance. It has long been controlled by the United States Seventh Fleet in the western part of the Pacific. As the rivalry increases between China and the United States, the Chinese government has started a significant program to develop a maritime power that can be projected over the world oceans to secure global maritime routes, exclusive economic zones, and confront other navies, such as the United States. The navy thus plays a crucial role in international affairs. Now, the United States again operates, by far, the largest Navy in the world, with close to half of worldwide capabilities in tonnage, followed by Russia and China, then other European countries (Figure 2.2).

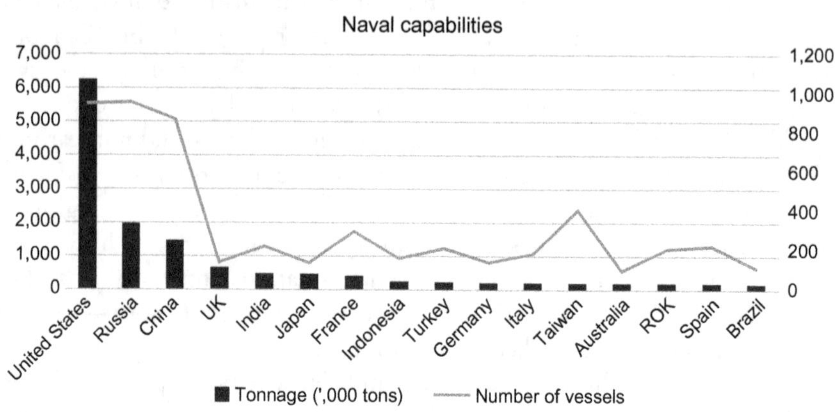

Figure 2.2 Naval capabilities (Global Security, 2019)

There are, however, different sorts of navy. Todd and Lindberg (1996) created a world naval hierarchy, splitting naval forces around the world between blue-water navies and green- or brown-water navies. While green-water navies have coastal projection capabilities, and brown navies are essentially inland riverine defense capabilities, blue-water navies have the capabilities to project forces globally, cruising through (blue water) oceans. They refined this hierarchy further by dividing blue-water navies between the very few countries able to project forces globally (namely the United States, France, and the United Kingdom) and those which have regional projection capabilities (including China, India, Japan, Australia, South Korea, Russia, Brazil, Germany, Spain, Italy, and Canada). Blue-water navies are those that matter when it comes to geopolitical impact, as they alone are able to control maritime routes and project forces. Another way to look at it is to check aircraft carrier capabilities across these blue-water navies. Indeed, aircraft carriers enable military power projection and only a handful of these countries have such capabilities. There are 10 aircraft carriers (and their fleet) in the United States Navy, by far the largest group in the world, as other countries have no more than two. In addition, most of them have conventional propulsion (diesel) that limits their ability to project very far. The "Charles De Gaulle" (French aircraft carrier) is the only aircraft carrier outside of the United States Navy with nuclear propulsion, hence practically unlimited range (Mizokami, 2016).

Blue-water navies enable countries to secure their maritime routes and project forces regionally or globally to secure their interests worldwide. It is an essential component of national security and an asset for only a few countries around the world.

China is still far away from having developed a blue-water navy with global projection capabilities. However, both the Chinese Navy (in the East China Sea and the South China Sea) and, to a lesser extent, the Indian Navy (in the Arabian Sea and the Indian Ocean) are growing in importance (Katyal, 2014; *The Straits Times*, 2017). The Chinese Navy is expected to have four aircraft carriers in operation by 2030, a similar number of nuclear ballistic submarines to the United States, double the amount of attack submarines, and three times more small surface ships. Concentrated in the South China Sea and the Pacific, the Chinese Navy would thus surpass the United States Navy in the region, transforming the balance of power in South and Eastern Asia. There does not seem to be anything that could hamper this development, and this is already leading to further tensions between the two giant economic and military powerhouses vying for domination in the South China Sea (Marshall, 2001). South-Eastern Asian countries are benefitting from this competition and their economic growth prospects are blooming. China argues that the development of its presence in the region should not be regarded as a threat as it tries to further tighten its relationship with South-Eastern Asian countries. Yet, despite the strong increase of economic interactions, the lack of Chinese "soft" power (especially with regards to the United States) has, so far, not pushed the balance further into this direction (Economy, 2018; Smil, 2008). This could change, and this is one of the key uncertainties going forward.

The Future of the Eurasian Plain

A landmark theory from the English geographer Halford Mackinder in 1904, "the Geographical Pivot of History," proposed that the heartland of the world would be the Eurasian plain (Garrity, 2008). This theory relied on the notion of a pivot around which world order would become organized, centered in Russia and Eastern Europe, Asia, and the Middle East. Mackinder summarized his theory as follows: "Who rules East Europe commands the Heartland, who rules the Heartland commands the World-Island, who rules the World-Island commands the world" (Garrity, 2008). This theory was based on resources and population distribution at the time of publication, so it is unsurprising that a number of things have changed when considering the hypothesis more than a century on. That being said, the vast resources available in the pivot area remain, and the people in Mackinder's identified region — Eastern Europe, the Middle East, Central Asia, Eastern Asia, Western Asia, and North Africa — represent two-thirds of the world's population. Even if dated, this geographical pivot invites us to reflect on the key relationships that exist within the Eurasian plain and possible expected developments, as well as relations to neighboring regions. More recently, Frankopan (2017) has revived this theory through his major history of the Silk Roads and the central role that these regions played in world history over the last 2,500 years. Will the Eurasian plain be destined to play a central role in future world affairs? The Chinese government's Belt and Road Initiative (BRI) — which we will return to — is a perfect example of tightening relationships within this pivot, reminiscent of Mackinder. What about Europe and Russia, then?

Marshall (2001) illustrated that the inherent complexity of the construction of European nations was due to the geography of mountains alternating with plains separated by rivers and impenetrable forests. The landscape of South Europe is slightly different with stronger limitations in Spain and Greece, with narrow coastal plains and vast plateaus in the middle. Rosenberg (2017) briefly summarized Europe's complex history, with a focus on the twentieth century, where two world wars left the continent immeasurably scarred. While Europe dominated the world economy in the nineteenth century, the first half of the twentieth century marked the brutal end of this dominance. One project of the European Union was to reconcile France and Germany, though the United

Kingdom did eventually join, perhaps because their foreign policy has always been to prevent a global power to emerge on the continent (Marshall, 2001). These relationships continue today, but the European Union's construction remains to be finalized, particularly with the United Kingdom's exit. There are various opinions on the course that this construction should take, whether it should further integrate, further enlarge, or on the contrary, regroup and give back authority to sovereign nations on some of the specific matters that were delegated to the Union. Yet, all would agree that it is far from being completed, no matter the form it should eventually take (Frankopan, 2018; Smil, 2008).

Another element at play is the complex relationship between the European Union and Russia. Today, the borders of the European Union meet those of Russia, especially since Baltic countries and Poland joined the Union in 2004. There is a long history of relations between Europe and Russia, and many argue Russia is culturally part of Europe (Smil, 2008). The history of Russia's western border has long been troubled, and there is significant resentment and worry from some of the countries at its borders, as they have often integrated into Russia over history. The root cause of this, as Marshall (2001) explains, is the geography of the continent. Europe is a vast plain with mountains in the south, with the narrowest point of the plain situated in Poland. Control of Russia to this point then guarantees its border from the west, at least in theory. There are two worlds, the Roman one and the Slavic one, on the two sides of this point.

Additionally, Russia is the largest country in the world, with over 17 million square kilometers, or around one-eighth of the inhabited land. Its history is complex, with its origins in some cities of what is now Ukraine and Western Russia, which eventually consolidated against the domination of invaders from the east, (notably the Mongols [or Tatars]), and expanded east to the Pacific coasts. The Ural Mountains represent the frontier between the European and Asian continents. Over 75 percent of the Russian population lives in Europe, while the territory covers only 25 percent of Russia's total landmass. There is thus a fundamental imbalance in the country and its population. Smil (2008) argues that the country is overstretched, while Marshall (2001) estimates that possible migrations from China to Russia are very likely in the future, since the Chinese, with rising needs for increased resources, live closer to Siberia than most Russians.

A final theme is the emergence of new sea routes across the Arctic Ocean. Global warming in the last decade has led to a significant reduction of the polar ice cap, making Arctic sea travel possible, at least in certain periods of the year. This had led to new maritime connections between Russia, Europe, and North America. While currently dominated by Russia, several countries in Europe (including Sweden, Finland, Denmark, and the United Kingdom) and Canada are trying to develop it, while the United States has not shown much interest thus far (Marshall, 2001). This could become a new theme in international relations going forward.

These themes will remain important in the coming decades and will likely be aggravated by continued developments. On the one hand, the absence of buffer at the western border of Russia confronts Western European nations with Russia. Would an alliance eventually be possible or, on the contrary, will defiance prevail? Such an alliance would carry a disruptive aspect to global geopolitical relations going forward and would certainly be a first in world history so it should not be underestimated. On the other hand, the vast resources of the Eastern parts of Russia will play a critical role for China's development in the decades to come. The control of this gigantic resources reservoir and underutilized landmass could become a major geopolitical prize in an era of scarcity and overpopulation. Finally, the way Russia, Europe, and China — and India, to a lesser extent — will cooperate together with the Middle East and Central Asia, particularly Iran, Turkey, and Pakistan will largely define the future of the Eurasian plain. There, the role of the Middle East and Central Asian nations will be central — a much more important issue than is usually considered (Frankopan, 2017, 2018).

Grand Plans: The Belt and Road Initiative

At the time of writing, global institutions are weakened. The set of multilateral organizations put in place post-World War II, notably the United Nations, the World Trade Organization, the International Monetary Fund (IMF), or the World Bank, to name just a few, have been prey to massive criticism from new economies (particularly China). For years, China has raised concerns about how slow international finance institutions were evolving. Important agreements on increasing resources to the IMF were, for instance, stalled by the US Congress. China also unsuccessfully promoted more focus from the World Bank on infrastructures and growth (Dollar, 2015). These institutions are also massively criticized by some prominent thought leaders in the west (Stiglitz, 2002), with many arguing that these organizations, despite their original design, end up working to the benefit of mature economies — particularly the ones devoted to economic stability and free trade. There have been few plans to accelerate the economic development of new economies or, at least, they have not been extremely effective.

In 2013, perhaps in response to the aforementioned realities, the General Secretary of the Communist Party Xi Jinping launched the Belt & Road Initiative (BRI) in China and proposed a vision of world economic exchanges that could facilitate the integration of a large number of new economies into global trade.

This initiative resonates with the earlier discussion on the future of the Eurasian plain. It targets almost 70 countries across the globe, which represents around 65 percent of worldwide population and one-third of world GDP (McKinsey & Company, 2016). These regions have historically remained isolated from global economic exchanges, at least in recent decades, despite previously forming the center of world exchanges (Frankopan, 2017). They also represent 50 percent of worldwide population growth by 2030 (United Nations, 2014), and their GDP per capita currently ranges from two to five times below that of mature economies in the Commonwealth of Independent States and the Middle East, India, and Central Asia, respectively (Organisation for Economic Co-operation and Development [OECD], 2018). The potential for development is considerable, and one could say that the ability of those regions to develop and integrate into the global economy is a defining challenge of the twenty-first century.

If the United States is the first commercial partner to 56 countries in the world (mainly in Europe and Latin America), China is the first commercial partner to 124 countries in Asia, Central, Eastern, Southern and South-Eastern Asia as well as Africa and some countries in Europe (particularly Eastern Europe and Germany; Desjardins, 2016). The BRI, then, is primarily an initiative that aims at simultaneously reinforcing and diversifying current Chinese trade positions, through bilateral agreements.

In 2016, the 65 countries identified by the BRI represented around 25 percent of global trade and 50 percent of total imports and exports to and from China (US$750 billion and US$1 trillion per year, respectively). They also represent the largest network of partners to China after Europe (UN Trade Statistics, 2018) making them a natural ground for Chinese geopolitics. Discounting Eastern Asia and South-Eastern Asia as part of the natural Chinese sphere of influence, the remaining countries represent only 8 percent of total imports to China (US$100 billion) and 15 percent of its exports (US$300 billion), a small share overall, yet, as stated, one with massive potential. The BRI has already proved a very sound economic strategy for China. The focus on infrastructures is crucial to enable sustainable growth in these regions as, on the one hand, the gap in investment is there (as previously mentioned), but on the other is the fact that it is generally admitted that 1 percent of investment in infrastructures yields around 2.5 percent GDP (Wijeratne *et al.*, 2017). The initiative is also a way to catch up with Foreign Direct Investments (FDI) from other regions and compete equally on such critical markets. World outward FDI flows reached US$1.5 trillion in 2016. They reached US$460 billion from Europe and US$300 billion from the United States. In China, the figure closed at US$200 billion, an eight-fold increase in 10 years (Chow *et al.*, 2015; OECD, 2018). This initiative is also a way to expand trade with Europe. Even though Europe represents close to 20 percent of trade exports of China (US$340 billion) already, it only represents 10 percent of imports from Europe, meaning the market share of China has room to expand in Europe.

It has also been said that the main root of the BRI is to solve a significant overcapacity issue in manufacturing that has built up in China. The Chinese government has identified overcapacity issues in a dozen of its sectors and, as a result, the BRI can be considered a way to export part of that overcapacity with a reasonably low opportunity cost (PwC's Growth Markets Centre, 2016). Yet, many analysts have identified that the BRI alone would not solve this issue. Several studies have shown that the initiative is estimated to have a positive impact on steel demand for only 7–10 percent of the current production, not enough to cope with production surplus (Dollar, 2015; Pu, 2016; Wijeratne *et al.*, 2017). Setser provides a thorough analysis for the Council of Foreign Relations (2016) pointing out that if the external surplus of China has actually grown as a percentage of worldwide GDP over the last decade, it has actually reduced significantly since the financial crisis of 2008 in terms of percentage of Chinese GDP, at around 5 percent — an indication that the issue is actually under control. It is, then, a fair assessment that the BRI is actually not aimed at coping with production surplus, or at least not entirely. Moreover, it has also been shown that the return on infrastructure investment has decreased over the last years in China, and that the BRI could actually amplify the phenomenon by pushing for more infrastructures' developments within China itself, as many regions are part of the initiative (Pu, 2016).

Instead, it is best to see this initiative as a global geopolitical move of China to reinforce its global leadership as part of complementary reforms that aim to accelerate local demand growth (Trachtman, 2011). The geographic aspect of this plan, which connects countries in between China and Europe, is also a way to economically connect Western regions of China, such as Xinjiang and Yunnan, to a global network of exchanges. The beauty of this vision is that it largely echoes ancient history's world order. Could this be the key to reviving the "old" world?

So, the question is whether this plan will work or not. Today, the BRI corresponds to around US$400 billion per year of project investments, and between US$100 and US$200 billion of mergers and acquisitions (M&A) in BRI countries (Wong *et al.*, 2017). The figure on projects has increased 25 percent since the project inception, with half of the increase coming from projects in China and half outside. This increase amounts to around US$100 billion per year. One can say this is the greatest output of the BRI initiative as of today. In terms of M&A, the figure varies from one year to another, so it is not possible to identify a clear acceleration. It does, however, represent over US$700 billion of M&A in BRI since 2011.

Examining these figures in further detail, Wong *et al.* (2017) has identified that M&A activity is poised by equity infrastructure underperformance, while the growth on projects is fueled by project costs growth, rather than an increase in the number of projects. The extent to which the BRI is more than a simple umbrella for existing activities remains a question.

The BRI is today supported by five main financial institutions (Chow *et al.*, 2015):

- The Asian Infrastructure Investment Bank, launched in 2015, with 50 countries participating, and US$100 billion in capital. China has 30 percent of the subscribed shares.
- The Silk Road Fund, launched in 2014, with first phase funding of US$10 billion.
- The New Development Bank, launched in 2014, with funding of US$100 billion, evenly shared across its member states.
- The China Development Bank (CDB), founded in 1994, with total assets around US$2.4 trillion in capital, and a US$250 billion commitment to BRI projects (Sun N., 2018).
- The Export-Import Bank of China founded in 1994, with US$45 billion injected by the Central Bank of China to boost the BRI.

In total, there is about US$500 billion of financing made directly available for the BRI in the coming years. In addition, state-owned enterprises (such as banks and companies from the infrastructure sector) are engaged in the initiative, with a reported US$200 billion of accumulated investments at the end of 2016 (Lau *et al.*, 2018). Over five years, these figures will match a global increase of US$100 billion investments per year. This is consistent with the Chinese commitment of US$1 trillion of investment in Belt and Road countries in the coming decade (Perlez and Huang, 2017).

The pace of change will obviously vary from one targeted country to another. The extent of success can be evaluated by looking at both the easiness and the attractiveness of each region (International Energy Agency, 2018; Lyn *et al.*, 2017; Shell, 2018; UN Trade Statistics, 2018; Worldstat.info, 2018). We can define them as:

- Easiness: The extent of trade between each region and China, and the GDP/capita can be evaluated. The higher the existing trade level and GDP/capita level, the easier the execution of the initiative.
- Attractiveness: Population growth is a key indicator of attractiveness. The higher, the better. Then, the level of development of infrastructures (e.g., electricity consumption per capita and railways network density) is also critical. The lower, the more attractive.

We have calculated average deviations in percentage and have averaged them across the different factors to come up with a combined index in percentage. The final result is presented in the Figure 2.3. It shows Western Asia (essentially the Middle East) and South-Eastern Asia as primary targets for the BRI. Their easiness

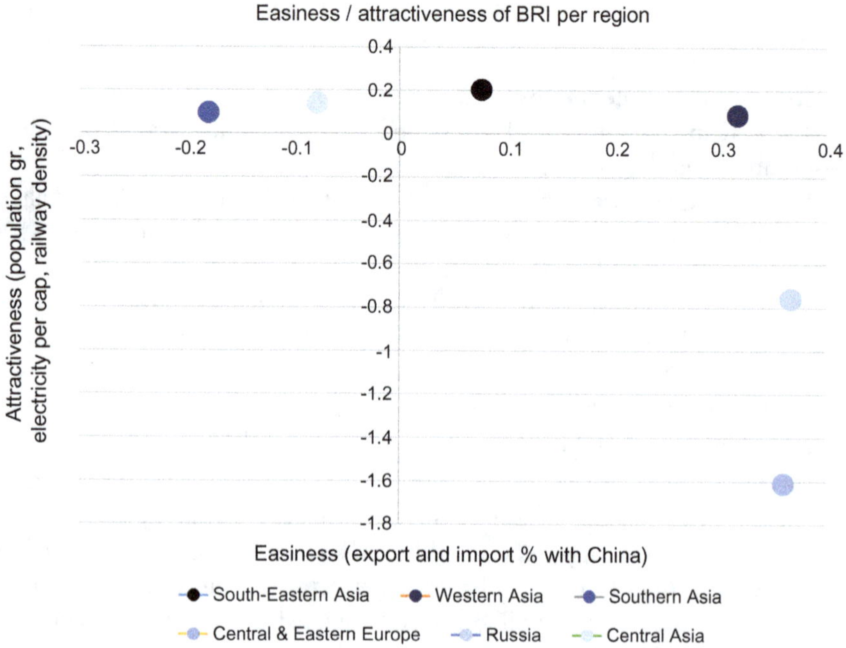

Figure 2.3 Easiness and attractiveness of different Belt and Road Initiative routes

is high due to already significant levels of development and trade exchanges with China, as well as their attractiveness in dynamic population growth, and relatively low levels of railway density and electricity consumption per capita. Russia soon follows as the next frontier of development of the initiative, followed by Europe, which is most likely an end destination in this case. Southern Asia and Central Asia present significant challenges in terms of easiness going forward (Figure 2.3).

When looking at the six main routes of the BRI, these conclusions suggest that not all routes will be as fast to implement. The China–Indochina Peninsula economic corridor is likely one of the top priorities as it helps connect and accelerate exchanges with South-Eastern Asia. The New Eurasian Land Bridge and the China–Mongolia–Russia economic corridor are "easier" to implement, but their attractiveness lies in the potential to extend connections with Russian and Eastern European economies to accelerate trade exchanges. This is also likely a priority of the initiative. The China-Central and Western Asia Economic Corridor and the Bangladesh, China, India, and Myanmar Economic Corridor (BCIM) are probably the most complex networks to develop, because of the development difficulties associated in the regions concerned. Finally, the China–Pakistan Economic Corridor is a focused project, which connects the main "road" to the Indian Ocean, and to the "maritime" routes of the Belt and Road.

The BRI corresponds to around US$400 billion of projects per year, a significant increase compared to the status at the inception of the initiative (25 percent), yet the volume of projects have stayed stable or only grown slightly since the first years of the initiative. The BRI is not significantly expanding thus far. Yet, China has deployed a number of financial tools, which helped to pour roughly US$100 billion per year into the initiative, in line with their commitment to inject more than US$1 trillion over time. This volume of investments needs to be compared to the US$2–US$3 billion needed annually for infrastructure developments in those regions (McKinsey & Company, 2016). In addition, there is currently a significant investment gap in those regions. The expected investment in new economy infrastructures is expected to grow by a factor of 2.5 by 2030, but two-thirds of it could lack financing as previously discussed (New Climate Economy, 2016; Bhattacharya *et al.*, 2016). The BRI is thus an accelerator of development for those regions, but it will not close the capital cliff alone.

For the BRI to yield the expected benefits, the volume of public and private external financing — such as FDI — needs to increase in these regions. For this to happen, the profitability and bankability of these projects need to be proven, while traditionally these projects are considered high risks resulting in high transactional costs (New Climate Economy, 2016). Therefore, the BRI still needs to prove that these projects can provide good yields. Doing so would not only enable the Initiative to attract a larger volume of investments from other regions (notably Europe) but an increased share of private investments — a critical contribution to reach the targeted figures. The study from PricewaterhouseCoopers (Wijeratne *et al.*, 2017) has shown that, up until now, the cost of projects has risen 47 percent in Belt and Road countries (and 14 percent in China) since the inception of the initiative. Additionally, many bankers have indicated that the debts in Belt and Road countries are way above safety levels, with liability ratios at 35 percent on average (vs. the 20 percent safety level) and debt ratios 126 percent (vs. 100 percent) (*South China Morning Post*, 2018). Yet, as discussed, regions differ in essence, and it is somewhat expected to see tremendous differences in development between the six routes (corridors) that are part of the initiative.

The world is in great need of a plan to accelerate the economic integration of new economies, especially as they face a significant rise in the constraints that apply to them. The BRI is the only large-scale plan that exists today, and it confronts multilateral organizations developed by mature economies that have been durably weakened. The extent of this Initiative's success will play heavily in the race toward global leadership in the decades to come.

Key Interaction Points: The System Map

Four key uncertainties have been explored here. The first one relates to how sustainable the position of the United States is, especially in light of internal

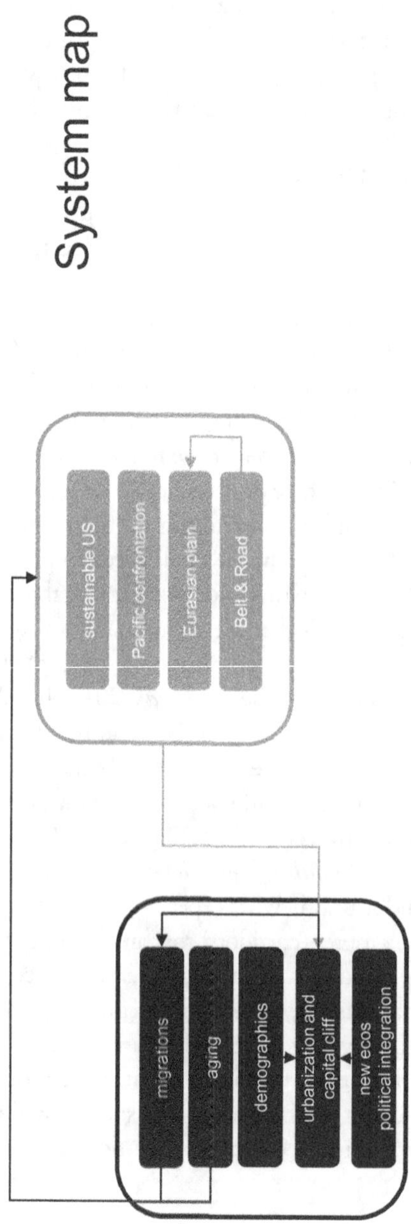

Figure 2.4 System map

policy considerations. The second one relates to the inevitable confrontation in the Pacific and the extent of its development. The future of the Eurasian plain is the next uncertainty, particularly as it relates to the future of Europe and its relations with Russia. Finally, the level of success of the BRI is the last uncertainty reviewed, with some implications for the development of a larger Eurasia.

All of these uncertainties will deeply affect the Future of the Global Order, hence new economies and their level of development (urbanization, the capital cliff, among others). On the flip side, migration could become a significant phenomenon of our time and impact global geopolitics. Aging is also a constant in mature economies, and its impact on both the global economy and global geopolitical stances remains a question. Finally, the extent of the success of the BRI will certainly play a role in how Europe will develop, particularly as it regards its relations with Russia (Figure 2.4).

Summary

The competition for supremacy has been ongoing for centuries. For three decades, the world has been dominated by the United States, whose military power surpasses largely that of all other nations, to the point where some could argue that it is virtually invincible and the current position unchallengeable. From a budget perspective, it devotes three times more money per year in its military than China, the second in line, and twice more than all Europeans put together. It has more troops and foreign bases worldwide than anybody else, and naval capabilities that are 10 times that of other nations. The United States has engaged in global foreign affairs since the advent of World War II and has not withdrawn since. Yet, it has always been balanced about the role it should play on the international scene. Traditionally, states from the south and center of the country have been more conservative, favoring an inner focus. The states from the east, and particularly the northeast, have always been turned to Europe, which represented their past history, and are therefore more internationally focused. Now, the structures of the country have been deeply evolving, and the share of citizens with Latin American roots is increasing, to the point that Spanish will become the main language in several states in the south. This is likely to revive tensions on what the international stance should be and if the Monroe Doctrine should be, to a certain extent, revived. Now, this should also not be extrapolated beyond reason. The democratic structure of the United States, with its two chambers, its two main parties of representatives, and indirect elections, prevents wildly unexpected moves from happening. Additionally, the critical economic interest in a more globalized world also prevents this from happening. Yet, a long-term trend toward an increased focus on internal affairs is apparent and raises some uncertainties on the foreign policy of the country in the coming decades.

At the very same time, China is reemerging as a global power in the twenty-first century. Although experts debate as to whether or not China will surpass the United States in economic terms before 2030 or after, it is highly likely that the country will become the first economic power by 2050. In a sense, this is a historic return to China's previous status after two centuries of a handful of Western countries dominating the world thanks to technology. China has never been a maritime power, except for a small period in the 1400s, which led to the establishment of many Chinese ports in South-Eastern Asia and accelerated trade exchanges at the time. Yet, the country spent a considerable amount of effort in its long history to remove threats from the west and the north, consolidating its position as a vast empire over centuries. In the globalized world of the twenty-first century, it has been necessary to evolve this stance, and China, as its economic power grows alongside its dependencies to others, has started to catch up from a military standpoint. Its naval forces could surpass those of the United States in the Pacific by 2030. The Pacific will indeed be the critical geopolitical space for decades to come, with a large chunk of the global population, of the global GDP, and of global resources of all sorts. Domination of trade routes, of economic dependencies, on access to resources, will prove critical for global domination. South-Eastern Asia will notably be a critical area of what will likely end up in a confrontation, which could be resolved peacefully or not.

Halford Mackinder, however, thought in the early 1900s that the key to global supremacy was the domination of the Eurasian plain. This view could be challenged today, with the tremendous importance that the geopolitics of the sea and that maritime routes have on global affairs. Yet, it invites a reflection on the future of Europe and its relationship with Russia, and beyond with its close neighbors, such as Western Asia and Africa. First, Europe and Russia have largely shared a common history for centuries, with the exception of a long period of domination by the Tatars from the thirteenth to sixteenth century, and, of course, the Soviet Union. Yet, Russia has always had a confrontational relationship with most Eastern European countries. The geographic situation partly explains this, as there is a clear geographical divide between the European and Slavic worlds. Now, Russia has extended east toward the Pacific and is the largest country in the world, a country too large for its inhabitants with 75 percent of the population living on the European side of the country. A relatively small Russian population, therefore, administrates the largest territory of the world, right in between the powerful China and dense European Union. The unstable balance that has been at play for decades has reemerged, and the future of Russia heading east or west is a critical question for the global order going forward. Will the country strengthen its ties with Europe, stretching toward the Pacific while providing critical resources to its population, or disaggregate in one way or another to the profit of China? This will also define the future of the European bloc on the international scene.

Finally, peripheral powers will take part in the global competition for supremacy. There are few large plans to support their integration within global economic exchanges and support their internal development. Most global institutions have supported this for decades, yet they are often seen as favorable to acting in mature economies' interests — those of the United States in particular. This concern has been voiced particularly by China in recent years. The BRI can, therefore, be considered as an attempt to preempt this space and win the battle of economic development while significantly increasing the relative position of China in these new economies. The question is whether this initiative will prove successful and overcome some of the inherent issues within new economies, which have, so far, limited their ability to integrate within global economic exchanges and reap benefits of their own. The role of minorities and ethnic disparities within most countries of the Middle East and Sub-Saharan Africa are, for instance, a critical topic that no large infrastructure project will ever be able to overcome. Also, the current lack of support from other mature economies, primarily the European Union, divided on this front, might prevent this initiative from accelerating. The recent history of the BRI shows that proof still needs to be made. Yet, it could be a powerful accelerator for development going forward. If this proved successful, this could also contribute to reshaping global institutions as we have known them in the recent past. This is another critical, yet unknown, eventuality.

To conclude, this competition for supremacy carries a lot of uncertainty. On the one hand, the position of the United States appears, on paper, to be immovable. Rising geopolitical tensions in the Pacific will be an interesting test to this assertion. The extent to which China manages to successfully secure its key dependencies will be critical in the extent to which the country creates a global position for itself. Also, the appetite of the United States to control its historic position will be tested. Finally, the future of Europe is deeply tied to that of Russia, and vice versa. Russia is a strategic opportunity for two massive economic powers, and the one that will eventually prevail will most certainly take a critical position in the new global order. Overall, this could transform global order significantly. Will the world of 2050 be dominated by China and the United States, with a weak Europe pushed away from the famous pivot of Mackinder, or will Europe, on the contrary, have a renewed role in global affairs? Will global institutions fade away to the profit of bilateral confrontations, or will they be revived? Finally, is there a risk for a more systemic crisis in the globally integrated economic and political landscape, which could lead to a more brutal disaggregation of global governance, and some kind of balkanization?

References

Arms Control Association. (2019). *Nuclear Weapons: Who Has What at a Glance.* Available from: https://www.armscontrol.org/factsheets/Nuclearweaponswhohaswhat [Accessed: November 2019].

Bhattacharya, A., Meltzer, J., Oppenheim, J., Qureshi, Z. and Stern, N. (2016). *Delivering on Sustainable Infrastructure for Better Development and Better Climate.* Washington, DC: Brookings Institute. Available from: https://www.brookings.edu/wp-content/uploads/2016/12/global_122316_delivering-on-sustainable-infrastructure.pdf [Accessed: April 2019].

Borger, J. (2019). "Donald Trump Confirms US Withdrawal from INF Nuclear Treaty," *The Guardian*, 1 February. Available from: https://www.theguardian.com/world/2019/feb/01/inf-donald-trump-confirms-us-withdrawal-nuclear-treaty [Accessed: April 2019].

Bush, R., Felbab-Brown, V., Indyk, M., O'Hanlon, M., Pifer, S. and Pollack, K. (2010). *U.S. Nuclear and Extended Deterrence: Considerations and Challenges.* Massachusetts: Brookings. Available from: https://www.brookings.edu/wp-content/uploads/2016/06/06_nuclear_deterrence.pdf [Accessed: April 2019].

Cebul, D. (2018). "US Remains Top Military Spender, SIPRI Reports," *Defense News*, 2 May. Available from: https://www.defensenews.com/industry/2018/05/02/us-remains-top-military-spender-sipri-reports/ [Accessed: April 2019].

China Power. (2018). *How Much Trade Transits the South China Sea?* Available from: https://chinapower.csis.org/much-trade-transits-south-china-sea/ [Accessed: April 2019].

Chow, L., Ho, M. and Zhao, N. (2015). *Navigating the Belt and Road — Financial Sector Paves the Way for Infrastructure.* Ernst & Young. Available from: https://www.ey.com/cn/en/services/specialty-services/china-overseas-investment-network/ey-navigating-the-belt-and-road [Accessed: May 2019].

Desjardins, J. (2016). *Four Maps Showing China's Rising Dominance in Trade.* Visual Capitalist. Available from: https://www.visualcapitalist.com/four-maps-showing-chinas-rising-dominance-trade/ [Accessed July 2019].

Dollar, D. (2015). "China's Rise as a Regional and Global Power: The AIIB and the 'One Belt, One Road,'" *Horizons*, Summer 2015 (4). Available from: https://www.brookings.edu/wp-content/uploads/2016/06/China-rise-as-regional-and-global-power.pdf [Accessed May 2019].

Economy, E. (2018). *The Third Revolution. Xi Jinping and the New Chinese State.* New York: OUP USA.

Flores, A. (2017). "How the U.S. Hispanic Population Is Changing," *Pew Research Center*, 18 September. Available from: http://www.pewresearch.org/fact-tank/2017/09/18/how-the-u-s-hispanic-population-is-changing/ [Accessed: May 2019].

Frankopan, P. (2017). *The Silk Roads: A New History of the World.* New York: Vintage Books.

Frankopan, P. (2018). *The New Silk Roads: The Present and Future of the World.* London: Bloomsbury.

Garrity, P. (2008). "The Geographical Pivot of History by Halford J. Mackinder (1919)," *Classics of Strategy*, 9 October. Available from: https://www.classicsofstrategy.com/2008/10/the-geographical-pivot-of-history.html [Accessed: June 2019].

Global Security. (2019). *Rest of World Ships Resources*. Available from: https://www.globalsecurity.org/military/world/links-navy.htm [Accessed: June 2019].

Holmes, J. (2014). "Everything You Know About Clausewitz Is Wrong," *The Diplomat*, 12 November. Available from: https://thediplomat.com/2014/11/everything-you-know-about-clausewitz-is-wrong/ [Accessed: November 2019].

International Energy Agency. (2018). *Electricity Power Consumption (kWh Per Capita).* ©OECD/IEA publishing. All rights reserved. License: www.iea.org/t&c, as modified by V. Petit. Available from: https://data.worldbank.org/indicator/EG.USE.ELEC.KH.PC [Accessed: June 2019].

Jacobs, F. (2017). "The World's Five Military Empires," *Big Think*, 10 July. Available from: https://bigthink.com/strange-maps/the-worlds-five-military-empires [Accessed: June 2019].

Katyal, R. (2014). "Why India's 'Blue Water' Ambitions Matter," *The Southern Asia Channel*, 4 August. Available from: https://foreignpolicy.com/2014/08/04/why-indias-blue-water-ambitions-matter/ [Accessed: June 2019].

Lau, H., Sun, M. and Li, J. (2018). "China's Belt and Road Initiative: Projects Pave the Way," *Herbert Smith Freehills*, Legal Briefings. [Online]

Lyn, F., Wu, D., Huang, E., Wong, G., Zhao, G. and Tan, C. (2017). *Prospects for Future Economic Cooperation Between China and Belt & Road Countries.* PricewaterhouseCoopers. Available from: https://www.pwccn.com/en/research-and-insights/publications/prospects-china-b-and-r/prospects-for-future-economic-cooperation-between-china-and-b-and-r-countries.pdf [Accessed: June 2019].

Marshall, T. (2001). *Prisoners of Geography: Ten Maps That Tell You Everything You Need to Know About Global Politics*. London: Elliott & Thompson.

McKinsey & Company. (2016). *China's One Belt, One Road: Will It Reshape Global Trade?* Available from: https://www.mckinsey.com/featured-insights/china/chinas-one-belt-one-road-will-it-reshape-global-trade [Accessed: June 2019].

Mizokami, K. (2016). "Here Is Every Aircraft Carrier in the World," *Popular Mechanics*, 25 January. Available from: https://www.popularmechanics.com/military/navy-ships/g2412/a-global-roundup-of-aircraft-carriers/ [Accessed: June 2019].

New Climate Economy. (2016). *The Sustainable Infrastructure Imperative.* New Climate Economy. Available from: http://newclimateeconomy.report [Accessed: July 2019].

OECD. (2018). *FDI Flows.* Available from: https://data.oecd.org/fdi/fdi-flows.htm [Accessed: June 2019].

Perlez, J. and Huang, Y. (2017). "Behind China's $1 Trillion Plan to Shake up the Economic Order," *New York Times*, 13 May. Available from: https://www.nytimes.com/2017/05/13/business/china-railway-one-belt-one-road-1-trillion-plan.html [Accessed: July 2019].

PricewaterhouseCoopers. (2017). *Global Defense Perspectives 2017. Updating the Map of Defense Prioritization and Posture in a Challenging World.* PricewaterhouseCoopers. Available from: https://www.PwC.com/gx/en/government-public-sector-research/pdf/global-defense-perspectives-2017.pdf [Accessed: July 2019].

Pu, X. (2016). "One Belt, One Road: Visions and Challenges of China's Geoeconomic Strategy," *Mainland China Studies*, 59, 111–132.

PwC's Growth Markets Centre. (2016). *China's New Silk Route: The Long and Winding Road.* PricewaterhouseCoopers. Available from: https://www.PwC.com/gx/en/growth-markets-center/assets/pdf/china-new-silk-route.pdf [Accessed: July 2019].

Ranger, S. (2018). "What Is Cyberwar? Everything You Need to Know About the Frightening Future of Digital Conflict," *ZDNet*, 4 December. https://www.zdnet.com/article/cyberwar-a-guide-to-the-frightening-future-of-online-conflict/ [Accessed July 2019].

Rosenberg, M. (2017). *Strategy and Geopolitics: Understanding Global Complexity in a Turbulent World.* Bingley: Emerald Publishing Limited.

SaxManSteve. (2017). "Number of Overseas Military Bases by Country [6434x3340]," *Reddit.* Available from: https://www.reddit.com/r/MapPorn/comments/52xkgs/number_of_overseas_military_bases_by_country/ [Accessed: July 2019].

Setser, B. (2016). "Just How Big Is China's External Surplus? Measurement Matters," *Council on Foreign Relations*, 27 July. Available from: https://www.cfr.org/blog/just-how-big-chinas-external-surplus-measurement-matters [Accessed: July 2019].

Shell (2018). *Sky Scenario.* Available from: https://www.shell.com/energy-and-innovation/the-energy-future/scenarios/shell-scenario-sky.html [Accessed: July 2019].

Smil, V. (2008). *Global Catastrophes and Trends: The Next Fifty Years.* Massachusetts: MIT Press.

South China Morning Post. (2018). "Is China's Belt and Road Infrastructure Development Plan About to Run Out of Money?" *Huifeng He.* Available from: http://www.scmp.com/news/china/economy/article/2141739/chinas-belt-and-road-infrastructure-development-plan-about-run [Accessed: November 2018].

Stiglitz, J. (2002). *Globalization and Its Discontents.* New York: W. W. Norton & Company.

The Straits Time. (2017). *China's 'Blue Water' Navy Catching Up with the US*. Available from: https://www.straitstimes.com/asia/east-asia/chinas-blue-water-navy-catching-up-with-the-us [Accessed: July 2019].

Sun, N. (2018). *China Development Bank commits $250bn to Belt and Road*. Nikkei Asian Review. Available from: https://asia.nikkei.com/Economy/China-Development-Bank-commits-250bn-to-Belt-and-Road [Accessed July 2019].

Todd, D. and Lindberg, M. (1996). *Navies and Shipbuilding Industries: The Strained Symbiosis*. Connecticut: Praegar Publishers.

Trachtman, S. (2011). "Understanding China's Trade Surplus: Going Beyond Currency Manipulation," *China Research Centre*, 10(2). [Online]

United Nations. (2014). *World Urbanization Prospects*. New York: United Nations. Available from: https://population.un.org/wup/Publications/Files/WUP2014-Report.pdf [Accessed: July 2019].

UN Trade Statistics. (2018). "Analytical Tables." Available from: https://unstats.un.org/unsd/trade/data/tables.asp#annualworld [Accessed: July 2019].

Wijeratne, D., Yau, J., Wong, G., Rathbone, M., Ling, N. and Lau, S. (2017). *Repaving the Ancient Silk Routes*. Available from: https://www.pwc.com/gx/en/growth-markets-centre/assets/pdf/pwc-gmc-repaving-the-ancient-silk-routes-web.pdf [Accessed: July 2019].

Wong, G., Booker, S. and Barthe-Dejean, G. (2017). *China and Belt and Road Infrastructure*. PricewaterhouseCoopers. Available from: https://www.PwChk.com/en//consulting/br-watch-infrastructure.html [Accessed: July 2019].

World Bank. (2018). *Military Expenditure (Current USD)*. Available from: https://data.worldbank.org/indicator/MS.MIL.XPND.CD [Accessed: July 2019].

Worldstat.info. (2018). *List of Countries by Density of Railways*. Available from: http://en.worldstat.info/Asia/List_of_countries_by_Density_of_railways [Accessed: July 2019].

CHAPTER 3

Change 3 — A World of Resource Scarcity

Smil (2015) explains how the United Kingdom reinvented its industry with coal in the eighteenth century at a time where its resources in wood (and charcoal) were fundamentally depleted, and there was massive deforestation of the country, threatening the future prosperity of the nation, alongside living standards and habits. At this time, the United Kingdom was importing vast quantities of wood before it turned to its large reserves of coal, giving the country the necessary energy independence to enable its rise as one of the dominant nations during the nineteenth century, ushering in the Industrial Revolution. The story is an interesting introduction to this chapter as it outlines how critical resources are to the development of a country. The development of modern economies has seen a surge of needs in terms of raw materials and all types of energy resources, and these are not evenly distributed across the globe. Over the last century, the consumption of resources has skyrocketed: the consumption of energy, for instance, has multiplied by a factor of 10, that of iron ore by 6, and copper by 30. With this rise of consumption, mature economies often had to procure the necessary resources from other countries in order to sustain the development of their economy, leading to new trade relationships and dependencies across countries. It is these dependencies that we are investigating in this chapter.

Over the past 20 years, the world has been consuming more resources than the planet is able to generate (Raisson, 2010), a trend that is accelerating. Material resource scarcity is likely to become a critical topic in the upcoming decades. It is expected that, with current forecasts, material extraction could increase 55 percent by 2030, from a 2010 baseline (KPMG, 2012). A result of this growing demand is possible scarcity, leading to diversification of supply, pressure on prices, and risks to supply chains. This will weigh heavily on regional dependencies, especially as the level of development in new economies and urbanization increases (Figure 3.1).

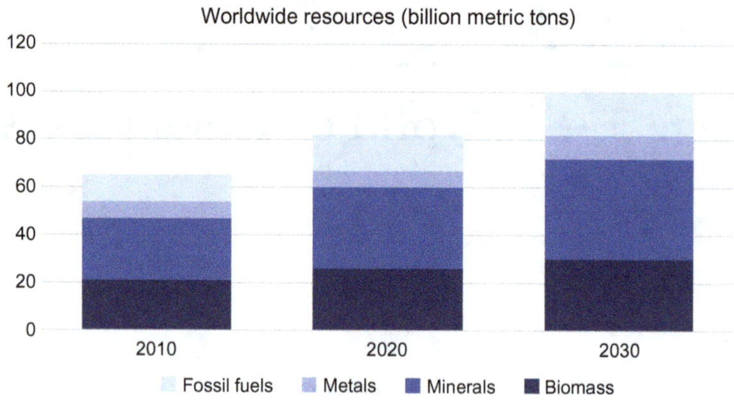

Figure 3.1 Worldwide resources (KPMG, 2012)

Shifting Geopolitics of Raw Materials

A quantified analysis of raw material production and demand is required to understand to what extent these dependencies will be exacerbated as pressure mounts on demand. In this analysis, several raw materials critical for the proper functioning of modern economies have been selected: bauxite (aluminum), copper, iron ore (steel), lead, zinc, manganese, nickel, lithium, cobalt, and rare earth materials.

The data on production, imports, and reserves has been collected from various sources and assembled into one coherent stream. The share of reserves, the production in key regions as a share of global production, and the number of years of remaining production (at a constant pace) are the supply dynamics being analyzed. The share of imports complements this with an indication of demand dynamics. For each material, we predominantly look at identifying the growing risk of scarcity from global reserves and the shift in dependencies across key regions. The growing demand for materials intensifies these existing issues. Figure 3.2 summarizes all of this data, which is based on current volumes of production and consumption.

The aggregation of different streams of data is obviously prey to challenge as data often differs from one source to another. The table below is a best estimate of the current situation based on a thorough analysis of the information at hand.

Bauxite (Aluminum)

At the current pace of production, there are around 65 years of reserves left, meaning a large disruption on Bauxite (Aluminum) is not expected in the

Resource	Metric	Australia	Brazil	Rest of Latin America	China	India	Rest of Asia and Pacific	Europe	Russia	Kazakhstan	Middle East	North Africa	Sub-Saharan Africa	Canada	USA	World
Alumina & Bauxite	Share of reserves	25%	10%	14%	4%	2%	12%	0%	1%	1%	0%	0%	30%	0%	0%	
	Years of reserves, at current production	63	57	192	9	24	78	0	25	27	0	0	394	0	0	66
	Production as % of total	26%	12%	5%	30%	7%	11%	0%	2%	2%	0%	0%	5%	0%	0%	
	Imports as % of total	0%	0%	0%	-56%	-2%	0%	-21%	0%	0%	0%	0%	0%	-4%	-17%	
Copper	Share of reserves	14%	2%	54%	5%	0%	8%	0%	10%	0%	0%	0%	0%	2%	5%	
	Years of reserves, at current production	91	20	27	18	83	53	0	71	0	0	0	0	15	0	35
	Production as % of total	5%	3%	69%	9%	0%	5%	0%	5%	0%	0%	0%	0%	4%	0%	
	Imports as % of total	0%	-2%	-4%	-48%	0%	-28%	-16%	0%	0%	0%	0%	0%	0%	-3%	
Iron & Steel	Share of reserves	41%	17%	0%	16%	6%	0%	0%	19%	0%	0%	0%	0%	0%	0%	
	Years of reserves, at current production	72	55	0	14	62	0	0	245	0	0	0	0	0	0	43
	Production as % of total	25%	14%	2%	50%	4%	0%	0%	3%	0%	0%	0%	0%	1%	0%	
	Imports as % of total	0%	0%	0%	-66%	-1%	-15%	-13%	0%	0%	-4%	0%	0%	-1%	0%	
Lead	Share of reserves	44%	0%	15%	21%	2%	0%	0%	8%	2%	0%	0%	0%	0%	6%	
	Years of reserves, at current production	48	7	18	6	19	0	0	28	53	0	0	0	108	14	16
	Production as % of total	15%	0%	13%	57%	2%	0%	0%	5%	1%	0%	0%	0%	0%	7%	
	Imports as % of total	-4%	0%	0%	-26%	0%	-29%	-26%	0%	-4%	0%	0%	0%	-11%	0%	
Zinc	Share of reserves	34%	1%	25%	21%	6%	0%	1%	0%	5%	0%	0%	0%	2%	5%	
	Years of reserves, at current production	41	14	18	8	16	0	2	0	29	0	0	0	12	12	16
	Production as % of total	13%	1%	21%	40%	6%	0%	7%	0%	3%	0%	0%	0%	3%	7%	
	Imports as % of total	-5%	-2%	0%	-19%	0%	-29%	-33%	-1%	-2%	0%	0%	0%	-8%	0%	
Manganese	Share of reserves	14%	17%	1%	7%	7%	0%	20%	0%	1%	0%	0%	34%	0%	0%	
	Years of reserves, at current production	12	46	0	15	19	0	214	0	2	0	0	30	0	0	25
	Production as % of total	28%	9%	0%	12%	9%	1%	2%	0%	10%	0%	0%	29%	0%	0%	
	Imports as % of total	0%	0%	-2%	-61%	-7%	-13%	-11%	-3%	0%	0%	0%	0%	0%	-3%	
Nickel	Share of reserves	25%	17%	11%	3%	0%	23%	0%	10%	0%	0%	0%	7%	3%	0%	
	Years of reserves, at current production	78	83	0	26	0	19	0	30	0	0	0	0	11	37	34
	Production as % of total	11%	7%	0%	5%	0%	42%	13%	12%	0%	0%	0%	0%	11%	0%	
	Imports as % of total	-1%	0%	0%	-54%	0%	-13%	-10%	-2%	0%	0%	0%	-13%	-6%	0%	
Lithium	Share of reserves	11%	0%	67%	22%	0%	0%	0%	0%	0%	0%	0%	0%	0%	0%	
	Years of reserves, at current production	72	240	475	1,067	0	0	0	0	0	0	0	0	0	0	321
	Production as % of total	48%	0%	45%	7%	0%	0%	0%	0%	0%	0%	0%	0%	0%	0%	
	Imports as % of total	0%	0%	0%	-21%	-1%	-40%	-26%	0%	0%	-3%	0%	0%	-1%	-9%	
Cobalt	Share of reserves	18%	1%	8%	0%	0%	5%	0%	4%	0%	0%	0%	60%	4%	0%	
	Years of reserves, at current production	179	33	0	0	0	0	0	40	0	0	0	49	63	0	65
	Production as % of total	6%	3%	0%	0%	0%	0%	0%	7%	0%	0%	0%	80%	4%	0%	
	Imports as % of total	0%	0%	0%	-90%	0%	0%	-10%	0%	0%	0%	0%	0%	0%	0%	
Rare earths materials	Share of reserves	3%	18%	0%	36%	6%	18%	1%	15%	0%	0%	0%	1%	1%	1%	
	Years of reserves, at current production	266	22,000	0	414	4,118	3,385	0	6,429	0	0	0	0	0	254	895
	Production as % of total	9%	1%	0%	78%	1%	5%	0%	2%	0%	0%	0%	0%	0%	4%	
	Imports as % of total	0%	0%	0%	0%	0%	0%	0%	0%	0%	0%	0%	0%	0%	-100%	

Figure 3.2 Raw materials (Author's evaluation based on data from Asian Metal, 2018; Barrera, 2017, 2019a, b; Bauxite Index, 2018; Da Silva, 2019a, b; Fastmarkets MB, 2014; Kay, 2018a, b; McLeod, 2019; National Minerals Information Center, 2018; *SMM*, 2018; The Observatory of Economic Complexity, 2018; Top 5 of Anything, 2018; Williams, 2019a, b)

short term. Major production today is in China and Australia, with China also representing 50 percent of worldwide imports, making it the largest consumer of Bauxite worldwide. The critical shift to understand is that there is less than a decade's worth of reserves in China. A significant shift in China's dependencies toward Australia, Latin America, and Africa is to be expected.

Copper

At the current pace of production, there are 35 years of reserves left, with all fields around the world depleted (with the exception of Australia), leading to possible scarcity in the coming decades. Copper is mainly produced by Latin America, which also has the largest reserves historically. China, Europe, and the Asia Pacific are major importers of copper and share dependencies with Latin America as a result. In the future, dependencies will partially shift to Australia, which is the only region that still has 90 years of reserves at the current pace of production.

Iron (Steel)

Overall, there are around 40 years of reserves at current levels of production. Production is largely dominated by China, which represents 50 percent of world production, as well as 60 percent of imports. Local iron ore extraction has represented two-thirds of its needs so far. Yet, with only 14 years of reserves left, a significant shift of dependencies is expected to happen toward Australia, Brazil, and more importantly, Russia — with cumulated reserves representing four times the amount of China's current ones.

Lead

The current reserves do not account for more than 15 years of production at the current pace, meaning scarcity could emerge in the coming decades. Once again, China represents more than half of worldwide production and consumption. And, as in other cases, China has limited reserves available — less than a decade's worth — though it relies on them for two-thirds of its needs. Major shifts of dependencies toward Australia and Latin America (particularly Peru and Mexico) are expected in the coming decade.

Zinc

Worldwide reserves of zinc are not estimated to exceed more than two decades, meaning zinc could also face scarcity in the coming decades. China represents around 40 percent of total worldwide consumption today. Again, the largest chunk of its needs is met by local reserves, with less than a decade of reserves. Significant shifts are expected, notably toward Australia, which has 40 years of reserves left at current production rate, and Latin America.

Manganese

Overall, there are 25 years of reserves at the current pace of production. Production is essentially located in Sub-Saharan Africa (30 percent), specifically South Africa, Gabon, and Ghana, and Australia (30 percent). Key consumers are China, India, Asia, and Europe. The reserves are more balanced and further localization of production in China, India, and Europe could be expected.

Nickel

There are around 30 years of nickel reserves worldwide. The largest reserves are in Australia, the Asia Pacific (Indonesia and the Philippines particularly), and Brazil, followed by the rest of Latin America (Cuba, Guatemala, Colombia), and Russia. Asia is the primary region where all production and consumption of Nickel occurs. There are significant trade exchanges between the Philippines, Indonesia, and China, but there are less than two decades of reserves available in the region. Diversification of resources is thus necessary, notably toward Australia, Latin America (Brazil in particular), and Russia, which hold significant reserves.

Lithium

There are over 300 years of reserves available from the current pace of production, but in a context of rapidly growing consumption from the development of electric vehicles and lithium-ion technologies, this may change. The current 10 percent compound annual growth rate estimate (Financialbuzz.com, 2018) would cause consumption to multiply by three times its rate within the coming decade. Though there would not be a major issue of scarcity in the coming decades if this projection were to come true. Most mature economies are dependent on Australian and Latin American imports today, and local production capacities are likely to increase in China going forward.

Cobalt

Sixty percent of cobalt reserves are located in Sub-Saharan Africa (namely the Democratic Republic of Congo, Zambia, and Tanzania). Another 20 percent is located in Australia, with the remainder spread across the globe. There are around 65 years of production left at the current pace. The development of energy batteries using cobalt could sharply reduce this figure. The development of alternative sources of cobalt could thus be expected in the coming decades, particularly in Australia. The major importer is China, leading to significant ties with Africa currently and Australia going forward.

The first conclusion from this analysis is that many of the raw materials on which global economic development is founded are reaching worryingly low levels of remaining reserves. Copper, lead, zinc, manganese, nickel will not have more than 30 years of reserves left at the current pace of production. As the demand for new materials continues to increase, the decades leading to 2050 should see growing levels of scarcity if nothing is changed. Of course, one can hope that further exploration will unveil new fields that raise the overall level of reserves. Nevertheless, it is plausible to see a tremendous increase in pressure on supply, with rising prices and intensified competition.

The second key outcome of this analysis is the major role that China plays in global raw material exchanges. China accounts for 30–50 percent of global production of many key materials today, particularly bauxite, iron ore, lead, and zinc. Over the last 40 years, China has, to a large extent, founded its economic development through its own resources, and, to a lesser extent, on imports from the Asia Pacific. Yet its reserves are facing depletion, leading to a rise in imports. China already represents more than 50 percent of global imports for many of these resources. As economic development continues to intensify, China's reliance on imports will keep rising and could lead to the country developing strong bilateral relationships with major exporters of those resources, in particular the two global "mines" of the twenty-first century — Latin America and Australia, both of which hold very significant reserves in most of these materials. As discussed in Chapter 2, the two regions with a window over the Pacific Ocean will likely be a critical stake for twenty-first century economic powerhouses. While Latin America has been a stronghold of American influence for decades, it is easy to predict that the competition between the two global economic giants will increase in the region. Australia, which is traditionally tied to the Western world, will also be critical for China's economic development. The evolution of relationships between the two countries is a major uncertainty going forward. The evolution of relationships with Latin America and Australia is less frequently discussed in comparison to the partnerships that China is building with Russia or African countries, which are also notable potential providers of resources, though to a lesser extent.

The Critical Topic of Rare Earth Materials

Finally, we will shed light on a very specific set of resources: rare earth materials. These materials have very powerful properties. They are usually found as dust, mixed in with other resources. Their process of extraction is, therefore, extremely complex, with critical impacts on the environment. Yet, they offer critical benefits once used. These materials are notably used as powerful magnets that enable the manufacture of electric motors with lighter weights. They can also be used in batteries and various chemical products, making them a critical resource to the energy industry. They are also widely used in the developing IT industry and represent a critical resource for technological advancements in sensors and computing systems, among many devices (Pitron, 2018).

There are no overall issues of reserves of rare earth materials in the coming decades, even if production increases significantly. There would, indeed, be several centuries of reserves available. China represents close to 40 percent of reserves available, with the rest being fairly evenly distributed between Brazil, the Asia Pacific, and Russia. The main topic today is that around 80 percent of production (and exports) is dominated by China. No other country has truly started developing a rare earth mining industry. This high dependency is expected to soften over decades to come as alternative sources are put in operation. This situation creates significant dependencies with the United States, as the main importer of these materials (even though the figure in the table is exaggerated, due to lack of data) — a point we will return to when analyzing the geopolitics of the digital industry.

Is There a Way Out?

These rather bleak perspectives could potentially be reversed, and one can reasonably assume that they will be as the world has historically demonstrated its capability to adapt. Forecasts should, therefore, be taken with caution. The demand for resources has increased considerably to meet the growing needs of a growing population. Yet, most of these materials end up being wasted, be it in the process of transformation or manufacturing or once a product reaches end of life. Nearly 99 percent of the consumer goods produced are being trashed within six months (The World Counts, 2018). Kaza *et al.* (2018) extensively researched the topic of waste. They found that over two billion tons of waste is generated each year and that this figure will increase to 3.4 billion tons by 2050, mainly from Asia and Africa. The waste per capita remains very different across regions. North America tops two tons per capita per year, while that of Asia or

Africa barely reaches 0.5 tons per capita per year. It is reasonable to assume that, if nothing changes, these ratios will also increase in new economies as the level of development increases.

Food waste accounts for nearly half of global waste. This means that the other half (one billion tons) is harder for the planet to absorb or complex to recycle. Hence, it keeps accumulating in landfills. Plastics are a good contemporary example, with their usage being strongly debated at the time of writing (Figure 3.3).

The growing resource scarcity and the piling up of waste and its environmental consequences have led to a number of organizations in the recent years investigating new ways of manufacturing products and dealing with them throughout their lifecycle. A range of solutions exist and, combined, could help reduce the overall consumption of resources (therefore mitigating strategic dependencies). This is what has often been defined as circularity. A circular economy is one that adopts a 5-R approach: Reduce, Reuse, Refurbish, Repair, and Recycle. The "Reduce" corresponds to mitigating demand. As unlikely as it may seem, the demand for resources can be mitigated. A good example of this would be how modal shifts in transportation enable us to reduce the number of vehicles. A similar approach could be applied to a number of the products we use daily. The "Reuse" and "Refurbish" correspond to extending the lifetime of

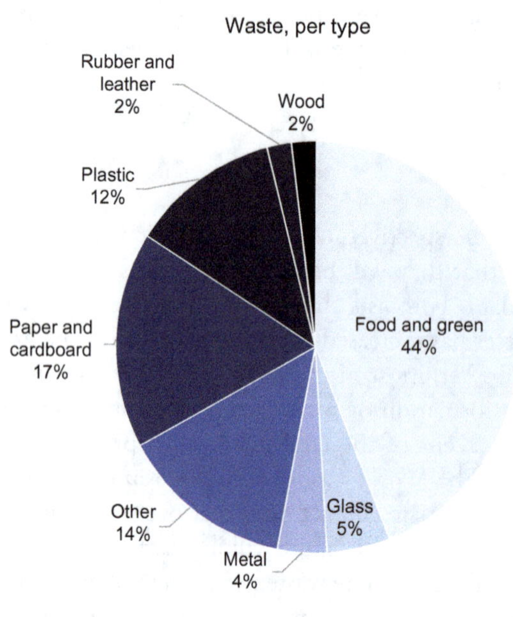

Figure 3.3 Waste by type (Kaza *et al.*, 2018)

products (like cars or phones, for instance), either as-is or through partial upgrades. "Repair" stands for all the damaged goods that are today disposed of as waste and could be, to a large extent, reused if properly repaired. Finally, "Recycle" consists of extracting from products the initial materials to reuse them in new products. This exhaustive circular approach would help reduce and mitigate demand for resources, and is starting to gain traction, most notably in Europe and more slowly in Asia and in North America, although significant improvements have been noticed recently.

The Energy Transition Commission (2018) has estimated that adopting a truly circular economy could help reduce primary plastic production by 56 percent, steel by 37 percent, aluminum by 40 percent, and cement by 34 percent, while helping to reduce emissions from these sectors by 40 percent. Beyond a circular economy, the design of new materials and the optimization of manufacturing processes are solutions to limit the impact of resource scarcity. Think, for instance, of bioplastic to replace traditional plastic, timber to replace cement, nanomaterials, among many more.

Overall, a range of approaches and solutions are in place to cope with growing resource scarcity, and they will likely all be developed at some stage, notably by Asian countries, with China certainly leading the effort. It is only a matter of time. The pace of change will, however, be critical to mitigating growing demand, fueled by new economies' development and urbanization.

Shifting Geopolitics of Energy

The shift to coal in the eighteenth century in the United Kingdom triggered the Industrial Revolution in Europe and North America, which expanded in the nineteenth century with the discovery of oil, a liquid fossil fuel with greater energy density. These shifts had a massive impact on geopolitics, leading Western economies to dominate globally for over two centuries.

Today's world is very much a product of these revolutions as it runs almost exclusively on fossil fuels, and there is no economic development without securing access to these resources. They are used to produce electricity, to provide heating, gasoline for engines, among several other uses. By-products of fossil fuels are plastic as well as key chemicals and gases that are used in consumer goods or certain industrial applications. They represent 81 percent of the total primary energy demand today (International Energy Agency, 2018).

In the last four decades of the century, a progressive catchup from new economies has started, particularly in China and, to a lesser extent, in India and South-Eastern Asia. This development has created maximum pressure on energy resources. Over a century, global primary energy consumption has increased by a factor of 10, while energy per capita has increased by a factor of 3 (Richie and Roser, 2019), and this trend is likely to continue.

We have decided to reproduce here forecasts from the International Energy Agency (2018) and particularly those from the Current Policies Scenario (CPS), which project the evolution of primary energy demand based on current policies. Again, these forecasts need to be taken with caution, as they essentially assume a continuation of current trends. Many scenarios and alternative forecasts exist and have been published in recent years. The International Energy Agency (2018), for instance, publishes alternative forecasts, for example, the New Policy Scenario (NPS), which assumes a number of policies are put in place in the coming years, or the Sustainable Development Scenario (SDS), which looks at the required evolution of the energy system to remain within a global carbon budget (the cumulated volume of CO_2 emissions) that is compatible with evaluations of global warming below two degrees. Other organizations like Shell, Equinor, BP, the International Renewable Energy Agency (IRENA), Greenpeace, the International Institute for Applied Systems Analysis (IIASA), to name but a few, also publish detailed transition forecasts. These vary depending on the assumptions that are being made. Most forecasts make different assumptions in terms of energy efficiency, the level of fuel switch across energy vectors, or the pace of decarbonization of various energy sources. These assumptions weigh heavily in global projections of energy demand to 2040. For this example, we have decided to use the Current Policy Scenario (CPS) from the International Energy Agency to provide a glimpse of the changes at play from a geopolitical standpoint, provided that "business as usual" approaches continue to prevail. Although an imperfect exercise (as is always the case with forecasts), we believe the conclusions continue to apply to a large array of existing published scenarios that assume a relative continuation (or slight inflection) of current trends. We will then challenge these results and explore some of the forecasts that predict significant transformations of the energy system within the coming two decades.

In the CPS, primary energy consumption is expected to increase by around 40 percent by 2040, a slightly lower growth rate than the one observed in the last two decades (60 percent). It will mainly increase in new economies, which will account for 95 percent of the total consumption increase. Asia in general would represent two-thirds of the increase, and China alone 26 percent of the increase (Figure 3.4).

This growth is driven by an increase of the population in new economies, but also the increase of the energy consumption per capita, led by the economic development of new economies, fostered by urbanization. North America and Eurasia stand out with levels of energy consumption per capita significantly above

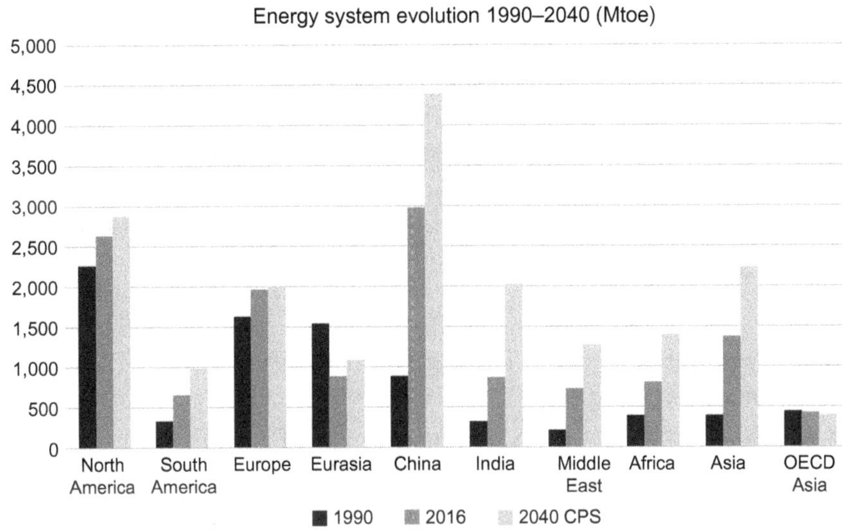

Figure 3.4 Primary energy consumption evolution 1990–2040 (International Energy Agency, 2018)

the world average. Both regions have experienced a reduction of their energy consumption per capita in the last decades, although Eurasia, which underwent a significant economic readjustment when the Soviet Union collapsed, is once again on an upward trend. New economies have significantly lower levels of energy consumption per capita, and the last 20 years have seen a progressive catchup, particularly in China and the Middle East. The evolution in this ratio is China, which is expected to grow 50 percent in the coming 20 years, leading to more than 1,500 millions of tons of oil equivalent (Mtoe) of additional primary energy demand. This shows the massive potential impact of new economies over the actual energy system. If all new economies reached similar energy consumption per capita to Europe, the worldwide primary energy consumption would reach 30,000 Mtoe, compared to 13,300 Mtoe in 2016 and around 18,700 Mtoe in 2040, according to the CPS. To a large extent, the dynamics of economic development will largely define worldwide energy consumption evolution in the coming decades. In this scenario, fossil fuels are expected to represent 70 percent of the total primary energy consumption growth by 2040.

A key question that arises, then, is whether the world has enough resources to fuel this growth of demand. Certain energy reserves are classified as being retrievable or proven. Retrievable reserves correspond to overall worldwide reserves, and these are only estimated figures. Proven reserves are those that have been identified and measured and typically correspond to fields already in operation. The main difference is that retrievable reserves have not been confirmed that they can be extracted, at least at a certain cost of production, with current technologies available. The ratio R/P (reserves over production) measured in years, estimates the remaining years of production at a given level of consumption. The R/P of proven reserves has shown roughly 50 years of remaining production at current consumption level for oil and natural gas, and around 170 years for coal. Thus, there is no major issue in terms of resource availability in the coming decades. This is all the more relevant when computing the R/P using retrievable reserves. Current estimates show that retrievable resources represent more than 200 years of production at current consumption level, and around 120 years for both oil and natural gas by 2040 (International Energy Agency, 2018; Petit, 2017). This is also what explains why proven reserves R/P have remained unchanged in the last 40 years. Retrievable reserves are progressively turned into proven ones as exploration expands. The world is not facing any shortage of energy resources in the coming decades, at least from a reserve standpoint. The cost of extraction of some of those resources could, however, prove to be prohibitive and prevent sustainable usage of them.

The geographical mix shows significant differences across regions. In terms of proven reserves, the Middle East represents the first region of the world for both oil and natural gas, with around 50 percent of worldwide reserves (60 percent for oil, 40 percent for natural gas), followed by the Americas for oil (30 percent), and Eurasia for natural gas (30 percent). In terms of retrievable reserves however, the picture is very different. The discovery of nonconventional oil reserves has placed North America as the first region of the world in terms of total reserves (40 percent of total), the Middle East dropping at 20 percent of total reserves. This could lead to a significant change of geopolitical paradigm, of which the consequences are yet to be seen. Natural gas resources are more balanced across geographies, which fits well with the regional characteristic of this market, as costs of transport of natural gas represent around half of the total cost of resource extraction and distribution. Around 60 percent of total reserves of natural gas are equally shared across North America, Eurasia, and the Middle East (Petit, 2017), the rest being well-balanced between South America, Europe, Africa, and the Asia Pacific.

These geographical particularities lead to significant dependencies between regions that produce and regions that consume energy. The influence ratio measures this level of dependency by looking at the share of imports of energy from one region to another (Petit, 2017). It shows that Asia, in general, is extremely dependent on oil exports from the Middle East and natural gas, though less so. India, in particular, relies on nearly 70 percent of its consumption of exports from the Middle East. What could also be surprising for nonspecialists is the relatively low level of dependency of North America on oil imports from the Middle East. For over 70 years, since World War II, the United States has had a presence within the region to secure political order, in order to maintain access to the vast oil reserves of the region. Several decades later, following the oil crisis of the 1970s, North America has expanded its own industry and has virtually become independent from oil imports from the Middle East, with less than 10 percent of those coming from the region (Petit, 2017). Again, the consequence of such a shift in dependencies is yet to be seen. The other critical dependency is Europe, which relies heavily on imports from Eurasia for natural gas, with 40 percent of its consumption coming from the region (Petit, 2017).

While energy consumption in Europe is not expected to significantly rise in the coming decades, this is not the case for India and Asia, where energy consumption is expected to skyrocket. It is expected to more than double in India and grow by over 60 percent in Asia if the projections from the CPS from the International Energy Agency (2018) materialize. This would lead to a significant increase in dependency and increased pressure on some bilateral relationships, which could endanger the sustainable economic development of importing regions. Obviously, one could argue that the oil market is global in nature — which is not the case for natural gas, which remains primarily regional, despite recent developments in liquefied natural gas (LNG) — and it is true that oil prices across regions are set largely by global market supply and demand balance. Yet, the very existence of a global market assumes a multilateral environment that enables free trade across regions. If critical confrontations emerge across some regions, this situation could evolve, leading to dependencies on oil or natural gas becoming an instrument of power in bilateral relationships.

To summarize, the energy sector could see a significant rise in dependencies across regions. Primary energy consumption could grow by as much as 40 percent in the coming 20 years, following a similar trend to the last 20 years. This growth is mainly driven by the increase of energy consumption per capita as a result of economic development. The potential for growth is, however, stronger. The increase in demand will be concentrated in new economies. There are no problems with reserves at a global level, even though the level of proven reserves remains limited to around 50 years of consumption. This level depends significantly on the investments realized in exploration and production, and there is no risk on fossil fuel procurements in the coming decades.

The geopolitics of energy has long been dominated by a market that the United States made global, with Western economies being the primary destination. In the past, these economies largely depended on cheap oil from the Middle East and less so on natural gas from Eurasia for Europe. This situation is evolving considerably, with two distinct factors that could reshape global relationships. On the one hand, the rise of demand from new economies in Asia (particularly China and India) could lead to an intensification of exchanges with the Middle East (oil) and Eurasia (natural gas). The levels of dependencies currently observed are worrisome for the global stability of Asian economies and should lead to strengthened bilateral agreements between the regions over the next decades. As the political situation has remained unstable for decades in the Middle East, it is also quite likely to see Asian powers (like China and India) take a greater role in the region. On the other hand, the massive discovery of unconventional reserves in North and South America means the continent is almost entirely independent from an energy standpoint. The fact that North America has become independent from an energy standpoint challenges the current "status quo" given the large presence of the United States in the Middle East. The "War on Terror" has intensified in the last decade, leading to an even greater engagement from the United States. Yet, more and more people in the United States, particularly the current administration, are beginning to advocate against this. President Trump recently said that the "US military presence in the Middle East [was] tied to the region's oil" and that "all of a sudden it gets to a point where you don't have to stay there" (Choi, 2018). This echoes the conclusions of Chapter 2 on the international stance that the United States could take going forward. Additionally, North America could become a net exporter of fossil fuels to the rest of the world, in particular to Europe. With a high share of natural gas coming from Russia, Europe could decide to relieve part of its dependency to the benefit of the US LNG imports, although the economics of this potential eventuality has not yet been worked out (Shriyaevskaya and Malik, 2018).

Will This Happen as Expected?

The world is not a prisoner from its past. If global economic growth in the twentieth century has largely been sustained by a significant recourse to fossil fuels, and oil in particular, the last decade has seen the beginning of a new energy revolution promoting an alternative pathway to fossil fuels. This transition was initiated following the discovery of the impact of fossil fuels on the concentration of carbon emissions, leading to global warming (Petit, 2017). Over the last decade, three solutions were unveiled, which combined would enable to mitigate the rise of carbon emissions and, even in most aggressive scenarios, mean the world could reach a zero-carbon economy by the mid twenty-first century (Energy Transitions Commission, 2018).

The first solution is the implementation of significant energy efficiency measures. Over the last few decades, there have been some efforts to optimize energy consumption. Massive benefits have been realized in a number of domains, leading the energy intensity to drop by 0.8 percent per year between 1990 and 2010 on average, while the baseline scenario from the International Energy Agency (2014) estimates a further drop of 1.49 percent per year until 2040. In the aforementioned International Energy Agency's SDS (2018), global energy consumption could remain flat up to 2040, through the deployment of massive energy efficiency measures (among others), against an almost 40 percent increase in the CPS.

The second solution consists of decarbonizing the power sector. Production of electricity accounts for 40 percent of total fossil fuel consumption today. Governments around the world have encouraged the development of alternative electricity production solutions, mainly based on renewable energies, with wind and solar power at the forefront. The aggressive subsidies provided by several countries (in particular OECD [Organisation for Economic Co-operation and Development] countries and China) have enabled this industry to ramp up, meaning costs have fallen as a result of mass production, leading these new forms of energy to reach today cost parity with most conventional power sources (BloombergNEF, 2018). Most of the decline of costs has come from the gigantic scale-up of the industry in China, for example, around 50 percent of the solar panels sold in the United States today come from China (EnergySage, 2018). According to BloombergNEF (2018), solar and wind, which accounted for 12 percent of installed power capacities in 2016, could reach 50 percent of the total by 2040. Shell (2018) also estimates that 45 percent of power generation could be supplied by solar and wind alone by 2040. This transition would, in turn, create a new dependency to the Chinese industry.

The third solution has made its way to global awareness in 2018 and is a natural enhancement of the previous one. It is the actual electrification of the energy system, including the migration of traditional energy uses for heating and mechanical propulsion to electrified solutions. The emblematic example of this shift is the dramatic acceleration in electric transportation. Electric vehicles are increasingly considered as an obvious choice for the future, as they progressively reach parity with conventional combustion engine vehicles. The benefit of electric vehicles is that, on the one hand, they are much simpler to manufacture and maintain with around 100 times fewer parts, and, on the other hand, their efficiency ratio is three times higher, meaning it takes three times less energy to run a car, leading to a strong competitive equation on fuel costs. Beyond electric vehicles, other applications are also considering electrification. Heat pumps also present a significant improvement in terms of efficiency versus traditional systems and could be deployed at large scale in homes, buildings, and manufacturing industries. Again, new scenarios emerge with aggressive electrification assumptions. The International Energy Agency (2018) has, for instance, developed a "Future is Electric Scenario" (FiES) in 2018 with aggressive projections of the share of electricity in the global mix. Shell (2018) also considers it in one of its recent scenarios, with a share of electricity in the mix lifted from 20 percent in 2016 to up to 40 percent by 2050, and 60 percent by the end of the century.

These three solutions combine to form the base of a global energy transition. Energy efficiency measures, on the demand side, help curb the rise of energy demand, while power decarbonization and electrification (clean electrification) enable a more efficient and carbon-free energy supply.

It is not the purpose of this book to go further in the details of this transition. What matters here is to understand to what extent this shift would impact on the forecasts and dependencies described above. Three forecasts have been plotted from the International Energy Agency (2018) and Shell (2018). They demonstrate the global oil demand uncertainty across scenarios, and that natural gas demand is expected to continue to rise (Figure 3.5).

If we focus on Asia Pacific, which is expected to become the new epicenter of energy geopolitics, all forecasts show that oil dependency will remain a key topic in the coming decades for the region, and natural gas will increase in the period.

If this transition eventually enables the region to mitigate its dependency on fossil fuels, it also creates new dependencies on specific raw materials. Think of

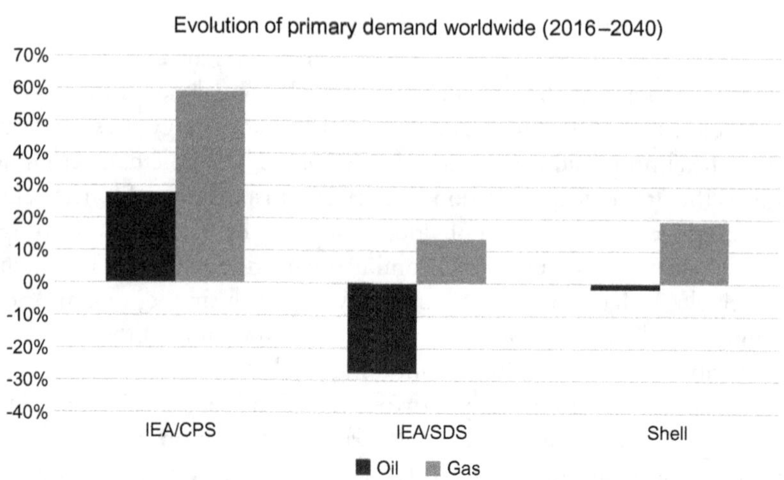

Figure 3.5 Evolution of primary demand worldwide (International Energy Agency, 2018; Shell, 2018)

lithium or cobalt resources that play a fundamental role in current battery technologies, or rare earth materials for electric motors. As the volume of those scales up, critical dependencies also increase on these raw materials. As was reviewed earlier, the dependencies and scarcity of some of these resources could also significantly slow down the energy transition as we see it today (Pitron, 2018), although ongoing research (BloombergNEF, 2018) suggests that upcoming innovations could mitigate these issues. Also, the reliance on China for rare earth materials could be balanced with rising production in other geographies with resources. The central role of the Chinese industry, within such a transition in the coming decades, would remain paramount and represent a new dependency for most economies around the world.

As an overall conclusion, it can be safely asserted that energy geopolitics will remain a key factor in the coming decades, even if (and as) they significantly evolve. A larger dependency on fossil fuels from the Middle East and Eurasia is likely to be expected from the Asia Pacific and Europe. In the meantime, North America is becoming virtually independent from an energy standpoint, something that could lead it to challenge its current level of support to the peace process in the Middle East. Finally, an accelerated energy transition, if it happens, could mitigate such dependencies, while simultaneously creating new dependencies, with China playing a prominent role.

Key Interaction Points: The System Map

Two uncertainties have been examined in this chapter. The first one relates to the future situation of raw materials: scarcity, dependencies, and alternative solutions. The second relates to the future energy system: based on fossil fuels, with evolving dependencies, notably with the rise of North America as a major energy supplier, or following a stringent decarbonization path that will lead to alternative dependencies.

The two uncertainties are connected with the geopolitical stance that key powerhouses will take going forward. Indeed, raw materials and energy resources are both matters of national security. The evolution of dependencies, the alternatives (or lack thereof) discovered on key materials or resources will all play heavily in global geopolitics. At the same time, the stance that key global powers will exchange between one another will also impact market developments of raw materials and energy resources. Confrontational stances would, for instance, foster innovation on new materials and circularity, while possibly limiting the development of the energy transition (due to higher capital costs and inefficient supply chains; Figure 3.6).

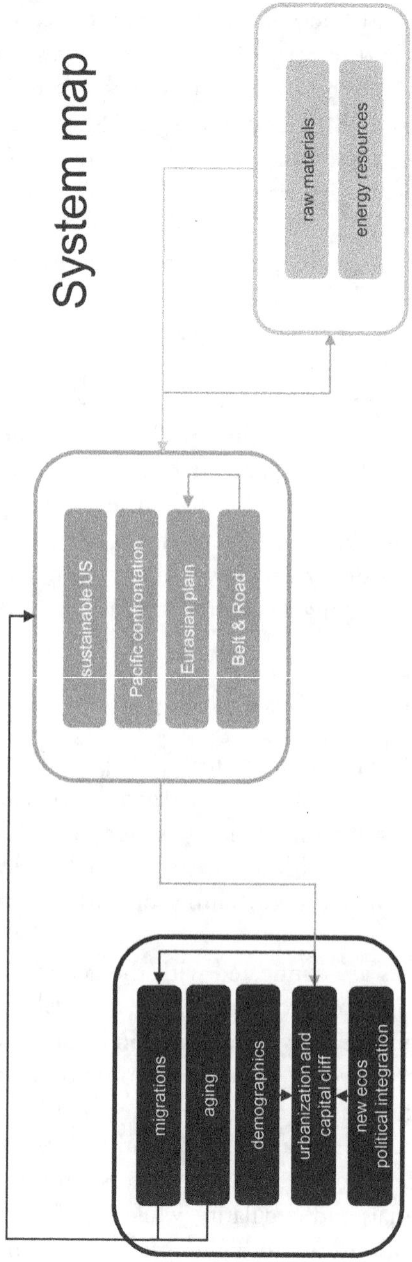

Figure 3.6 System map

Summary

For 20 years, the world has been consuming more resources than the planet is able to generate, and every year the "Earth Overshoot Day" (the day from which humanity consumes resources that are not ecologically renewed) comes a little earlier. Most of the essential raw materials in the proper functioning of the economy have, according to sources, only a few decades left of reserves at current paces of production, while production is set to increase with global economic development. There are, of course, possible reserves that are yet to be discovered, notably in the oceans, but it is reasonable to assume that significant pressure on global material supply chains will increase in the coming decades. Two regions that stand out with massive reserves of almost all materials are Latin America and Australia. Those two global mines of the twenty-first century will, therefore, play a critical role going forward. Also, though to a slightly lesser extent, the vast plains of Russia and Africa also present significant reserves. Clearly, the geopolitics of raw materials will intensify in the coming decades, revolving around these four regions. It will, therefore, not be a surprise if competition happens to control access to resources. This is notably apparent in Africa. The development of powerful naval capabilities in the Pacific Ocean by China is also a sign that the competition over control of the oceans, hence exchanges with Latin America and Australia, is also a major stake for the country. Beyond the critical status of these materials for the modern industry, there would be over one billion tons of waste, which are disposed of in landfills. A considerable opportunity for more circular models thus exists, which remains to be untapped.

This paradigm also exists for energy resources. For a century, the geopolitics of energy have been dominated by the risk of scarcity and cheap access to oil reserves in the Middle East, and, to a lesser extent, Russia — notably for natural gas. The development of military power of the United States, post-World War II, and its resolute engagement into world affairs has undoubtedly led to securing access to oil resources in the Middle East. Yet, this paradigm has also changed in the last decade or so. The discoveries of shale oil and gas have significantly transformed the balance of power on fossil fuels. Retrievable reserves have skyrocketed, and North America now stands with the largest reserves in the world, even ahead of the Middle East (at least for oil). This means that North America stands virtually independent from an energy standpoint, while the dependency from China, India, and the Asia Pacific has intensified and is expected to continue to do so. This results in a large shift from west to east in strategic dependencies, with potentially large implications from a geopolitical standpoint. Will the United States retreat from its bases of the Middle East, as was once suggested by President Trump? Though unlikely, the US energy independence and cheap access to fossil fuels implies that changes are yet to be seen. Another interesting dependency that could shift is Europe's move away from Russian gas, and the possible play of the United States as an alternative supplier. Simultaneously, an energy transition has started, with a focus on decarbonizing the current energy system. Renewable energies have been gaining traction and are emerging as strong economic alternatives to fossil fuels. In a number of scenarios, they could potentially disrupt oil and gas fuels by 2040. In doing so, they would reshuffle the current geopolitics of energy. China has taken critical steps to become the global industry leader of these new technologies. Should this transition happen, new critical dependencies to China would emerge by 2040. The situation in the United States and this transition is very interesting and illustrates the complexity of understanding global issues such as this one. On the one hand, many actors (private technology companies, cities, citizens) advocate for clear solutions to be taken to fight climate change, such as deploying renewable energies, which for the largest part are technologies imported from China. But on the other hand, other players (including the government) push for the development of oil and natural gas infrastructures, in order to become the first energy provider of the world, ahead of the Saudis and Russians. Two worlds confront each other within the same country.

As a result, it seems clear that tensions are likely to be exacerbated in the coming decades. The world may not face scarcity, but geopolitical dependencies in key regions could increase significantly, while critical geopolitical shifts could occur. At the same time, a critical potential exists for innovation in circularity models and sustainable energy-efficient systems. Will a region lead the charge with these changes? Europe seems to have taken initial steps, followed by China, but the world of resources is likely to remain a key uncertainty moving forward in a complex game that could unfold in several ways.

References

Asian Metal. (2018). *Zinc: Resource Distribution and Production.* Available from: http://metalpedia.asianmetal.com/metal/zinc/resources&production.shtml [Accessed: June 2019].

Barrera, P. (2017). "Top Lead Reserves by Country," *Investing News.* Available from: https://investingnews.com/daily/resource-investing/base-metals-investing/lead-investing/lead-reserves-by-country/ [Accessed: June 2019].

Barrera, P. (2019a). "Top Lithium Reserves by Country," *Investing News.* Available from: https://investingnews.com/daily/resource-investing/battery-metals-investing/lithium-investing/lithium-reserves-country/ [Accessed: June 2019].

Barrera, P. (2019b). "Top Cobalt Reserves by Country," *Investing News*. Available from: https://investingnews.com/daily/resource-investing/battery-metals-investing/cobalt-investing/cobalt-producer-cobalt-reserves/ [Accessed: March 2020].

Bauxite Index. (2018). *The Bauxite Index*. Available from: https://thebauxiteindex.com/en/cbix/industry-101/bauxite-101/bauxite-reserves [Accessed: June 2019].

BloombergNEF. (2018). *New Energy Outlook*. Available from: https://about.bnef.com/new-energy-outlook/ [Accessed: June 2019].

Choi, D. (2018). "Trump Says US Troops May Not Need to be in the Middle East Because 'We're Producing More Oil Now'," *Business Insider*, 28 November. Available from: https://www.businessinsider.com/trump-withdraw-us-troops-in-middle-east-oil-2018-11 [Accessed: June 2019].

Da Silva, O. (2019a). "Top Copper Reserves by Country," *Investing News*. Available from: https://investingnews.com/daily/resource-investing/base-metals-investing/copper-investing/top-copper-reserves-country/ [Accessed: June 2019].

Da Silva, O. (2019b). "Top Iron Reserves by Country," *Investing News*. Available from: https://investingnews.com/daily/resource-investing/base-metals-investing/iron-investing/top-iron-producing-countries/ [Accessed: September 2019].

EnergySage. (2018). *Where Are Solar Panels Made and Should You Care?* Available from: https://news.energysage.com/where-solar-panels-are-manufactured/ [Accessed: June 2019].

Energy Transitions Commission. (2018). *Mission Possible Report: Reaching Net-Zero Carbon Emissions from Harder-To-Abate Sectors by Mid-Century*. Available from: http://www.energy-transitions.org/mission-possible [Accessed: June 2019].

Financialbuzz.com. (2018). "Lithium Demand Is Growing as Electric and Hybrid Vehicles Increase in Popularity," *PR Newswire*, 6 March. Available from: https://www.prnewswire.com/news-releases/lithium-demand-is-growing-as-electric-and-hybrid-vehicles-increase-in-popularity-675985693.html [Accessed: June 2019].

International Energy Agency. (2014). *World Energy Outlook 2014*. ©OECD/IEA publishing. All rights reserved. License: www.iea.org/t&c, as modified by V. Petit. Available from: https://doi.org/10.1787/weo-2014-en [Accessed: June 2019].

International Energy Agency. (2018). *World Energy Outlook 2018*. ©OECD/IEA publishing. All rights reserved. License: www.iea.org/t&c, as modified by V. Petit. Available from: https://www.iea.org/reports/world-energy-outlook-2018 [Accessed: June 2019].

Kay, A. (2018a). "Top Zinc Reserves by Country," *Investing News*. Available from: https://investingnews.com/daily/resource-investing/base-metals-investing/zinc-investing/top-zinc-producing-countries/ [Accessed: June 2019].

Kay, A. (2018b). "Top Nickel Reserves by Country," *Investing News*. Available from: https://investingnews.com/daily/resource-investing/base-metals-investing/nickel-investing/nickel-reserves-by-country/ [Accessed: June 2019].

Kaza, S., Yao, L. Bhada-Tata, P. and Van Woerden, F. (2018). *What a Waste 2.0: A Global Snapshot of Solid Waste Management to 2050. Urban Development.* Washington, DC: World Bank. Available from: https://openknowledge.worldbank.org/handle/10986/30317 [Accessed May 2019].

KPMG. (2012). *Expect the Unexpected: Building Business Value in a Changing World.* Available from: https://home.kpmg.com/xx/en/home/insights/2012/02/building-business-value.html [Accessed: June 2019].

McLeod, C. (2019). "Top Rare Earth Reserves by Country," *Investing News.* Available from: https://investingnews.com/daily/resource-investing/critical-metals-investing/rare-earth-investing/rare-earth-reserves-country/ [Accessed: June 2019].

National Minerals Information Center. (2018). "International Minerals Statistics and Information," *US Geological Survey.* Available from: https://minerals.usgs.gov/minerals/pubs/country/ [Accessed: June 2019].

The Observatory of Economic Complexity. (2018). *Observatory of Economic Complexity Data Sources.* Available from: https://oec.world/en/resources/data/ [Accessed: December 2018].

Petit, V. (2017). *The Energy Transition: An Overview of the True Challenge of the 21st Century.* Berlin: Springer.

Pitron, G. (2018). *La guerre des métaux rares: La face cachée de la transition énergétique et numérique.* Paris: Les Liens Qui Libèrent.

Raisson, V. (2010). *2033, Atlas des Futurs du Monde.* Paris: Laffont.

Ritchie, H. and Roser, M. (2019). "Access to Energy," *Our World in Data,* September. Available from: https://ourworldindata.org/energy-production-and-changing-energy-sources [Accessed: September 2019].

Shell. (2018). *Sky Scenario.* Available from: https://www.shell.com/energy-and-innovation/the-energy-future/scenarios/shell-scenario-sky.html [Accessed: June 2019].

Shriyaevskaya, A. and Malik, N. (2018). "Europe Shows It's Getting Serious About Buying U.S. LNG," *Bloomberg,* 9 August. Available from: https://www.bloomberg.com/news/articles/2018-08-09/europe-shows-it-s-getting-serious-about-getting-more-u-s-lng [Accessed: June 2019].

Smil, V. (2015). *Power Density: A Key to Understanding Energy Sources and Uses.* Massachusetts: MIT Press.

SMM. (2018). "China Nickel Imports and Exports Data Sep. 2017," *SMM,* 24 October. Available from: https://news.metal.com/newscontent/100763131/china-nickel-imports-and-exports-data-sep-2017 [Accessed: June 2019].

Top 5 of Anything. (2018). *The Top 5 Countries with the Most Iron Ore Reserves.* Available from: https://top5ofanything.com/list/f5ee694e/Countries-with-the-Most-Iron-Ore-Reserves [Accessed: June 2019].

Williams, G. (2019a). "Top Aluminum Reserves by Country," *Investing News.* Available from: https://investingnews.com/daily/resource-investing/industrial-metals-investing/aluminum-investing/aluminum-producing-countries/ [Accessed: September 2019].

Williams, G. (2019b). "Top Manganese Reserves by Country," *Investing News*. Available from: https://investingnews.com/daily/resource-investing/battery-metals-investing/manganese-investing/op-manganese-producing-countries-south-africa-china-austraia/ [Accessed: September 2019].

The World Counts. (2018). *A World of Waste*. Available from: https://www.theworldcounts.com/challenges/planet-earth/state-of-the-planet/world-waste-facts [Accessed: June 2019].

Zhang, R. (2014). *China's Supply and Demand of Zinc Mine and Refined Metal*. Fastmarkets MB. Available from: http://www.metalbulletin.com/events/download.ashx/document/speaker/7042/a0ID000000X0jtbMAB/Presentation [Accessed: June 2019].

CHAPTER 4

Change 4 — Climate Change Kicks In

The Intergovernmental Panel for Climate Change (IPCC), created in 1988, is dedicated to providing a scientific perspective on climate change and engages with scientists around the world, consolidating inputs from published literature, both peer-reviewed and not. Despite criticism, a vast majority of scientists today recognize its major contribution to providing a clear perspective on a complex issue.

Historically, recognition of global warming started with the measurement of the increase of the Earth's temperature. Scientists discovered that temperature had been rising for over a century, with a recent acceleration in the last decades (IPCC, 2014). This was also confirmed by the NASA Earth Observatory (2017), which showed that two-thirds of the temperature increase had occurred in the last four decades. The current increase is around 0.15–0.2 degrees per decade. Global warming is thus a demonstrated reality, and with it comes climate change.

There are many different factors that influence the Earth's temperature. The buildup of the atmosphere has a major impact, since it changes the Sun's radiative forcing. In broad figures, the planet receives around 340 W/m^2 of radiation every second and around a third of this is reflected back. The remaining radiation enters the atmosphere. Ultimately, it is also reflected back but the atmosphere's constitution helps maintain an ongoing volume of energy, which heats up the planet surface. With a higher greenhouse gas (GHG) concentration, it becomes more difficult for radiation to leave the atmosphere. They tend to concentrate and accelerating warming. Beyond atmospheric constitution, astronomic evolutions also have significant impacts. Gravitational attraction between the Earth and other planets, and the Sun's activity, all contribute to modifying temperature on the planet's surface (Milankovitch, 1920). Finally, volcanic activity or tectonic variations of the Earth's plates also have non-negligible effects.

All these factors have significantly impacted the Earth's temperature over its long history. Before an oxygen "explosion" 2.5 billion years ago, the atmosphere was saturated with methane and ammonia, and radiative forcing was extremely significant. When this event occurred, the temperature dropped dramatically with conditions on the Equator similar to current Antarctic ones. Nearly 500 million years ago, the temperature eventually stabilized around current levels. The emergence of life on Earth led to an increase in temperature due to CO_2 emissions, which lasted until 35 million years ago when the planet entered the Ice Age. This new climatic event is usually associated with the extinction of the *Azolla* fern, which led to a massive carbon capture and a reduction of radiative forcing. Since then, the temperature of the planet has remained within two degrees of current levels with most of these changes being explained by astronomic evolutions. Temperatures have started to rise since the twentieth century. The main difference today is the pace of the change, which appears to be unknown in history (Much Ado About Climate, 2013).

This brutal evolution can only be explained by a rapid evolution of the planet's atmospheric constitution, which is one of the most critical factors that can explain temperature changes. The IPCC has argued that "anthropogenic forcing," the evolution of the atmosphere mix related to human activity, is the main reason for change. GHG emissions from human activity stand at around 3 W/m^2 today, compared to the 340 W/m^2 of Sun radiative emissions (World Meteorological Organization [WMO], 2016). These gases are essentially made of methane (16 percent) and CO_2 (76 percent; Environmental Protection Agency (US) [EPA], 2020). Since the lifetime of methane in the atmosphere is typically around 10 years, while that of CO_2 ranges above 100 years, CO_2 has a much larger impact, notwithstanding its higher share. Other gases (nitrous oxide and various fluorinated gases) have very different lifetimes (from 100 years for nitrous oxide to several thousands of years for some fluorinated gases), yet their concentration in the atmosphere is so small that one can approximate CO_2 to be the main contributor to GHG emissions. This current forcing (3 W/m^2) corresponds to around 400 parts per million (ppm) of CO_2 concentration, where it never exceeded 280 ppm in the last 650,000 years (WMO, 2016). Scientists in the IPCC (2014) argue that this difference in concentration helps explain the fast-pace temperature increase on Earth. But does everybody agree?

The vast majority of scientists have recognized the acceleration of global warming. There is no debate on temperature increase and the underlying reality of climate change, but the debate still persists on its actual root cause. While many science academies worldwide have publicly acknowledged the relationship between climate change and human activities, or anthropogenic forcing, some scientists have raised concerns that the current accuracy of climate models prevents from actually proving the relationship undoubtedly (National Academies, 2009). Specifically, the role of oceans in regulating the CO_2 concentration within the atmosphere is still not fully understood in models (Institut français de recherche pour l'exploitation de la mer [IFREMER], 2019). Scientists generally recognize that the observed increase of GHG concentration in the atmosphere naturally leads to significant climate evolutions and have not yet identified another possible cause for the temperature increase, and, more importantly, its pace of change.

GHG concentration has significantly evolved over the last decades. The concentration of CO_2 has arisen from 280 ppm to above 400 ppm today. According to various sources, 50 percent of the increase in GHG concentration since preindustrial levels (1750) occurred over the last 40 years (IPPC, 2014; WMO, 2016). This has led to a significant impact of radiative forcing, which the WMO estimates have increased 60 percent in 30 years. A study of recent GHG emissions leads to a number of striking conclusions, starting with an 80 percent increase in annual emissions over the last 40 years, up to 40,000 Metric tons of carbon dioxide equivalent ($MtCO_2e$) today. This is mainly due to CO_2 emissions, which have more than doubled over this period. Other types of emissions have not increased at the same speed, except those of fluorinated gases, which have been multiplied by eight over the same period. Yet they still represent a minor share of total emissions, with CO_2 making up the bulk of GHG emissions.

According to the IPCC (2014), fossil fuels represent above 85 percent of total CO_2 emissions. While the amount of emissions related to forestry and land use have not increased in the last 40 years, those of fossil fuels have more than doubled over the same period. CO_2 emissions from fossil fuels form the bulk of the increase in emissions. Over this period, they gained 10 points in the total GHG mix, reaching 65 percent of total emissions. CO_2 emissions from fossil fuels are mainly driven by the generation and distribution of energy. Energy represents close to 100 percent of the emissions in the buildings and the transportation sector. In the industry sector, it represents close to 70 percent of total GHG emissions. The remaining 30 percent is split equally between natural CO_2 emissions associated to process operations and other emissions linked to waste or non-CO_2 emissions (International Energy Agency, 2019; IPCC, 2014). Most of these emissions are currently concentrated in OECD (Organisation for Economic Co-operation and Development) countries and Asia, with these regions representing around 80 percent of total emissions. New economies are expected to see their emissions growing faster than mature economies because of the growth of their economic activity. This makes Asia the cornerstone of the world's decarbonization.

Forecasts for the coming years are concerning. They correspond to the reference scenario (Current Policy Scenario [CPS]) from the International Energy Agency (2014). These projections show that CO_2 emissions are expected to increase by another 10,000 $MtCO_2e$ — or another 25–30 percent — in less than 20 years, similar to the total value of growth in the last 20 years. The IPCC (2014) has evaluated the possible evolution of CO_2 concentration in the

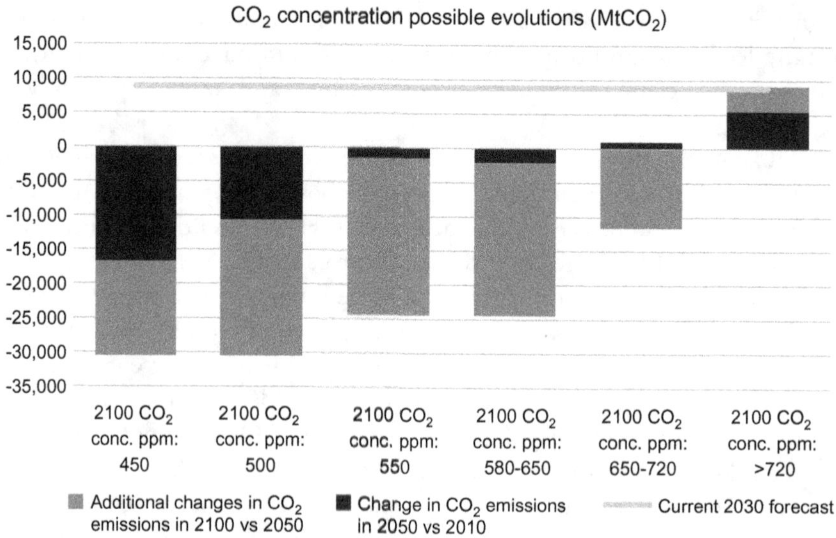

Figure 4.1 2100 CO_2 concentration scenarios (International Energy Agency, 2014; IPCC, 2014; Teske *et al.*, 2015)

atmosphere by 2100 based on the evolution of emissions in the coming decades. The striking conclusion of that analysis is that current patterns of CO_2 emissions evolutions would lead concentration to largely exceed 700 ppm by 2100, if nothing is done. The IPPC (2014) estimates that temperature would increase by four degrees or above by 2100 if this is the case (Figure 4.1).

One can still have doubts about conclusions from the IPCC on how these emissions translate into climate change. The maturity of climate models is yet to be improved, but most scientists agree that such an increase in anthropogenic emissions is likely to yield further climate impacts. With climate change being an already widely recognized reality, increased emissions are undoubtedly an aggravating factor. The level of these impacts, however, remains an uncertainty going forward.

At the same time, the economic development of new economies is likely to push CO_2 emissions upward in the coming decades. Energy consumption and decarbonization will, therefore, play a key role as it forms the bulk of emissions. This is why the energy transition previously described is a topic high on the agenda of many governments. The extent to which it will materialize, and the pace of the transition, will both play a key role in curbing CO_2 emissions. Yet, despite growing public awareness, governments around the world still struggle to activate collaborative strategies that are effectively implemented. Recently, the 2015 United Nations Climate Change Conference held in Paris was an important step in the right direction. But, at the time of writing, the United States stated that they would withdraw from the agreement, despite representing 20 percent of global emissions. There is still no global carbon pricing scheme in place. Will climate adaptation, as opposed to mitigation, be the new paradigm of the decades to come?

Global Consequences from Climate Change

What will the consequences of climate change be? In actuality they can prove difficult to predict. The IPCC (2014) has listed a number of eventualities as being "probable" or "highly probable." Primary consequences could be a significant evolution of snowpack, mountain lakes, and the intensification of runoffs and cyclonic activity. Seasons and the corresponding ecological balance could be modified in a number of regions due to the evolution of wind and marine streams (Amadeo, 2019). Fragile ecosystems, such as mountains, tropical forests, and some marine systems, would be threatened first, as they are unable to adapt to such a brutal change in climate conditions. New economies, in particular rural populations with low-income conditions, would also be the first ones to suffer from these changes through water stress, the transformation of forests into savanna in Africa, and the rise of sea level in some parts of Asia. Finally, things could even get worse. Although this is very uncertain, 20 percent of the living animal species could disappear beyond a global temperature rise of two degrees, and the more the temperature rises, the larger these extinctions (IPCC, 2014).

From an economic standpoint, there have been a number of studies trying to assess the impact of climate change. Scientists from Stanford University evaluated the impact of the Gross Domestic Product (GDP) by 2100 as ranging from 15 percent to 30 percent depending on the temperature rise (2.5–4 degrees; Amadeo, 2019). This could result in 1,200 million jobs being threatened, particularly in agriculture, fisheries, and forestry. They estimate that inflation on food would likely be inevitable and migration could reach up to 700 million people by 2050 (compared to 22 million in the last decade, or 10 times more). KPMG (2014) estimates this number at 200 million by 2050, or three times more than the observed rate in the last decade. A concurrent study published by Burke *et al.* estimated the impact of climate change on productivity and subsequently growth, excluding extreme weather impacts (Burke *et al.*, 2015; Worland, 2015). They estimated that human productivity peaks at an average temperature of 13 degrees Celsius and that the worldwide GDP per capita could be dropping in average by 23 percent by 2100. Finally, Wade and Jennings (2016) estimated an impact on GDP of 1 percent per year by 2050 (or 64 percent by 2100). Climate change would thus trigger inflation, a rise of insurance costs and permanent moves of capital from most concerned regions to less impacted ones. Models differ in magnitude, highlighting the uncertainties around climate change and its impacts, and it is likely that we will be unable to make precise estimates until late in the century due to the lack of global understanding of the Earth's current cycles. It is, however, quite clear that the increase in extreme weather events and the drop of productivity due to global warming would have consequences, at least on some, if not all, regions.

KPMG (2014) estimates that 75–80 percent of the adaptation costs would have to be borne by new economies, a conclusion confirmed by others (Burke *et al.*, 2015; Wade and Jennings, 2016). Wade and Jennings (2016) consider that most regional effects would concern new economies because they mostly rely on climate-sensitive activities (such as agriculture, fisheries, among others), the climate is warmer, thus negatively impacted by further warming, and that the cost of extreme weather events would hamper their capability to invest in developing the economy. It could be added that if extreme weather impacts are to be repetitive (or permanent), capital would likely flee from these regions durably impacting them from an economic standpoint. Wade and Jennings estimate that 80 percent of the damage would be concentrated in low-latitude countries: Africa, South-Eastern Asia, and Southern Asia mainly (Figure 4.2).

Despite the lack of precise estimations, it can be acknowledged with reasonable certainty that, if climate change impacts eventually materialize, they would lead to a growing divide between mature and new economies. Low-latitude countries around the Tropic of Cancer are likely to be the most impacted. Consequences on such economies, which also are the ones with the highest dynamic of population growth, could trigger massive migration. Around 40 percent of total migration today is related to climate change — this corresponds to around two million people a year. This figure, in worst-case scenarios, could be up 10 times in the coming decades.

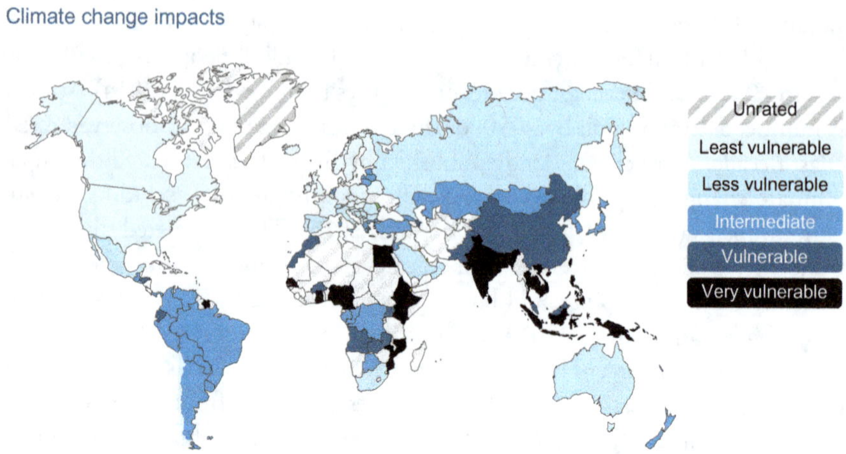

Figure 4.2 Climate change impacts (Wade and Jennings, 2016)

The Food and Water Problem

There are today around 800 million people who suffer from undernourishment. This is 200 million less than 25 years ago (Roser and Richie, 2018). This includes 16 percent of the total population of Southern Asia and 18 percent of that of Sub-Saharan Africa. Since 1960, the demand for food has been multiplied by nearly three times. With the growth of global population and the changes in consumption patterns, this picture is expected to evolve. Worldwide demand is expected to grow 70 percent by 2050 and 97 percent in new economies. Despite the standard caution that should be applied to forecasts, it is obvious that demand is on a clear upward trend.

In the last 50 years, cultivated land increased by only 12 percent. Rainfed lands have slightly decreased over the period (–0.2 percent), while irrigated lands have increased significantly (+117 percent). This shows that significant productivity yields have been reached, both around techniques on traditional rainfed lands and through the development of irrigated cultures, which typically provide twice the yield of traditional agriculture (The Food and Agriculture Organization of the United Nations, 2011).

Current projections show that land use is not expected to increase significantly. A critical indicator is the share of land per capita (hectares per capita or ha/cap). In mature economies, it is expected to drop from 0.62 to 0.45 ha/cap by 2050 in North America, remain stable around 0.25 ha/cap in Europe, but increase in Russia (from 0.8 to 1.03). This is a sign of continued productivity in agricultural yields. In new economies, it is expected to significantly drop everywhere, a counterintuitive outcome considering the current levels, current productivity yields, and expected growth in demand. It would notably yield levels as low as 0.1 ha/cap in Central America, Africa, Western Asia, and Southern Asia. In Central Asia, it could be halved (from 0.6 to 0.3 ha/cap) by that time (The Food and Agriculture Organization of the United Nations, 2011).

How can this disconnect between food demand growth and the limited evolution of cultivated land be explained? Land availability can, in part, explain it. Traditional agriculture, or rainfed agriculture, accounted for 83 percent of total cultivated lands in 2009. Some regions offer a greater potential for extending rainfed lands, such as Sub-Saharan Africa or Latin America. There, the increase in cultivated land seems a given and is properly reflected in projections. Other regions have much less ability to meet rising demand domestically (Citi GPS, 2018). This could be particularly acute for Northern Africa, the Middle East, and Central Asia, or Central America and Asia, which have already low levels of cultivated land per capita (Figure 4.3).

Many regions also face difficulties in extending their share of cultivated land, when available, because of the quality and accessibility of soils or because

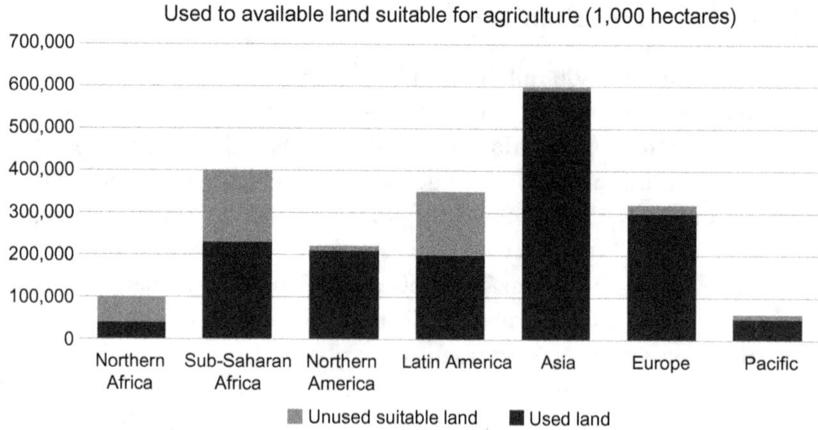

Figure 4.3 Used and available land suitable for agriculture (Citi GPS, 2018; The Food and Agriculture Organization of the United Nations, 2011)

the volume of rainfed land available is subject to change due to human activities. As an example, 40 percent of arable land in China would be polluted (Marshall, 2001), which further worsens the case of those regions.

The rise of food demand could lead, in some regions, to an inability to supply locally because of the low level of suitable land. Yet, a considerable potential for productivity improvements exist. Productivity is extremely uneven across regions. It can be as high as 10 tons per hectare (t/ha) for specific grains in Europe and as low as 0.5 t/ha in certain environmentally unfriendly regions of the Middle East, Central Asia, or Africa. As an example, maize production yields have evolved significantly across regions. It has doubled in Europe (2–5 t/ha) since 1960, tripled in South America (1–3 t/ha) but remained stable in Sub-Saharan Africa (1 t/ha). Today, most new economies (with the exception of East and South-Eastern Asia) have agricultural yields that are 50 percent below their optimal potential. For example, certain regions, like Northern Africa, Central America, or Central Asia, even experience gaps in yield below 40 percent. This is a critical theme for these regions that already have the lowest levels of cultivated land per capita. One of the ways to maximize crop yields is the use of fertilizers, mainly coming from phosphorus. With worldwide population increase, this resource becomes more and more critical to procure. Yet, 80 percent of the remaining phosphate rock reserves are located in Northern Africa (particularly in Morocco), and there are around 50 years of remaining reserves in the worst-case scenario at the current pace of production, though this figure remains highly debated (Cordell, 2017). Food demand increase thus creates new dependencies across regions, especially between Asia and Northern Africa.

The ability to significantly increase productivity yields of current cultivated lands remains an uncertainty, considering the relative availability of fertilizers and the massive gap that exists between regions. This is why the previous projections are worrisome, especially as they mainly concern regions with high population growth projections.

Climate change could also be an aggravating factor (The Food and Agriculture Organization of the United Nations, 2011). It could increase the productivity gap by 15 percent in North Africa and Central America, and nearly 10 percent in Sub-Saharan Africa and South America. In other regions, it would be lower, in the range of 5 percent in South and South-Eastern Asia for instance and could even benefit some regions like Central Asia with an estimated 20 percent improvement (The Food and Agriculture Organization of the United Nations, 2011). Again, projections are subject to challenges and the extent to which climate change will materialize remains a question. Yet, regions around the Tropic of Cancer, such as Central America, North Africa, or the Middle East combine all negative risks: low availability of land, potential drop in productivity yields because of climate change, and already low levels of productivity (Figure 4.4).

This shows that food scarcity could become more apparent in the coming decades.

On top of these issues is one of water availability. Freshwater withdrawals vary from one region to another and notably depend on agricultural patterns. Around 70 percent of water use is devoted to agriculture today (World Bank, 2018). Irrigation, which represents 17 percent of total cultivated land, offers double the traditional yield of rainfed land. They are a definite component of modern intensive agriculture yet depend largely on water availability. These

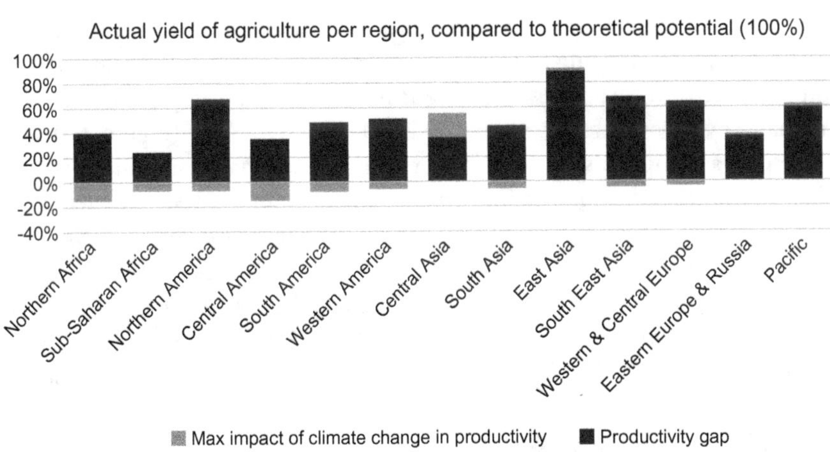

Figure 4.4 Actual yield of agriculture per region (The Food and Agriculture Organization of the United Nations, 2011)

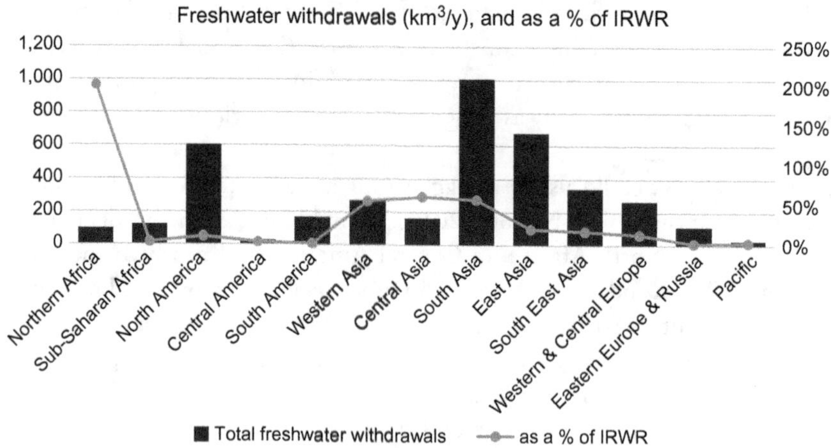

Figure 4.5 Freshwater withdrawals (World Bank, 2018)

withdrawals must be compared to the Internal Renewable Water Resources (IRWR), which is the maximum amount of water that can be sustainably withdrawn. Traditionally, it is estimated that above 20 percent of the IRWR ground water gets depleted, and water scarcity becomes apparent. Today, most of Asia (from Eastern Asia to the Middle East) and North Africa are facing ratios above 20 percent, even topping 200 percent for Northern Africa — a figure that is only going to get worse as the demand for food (and water) increases (Figure 4.5).

KPMG (2012) estimates demand to grow more than 50 percent between 2005 and 2030. Water scarcity is thus a critical phenomenon going forward for sustainable food production, particularly in Asia and North Africa, which accounts for close to 60 percent of the world population and a similar share of the increase of population going forward. Water scarcity can also be the result of a lack of proper water infrastructures. Again, estimates show that supply could be short on demand by as much as 40 percent by 2030 (KPMG, 2012) (Figure 4.6).

Despite assumptions on forecasts, it seems a reasonable statement that the problem of water stress, and its further consequences on food scarcity, will intensify in the coming decades. These issues will also transform regional geopolitics; something also known as hydropolitics (Lufkin, 2017). Today, there are 260 river basins that are shared by several countries (France Libertés, 2011; Castelo, 2018a; Friedman and Fedirka, 2017; Office of the Director of National Intelligence, 2012; Richey *et al.*, 2015). The most famous basins under pressure are those of:

- the Nile (between Egypt, Sudan, and Ethiopia);
- the Zambezi (between Zambia, Zimbabwe, and Botswana);
- the Euphrates (between Iraq, Syria, and Turkey);

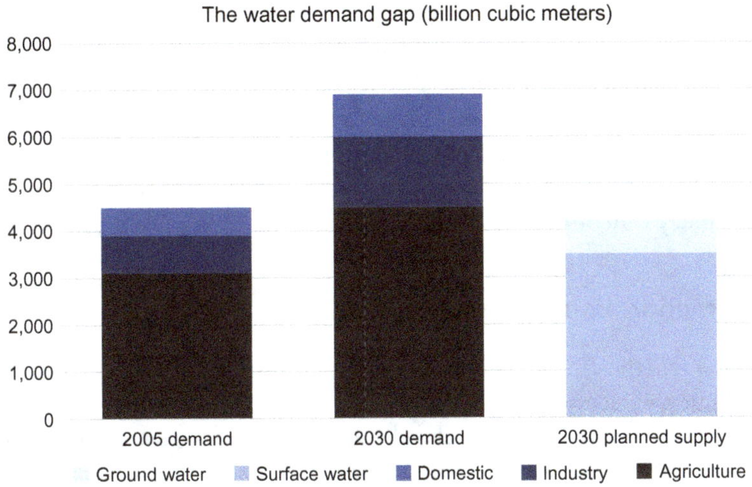

Figure 4.6 Water demand gap (KPMG, 2012)

- the Helmand River Basin (between Iran and Afghanistan);
- the Syr Darya (between Uzbekistan, Kazakhstan, and Tajikistan);
- the Indus basin (between Pakistan and India);
- the Ganges(between Bangladesh and India);
- the Mekong (between Cambodia, Laos, Thailand, and Vietnam);
- the Colorado (between the United States and Mexico).

The water stress associated with the depletion of reserves of these basins could lead to potential regional conflicts across those populations who are highly dependent on them.

Countries around the Tropic of Cancer (Central America, Northern Africa, the Middle East, Central Asia, the North of India, and a number of Eastern Asian countries) face significant risks of water stress and food scarcity going forward, and combine all negative potential impacts, from low land availability, lack of water resources, low productivity yields, and possible negative impacts from climate change. For these countries, a greater recourse to food trade would be necessary, although it would weaken these economies and create unsustainable dependencies; there are already 160 countries today, which would depend on imported food (Lufkin, 2017).

For these countries, a new paradigm for geopolitics of food and water is therefore emerging, with critical dependencies between neighbors sharing the same river basins and countries in a capacity to export excess food. The current extent and pace of changes, notably if climate change materializes rapidly, could trigger more massive migrations, away from "deserted" lands, turning local issues into global problems. These issues could materialize sooner than we think. The

Arabian Aquifer System would, for instance, be 80 percent depleted (Castelo, 2018b), and some projections expect that half of the world population could live in water-stressed areas as soon as 2025. At the time of the writing, a large migrant caravan left Central America to reach the United States, launching a violent antimigrant campaign and reaction from the United States administration. One of the factors that consolidated this sudden migration was food scarcity, a likely outcome of climate change (Milman *et al.*, 2018).

Key Interaction Points: The System Map

In this chapter, the first uncertainty explores global consequences on climate change, while the second dives deeper into global food and water issues. Climate change is an aggravating factor of the already apparent food and water problem, which is strongly pressured by inevitable demographics. These two issues could have a very significant impact on urbanization and migrations, hence impact further global geopolitics (Figure 4.7).

Summary

The work from the IPCC has projected anthropogenic forcing as a firm transformative factor of our time. This essentially takes the form of CO_2 emissions reduction, though they have grown 80 percent in the last decades. These CO_2 emissions are mainly related to the current energy system in which modern economies operate. Global economic development is leading to a projected rise of these emissions in the coming decades, and a significant energy transition appears to be the only solution to drastically reduce CO_2 emissions in a short period of time. These emissions translate into a greater level of concentration within the atmosphere, which increases the level of anthropogenic forcing. Already, concentration in the atmosphere has reached 400 ppm, compared to preindustrial levels that never exceeded 280 ppm. Most scientists agree that such levels of concentration could and likely will significantly impact the climate as we know it. Yet, the extent and pace of climate change is still an uncertainty.

The conclusions of the IPCC show that climate change could trigger massive irreversible transformations, from forests turning into savannas, the disappearance of mountain snowpacks, rising sea levels, and massive extinction of species. Several studies also show that climate change could lead to a significant economic downturn, although forecasts vary widely depending on the assumptions taken. Yet, all these studies seem to converge on the fact that most of the economic impact would have to be borne by countries situated in low latitudes, around the Tropic of Cancer.

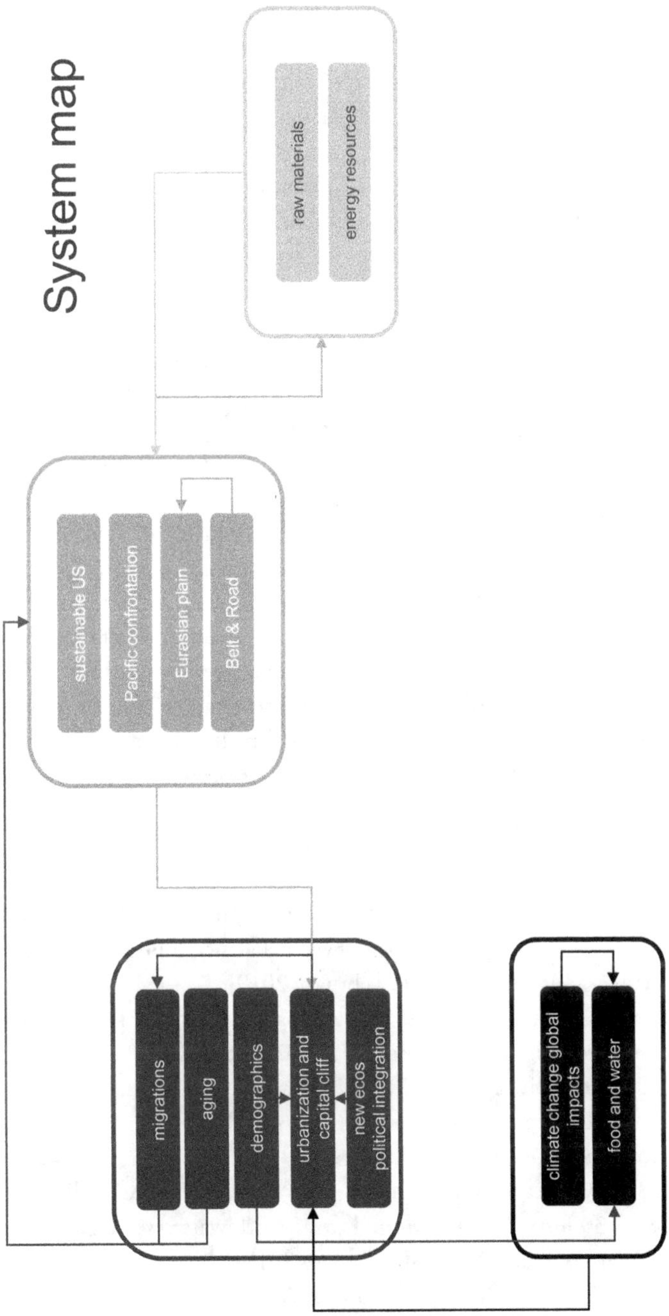

Figure 4.7 System map

A global food and water crisis is also upon us and, again, will mainly hit these countries. They combine all negative risks going forward: low agricultural productivity yields, low availability of land, already apparent issues of water scarcity, which is getting worse year after year. A clear global divide is emerging between these countries and the rest of the world, particularly between mature economies located in the Northern Hemisphere and new economies in the Southern Hemisphere.

The materiality of these changes is a major uncertainty that could bear enormous consequences to regional and global stability. From a regional standpoint, competition for water resources or suitable land could lead to large regional conflicts. From a global standpoint, the consequences of such a situation would lead to new geopolitics of food and water emerging, creating new dependencies across countries, which could weaken economies already catching up with their mature counterparts. While the population of these countries is expected to keep growing at a rapid pace in the coming decades, the impact of climate change could also trigger massive migrations toward mature economies from the Northern Hemisphere, notably Europe.

Forecasts and projections, as always, are prey to many challenges because of the assumptions they are based on. In this particular context, however, some of these changes are already visible. Depleted water basins, local conflicts over resources, and climate-related migrations are accelerating. Have we seen it all or is this just the beginning of larger transformations? What if this changes everything? More importantly, who could lead the global community into change? Which nation could build the technological and financial foundations for it? Ahead of this truly global challenge, coordination efforts have so far clearly not been up to task.

References

Amadeo, K. (2019). "Climate Change Facts and Effect on the Economy," *The Balance*, 27 January. Available from: https://www.thebalance.com/economic-impact-of-climate-change-3305682 [Accessed: February 2019].

Burke, M., Hsiang, S. and Miguel, E. (2015). "Global Non-Linear Effect of Temperature on Economic Production," *Nature*, 527, 235–239. doi: 10.1038/nature15725.

Castelo, J. (2018a). "10 Critical Water Scarcity Facts We Must Not Ignore," *World Water Reserve*, 14 November. Available from: https://worldwaterreserve.com/water-crisis/water-scarcity-facts/ [Accessed: February 2019].

Castelo, J. (2018b). "Causes of Water Conflict: Past Wars and Future Predictions," *World Water Reserve*, 30 June. Available from: https://worldwaterreserve.com/water-crisis/causes-of-water-conflict/ [Accessed: February 2019].

Citi GPS. (2018). Citi GPS: *Feeding the Future*. Available from: https://www.privatebank.citibank.com/home/fresh-insight/citi-gps-feeding-the-future.html [Accessed: February 2019].

Cordell, D. (2017). *The Story of Phosphorus*. Phosphorus Futures. Available from: http://phosphorusfutures.net/the-phosphorus-challenge/the-story-of-phosphorus-8-reasons-why-we-need-to-rethink-the-management-of-phosphorus-resources-in-the-global-food-system/ [Accessed: February 2019].

EPA. (2020). "Global Greenhouse Gas Emissions Data," *US Environmental Protection Agency*. Available from: https://www.epa.gov/ghgemissions/global-greenhouse-gas-emissions-data [Accessed: January 2020].

The Food and Agriculture Organization of the United Nations. (2011). *The State of the World's Land and Water Resources*. Available from: http://www.fao.org/nr/solaw/solaw-home/en/ [Accessed: February 2019].

France Libertés — Fondation Danielle Miterrand. (2011). *Geopolitics of Water*. Available from: https://www.france-libertes.org/fr/geopolitics-of-water/ [Accessed: February 2019].

Friedman, G. and Fedirka, A. (2017). "Water and Geopolitical Imperatives," *Geopolitical Futures*, 27 February. Available from: https://geopoliticalfutures.com/water-geopolitical-imperatives/ [Accessed: February 2019].

IFREMER. (2019). "Absorption de CO2: comment l'océan régule le climat?" *Institut français de recherche pour l'exploitation de la mer*, 4 December. Available from: https://wwz.ifremer.fr/L-ocean-pour-tous/Nos-ressources-pedagogiques/Comprendre-les-oceans/Ocean-et-climat/Absorption-de-CO2-comment-l-ocean-regule-le-climat [Accessed: December 2019].

International Energy Agency. (2014). *World Energy Outlook 2014*, ©OECD/IEA publishing. All rights reserved. License: www.iea.org/t&c, as modified by V. Petit. Available from: https://doi.org/10.1787/weo-2014-en [Accessed: February 2019].

International Energy Agency. (2019). *CO2 Emissions from Fuel Combustion Highlights 2019*, ©OECD/IEA publishing. All rights reserved. License: www.iea.org/t&c, as modified by V. Petit. Available from: https://webstore.iea.org/co2-emissions-from-fuel-combustion-2019-highlights [Accessed: February 2019].

IPPC. (2014). *Climate Change 2014 Impacts, Adaptation, and Vulnerability Part A: Global and Sectoral Aspects*. New York: Cambridge University Press. Available from: https://www.ipcc.ch/report/ar5/wg2/ [Accessed: February 2019].

KPMG. (2012). *Expect the Unexpected: Building Business Value in a Changing World*. Available from: https://home.kpmg.com/xx/en/home/insights/2012/02/building-business-value.html [Accessed: February 2019].

KPMG. (2014). *Future State 2030*. Available from: https://home.kpmg.com/xx/en/home/insights/2015/03/future-state-2030.html [Accessed: February 2019].

Lufkin, B. (2017). "Why Hydro-Politics Will Shape the 21st Century," *BBC Future*, 16 June. Available from: http://www.bbc.com/future/story/20170615-why-hydro-politics-will-shape-the-21st-century [Accessed: February 2019].

Marshall, T. (2001). *Prisoners of Geography: Ten Maps That Tell You Everything You Need to Know About Global Politics*. London: Elliott & Thompson.

Milankovitch, M. (1920). *Théorie mathématique des phénomènes thermiques produits par la radiation solaire*. Paris: Gauthier-Villars et cie.

Milman, O., Holden, E. and Agren, D. (2018). "The Unseen Driver Behind the Migrant Caravan: Climate Change," *The Guardian*, 30 October. Available from: https://www.theguardian.com/world/2018/oct/30/migrant-caravan-causes-climate-change-central-america?CMP=share_btn_link [Accessed: February 2019].

Much Ado About Climate. (2013). "4.5 Billion Years of the Earth's Temperature," *Much Ado About Climate*, 3 August. Available from: https://muchadoaboutclimate.wordpress.com/2013/08/03/4-5-billion-years-of-the-earths-temperature/ [Accessed: February 2019].

NASA Earth Observatory. (2017). *World of Change: Global Temperatures*. Available from: https://earthobservatory.nasa.gov/Features/WorldOfChange/decadaltemp.php [Accessed: February 2019].

National Academies. (2009). *G8+5 Academies' Joint Statement: Climate Change and the Transformation of Energy Technologies for a Low Carbon Future*. Available from: http://www.nationalacademies.org/includes/G8+5energy-climate09.pdf [Accessed: February 2019].

Office of the Director of National Intelligence. (2012). *Global Water Security*. Available from: https://www.dni.gov/files/documents/Special%20Report_ICA%20Global%20Water%20Security.pdf[Accessed: February 2019].

Richey, A. S., Thomas, B. F., Lo, M.-H., Reager, J. T., Famiglietti, J. S., Voss, K., Swenson, S. and Rodell, M. (2015). "Quantifying Renewable Ground Water Stress with GRACE," *Water Resources Research*, 51, 5217–5238. doi: 10.1002/2015WR017349.

Roser, M. and Richie, H. (2018). "Hunger and Undernourishment," *Our World in Data*. Available from: https://ourworldindata.org/hunger-and-undernourishment [Accessed: February 2019].

Teske, S., Sawyer, S. and Schäfer, O. (2015). *Energy [R]evolution — A Sustainable World Energy Outlook 2015*, Greenpeace, September 2015. Available from: http://www.greenpeace.org/international/Global/international/publications/climate/2015/Energy-Revolution-2015-Full.pdf [Accessed: February 2019].

Wade, K. and Jennings, M. (2016). "The Impact of Climate Change on the Global Economy," *Schroders*, 31 August. Available from: https://www.schroders.com/nl/sysglobalassets/digital/us/pdfs/the-impact-of-climate-change.pdf [Accessed: February 2019].

Worland, J. (2015). "Climate Change Could Wreck the Global Economy," *Time*, 22 October. Available from: http://time.com/4082328/climate-change-economic-impact/ [Accessed: February 2019].

The World Bank. (2018). *Water in Agriculture*. Available from: https://www.worldbank.org/en/topic/water-in-agriculture [Accessed: February 2019].

World Meteorological Organization. (2016). *WMO Greenhouse Gas Bulletin*. Available from: https://ane4bf-datap1.s3-eu-west-1.amazonaws.com/wmocms/s3fs-public/GHG_Bulletin_12_EN_web_JN161640.pdf?aZaKZhdpDfJdmHvtbSvLwbj6zb_PWwdz [Accessed: February 2019].

CHAPTER 5

Change 5 — Sustainable Global Economy

For nearly a decade, the world has operated in a very unusual economic context, characterized by a high level of globalization, low cost of capital, but limited inflation and growth from all major economies. Will this paradigm continue, or will it change in the coming years or decades? What are the key forces at play?

As a starting point, it is essential to present a theoretical framework to understand what will be examined at in this chapter.

There are typically four main factors that shape the economy of a country. The first one is the Gross Domestic Product (GDP), or the output from the "work" and "consumption" of a nation. The GDP is mainly driven by four types of inputs:

- Labor force participation: the number of people participating to the economic activity.
- Population demand: the demand (or consumption) from people.
- Productivity: the productivity yields in manufacturing or services. Traditionally, productivity has been more important in manufacturing than in services.
- Capital investments: investments in the economic activity to create more "supply" capacities to respond to evolving demand.

The slow economic growth of most mature economies today can be explained by a combination of these factors: slow increase to flat number of people participating in the economy; depressed demand; low technical productivity yields (because today's economy is more driven by services); and limited capital investment (due to depressed demand and the inherent limits of global trade). The growth in GDP in new economies is higher as the same inputs apply differently: the population today keeps expanding, demand is booming (notably with urbanization), and, since exports are on the rise, these economies also tend to see an increase in capital investments.

The second factor is the actual wealth of the population and of governments. This wealth is made of both real estate and financial assets. The product of the economic activity yields yearly savings that directly impact the wealth of a population. Global wealth distribution is a much less disclosed and obvious factor than the GDP, but is considerably more important, as it highlights the cumulated assets that a population or a government own. Wealth enables capital to be dispatched. In the following pages, we will refer to capital as pure financial assets. We consider real estate as a separate source of wealth, and financial capital is made of equity, bonds, and loans.

Part of a country's capital can be directly invested in the economy or lent through contracted debt. Debt plays a critical role in a modern economy as it enables to the acceleration of (capital) investments and fosters demand. When the use of debt is increasing, it is said that an economy is "leveraging." When, on the contrary, debt is being reduced, an economy is "deleveraging." Typical cycles of leveraging and deleveraging follow each other, roughly every 10–20 years (Dalio, 2018). The rationale for deleveraging is an excessive burden of debt interests on the economy, which usually yields slow economic growth because of a corresponding reduction of the capacity to invest, with the economic output being used to repay old debt.

Finally, economic activity has an impact on prices. If the balance of supply versus demand is not perfect, then prices tend to rise or deflate. The central bank of a country will regulate inflation and deflation through interest rates. These set points will influence the level of currency on global markets, hence global competitiveness. Then, an excess of available capital tends to pressure interest rates downward while scarcity will, on the contrary, pressure them upward. Interest rates are thus a complicated combination of various inputs. The world has been entering a period of low interest rates globally for a decade, essentially driven by an excess of capital available — this is what Ben Bernanke famously referred to as the "Global Saving Glut" in 2005 (Bernanke, 2005).

From the simple overview in Figure 5.1, things become slightly more complex as countries interact with one another. Essentially, countries around the world exchange:

- Goods and services through trade.
- Capital and debt through financial exchanges.

The balance of exchanges leads to what is known as account (im)balance(s). The balance of financial and trade exchanges impacts the currencies of each country that partakes in the economic interaction.

Trade enables the population of a given country to consume a product or service manufactured in another. As the good (or service) moves from

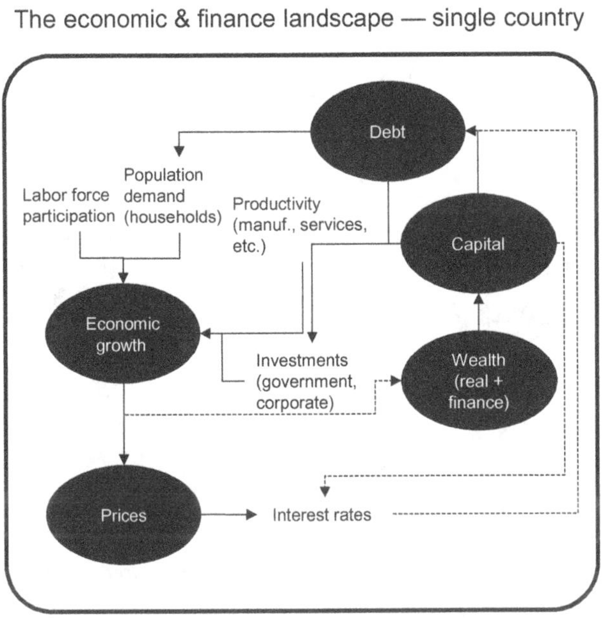

Figure 5.1 Economic and financial landscape for one country

country A to B, a financial transaction operates from country B to A. The more goods and services are exported, the more financial reserves are being accumulated.

Capital also navigates across countries, following a similar principle. Capital can be directly invested from country A into country B through foreign direct investment (FDI) or equity. It can also be lent as a debt between a creditor (country A) and a debtor (country B), the latter will then invest this money locally. A specific amount of money is transferred from country A to B and progressively reimbursed back from country B to A, with interest. Debt can take essentially two forms, loans (securitized or not) and bonds (government, corporate or financial). The volume of debt is critical, as interest can impact growth of the economy over a certain level, which triggers deleveraging. International capital flows and foreign asset positions are also fundamental, as they define what a country will inherit from capital revenues from economic activity in other countries and its own. Piketty (2014) has, for instance, explained that most of the revenue from capital in several Sub-Saharan African countries was leaving the country, significantly impacting their account balance and ability to generate wealth over the long term.

Both trade and capital exchanges have an impact on currency exchanges, alongside inflation/deflation and interest rates set by central banks — the higher

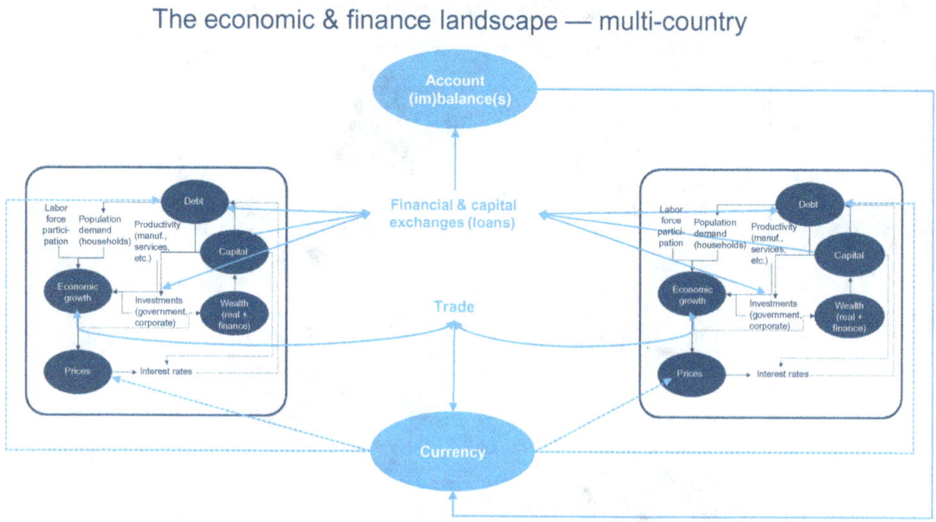

Figure 5.2 Economic and financial landscape between countries

the interest rate, the higher the exchange rate of a currency. This has several impacts, meaning the higher the inflation, the lower the exchange rate. This, in turn, means the higher the trade surplus, the higher the currency. Finally, the higher the capital inflows, the higher the valuation of the currency (Figure 5.2).

Four key topics will now be reviewed in this chapter. First, the evolution of global goods trade, followed by the evolution of capital distribution, then the status of financial globalization, concluding with a review on debt situations. These topics are good proxies for understanding the global economic situation and how sustainable it is.

The Future of Global Trade

Economics largely define the actual relationship between nations. Trading of goods has been around for millennia, even over large regions of the world (Frankopan, 2017), and it constitutes the primary set of relationships that countries establish in search of resources or products to fuel their economy. To a large extent, then, global goods trade defines geopolitics. Notable instances include the Anglo-Dutch wars in the seventeenth century; the Opium Wars in the nineteenth century between Western economies and China; and, more recently, the trade tariff conflicts that took center stage in 2018 between the United States and China.

Over the last 15 years, the world has become more intricate, with massive shifts in dependencies. Global goods trade exchanges represented around 10 percent of GDP in 2001, rising to 15 percent in 2016. During this period, trade expanded three-fold (to reach US$16 trillion in 2016), while GDP doubled (from US$60 trillion to US$100 trillion; Shell, 2018; UN Trade Statistics, 2018). The development has been significant everywhere, but particularly in Europe and Asia, which remain the most exporting economies. Overall, Europe is the largest exporting economy of the world in volume and percentage.

Yet, it is important to understand the destination of actual trade (UN Trade Statistics, 2018). About 40 percent of global trade occurs within the boundaries of a given region with country neighbors, called intraregional flows. For instance, 66 percent of global European trade occurs within Europe itself, and more than 30 percent of North America's trade is between Canada, United States, and Mexico. To understand the global landscape of trade and its impact on geopolitics, those exchanges must therefore be factored out, and the focus must be on interregional flows or trade exchanges across regions.

Once factored out, interregional flows represented close to US$10 trillion in 2016 (around 10 percent of global GDP), with a good balance across regions. Some regions, such as Western Asia or Europe, are slightly higher with 12 percent of the world average, while others stand slightly below, like China or North America who hold 8 percent. With 10 percent of GDP impact, interregional flows are critical to the economy, but these should not be exceedingly considered as crucial to economic development. The bulk of the economy remains local.

When looking at exports, two regions truly dominate the global landscape — Europe and China, at US$2 trillion and US$1.5 trillion, respectively; though China stands on par with Europe if we include commerce with its close neighbors in East Asia. North America comes in at a close third with around US$1.2 trillion of exports. The destination of these exports varies significantly and sheds light on key dependencies. China, for instance, has strong dependencies on North America and Europe, with 20 percent of total Chinese exports each. East and South East Asia are also strongly dependent on China with around 30 percent of their exports directed there. North America is strongly dependent on Latin America (20 percent) and Europe (20 percent) for its exports, yet not to China (7 percent). Around 50 percent of Latin America exports are, however, tied to North America, making it extremely dependent on its neighbor. Europe is more balanced and enjoys commerce with most regions of the world, even though 25 percent of its exports are directed toward North America. Europe is also the first trade partner of the Commonwealth of Independent States (CIS; 50 percent of CIS imports) and Africa (50 percent of Northern Africa, 26 percent of Sub-Saharan Africa), leading to significant ties with these regions (Figure 5.3).

The picture slightly changes when looking at import flows (UN Trade Statistics, 2018). There, North America largely relies on Europe, Latin America, *and* Chinese imports (around 20 percent each). Unsurprisingly, Europe essentially relies on imports from China and North America (at 20 percent of interregional imports each). Finally, China mostly relies on imports from Europe and Eastern Asia (Figure 5.4).

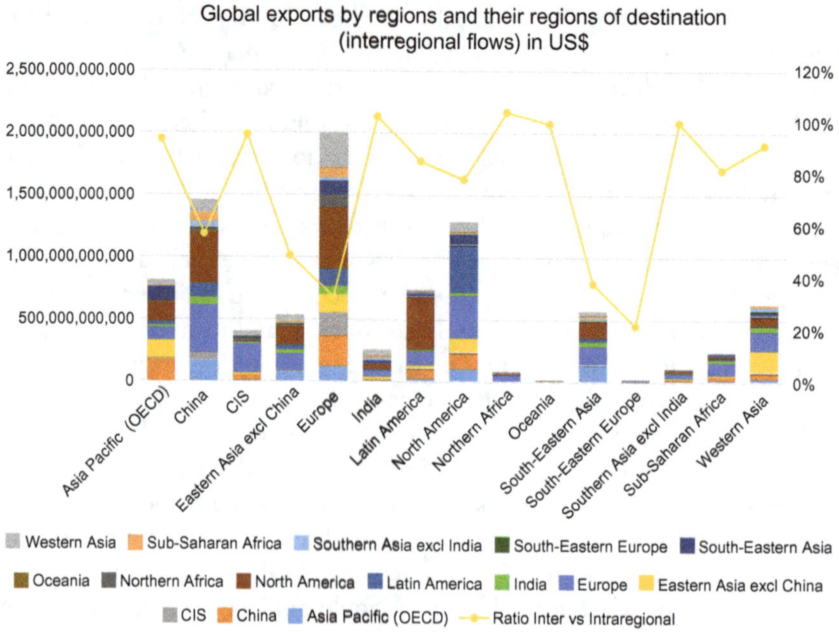

Figure 5.3 Global exports by region (UN Trade Statistics, 2018)

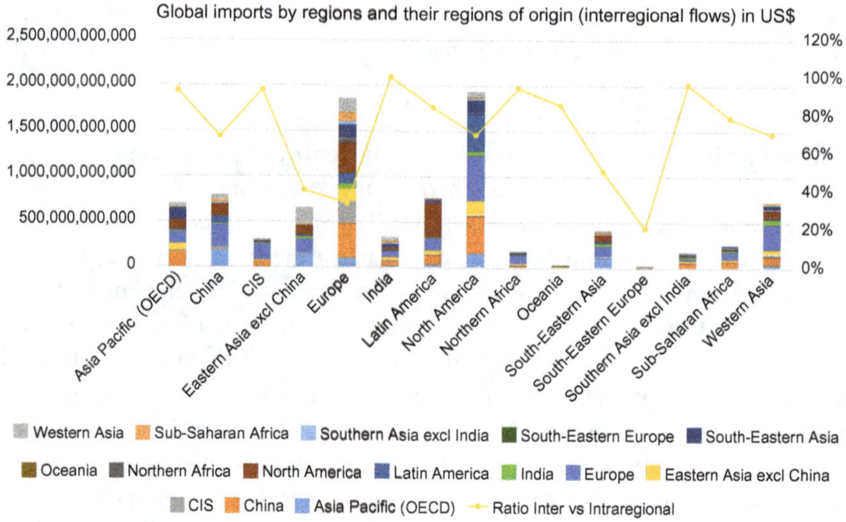

Figure 5.4 Global imports by region (UN Trade Statistics, 2018)

Another way to look at this is to evaluate the commercial balance of key regions, focusing on interregional export and import flows (Figure 5.5). At a global level, a major imbalance exists with China being a major exporter to the world and North America a major importer. This major difference drives commercial imbalances between China and North America to a large extent and, to a lesser extent, between Europe and North America, and Europe and China. Also interesting, though less important in volume of trade, Western Asia is a significant importer of goods from Europe, while at the same time significantly exporting to Eastern Asia and OECD Asia Pacific. India, Southern Asia, and Africa are net importers, from both Europe and North America, meaning they import more than they export.

The analysis of the evolution of trade balance across regions between 2001 and 2016 also shows that a significant part of this situation has materialized in the last 15 years.

These structural gaps in goods trade have had an obvious impact on the current account balance and size of total (cash) reserves. The current account balance is the result of the difference between flows as well as incomes coming from investments and cash transfers, like remittances for instance. The 2005–2016 current account balance evolution of the last 10 years shows that Europe, China, and North America have the largest positive account balance over the past decade, but for different reasons. Europe and China benefit from the size of their exports, particularly China, which has a positive balance of trade. Europe is also a primary destination for investments, and this impacts its account balance negatively with dividends leaving the region. North America is the largest recipient of primary incomes, a sign that the region actually lends capital to the rest of the world, and this is what primarily makes its account balance positive. Finally, most new economies have negative account balances, mainly driven by their net importer situations (World Integrated Trade Solutions, 2018).

As a consequence of these developments, total reserves have also evolved significantly. They have considerably increased in China, Eastern Asia, Western Asia, and Europe, reaching comfortable levels at around 15–20 percent of GDP. Beyond these, most other regions of the world show lower ratios of reserves, even though those have slightly increased over the past decade.

A new landscape has emerged in the last 15 years. Firstly, a global imbalance has appeared between China (in terms of trade credit and total reserves) and North America (in terms of trade deficit). This has significant geopolitical consequences that weigh heavily on China–US relations, as was exemplified by the recent trade conflicts between the two economic powerhouses. Since then, a global economic concentration revolving around three blocs has consolidated. The Americas are a paradigm that first expanded, with a stronger dependency of

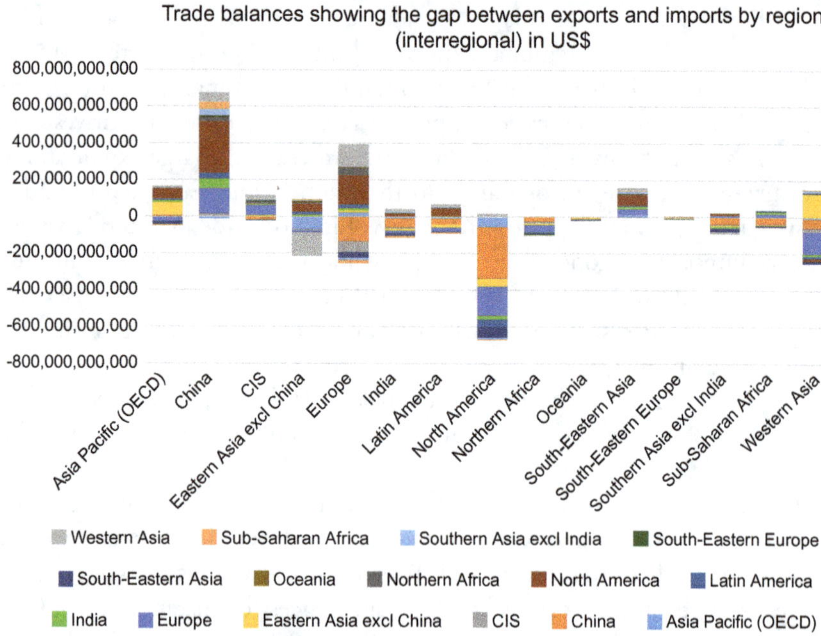

Figure 5.5 Trade gaps between exporting and importing (UN Trade Statistics, 2018)

Latin America to North America. Then, an Eastern (and South-Eastern) Asian bloc has emerged, revolving around China, with major dependencies from the countries of the region to China. This was followed by the continued integration of Europe, making it the first region in terms of global goods trade to be a true multilateral player, with limited dependencies to any specific region of the world. Western Asia has started to integrate within the global economy, with a significant rise of imports from Europe and exports to Asia. However, the region is massively imbalanced between Middle East oil exporting countries and others, notably in terms of current account balance and cash reserves. Finally, other regions of the world (Africa, India, Southern Asia) have so far remained relatively isolated from global economic interactions. Most new economies have recorded trade deficits over this period, a sign of their inability to actually integrate global economic competition, thereby limiting overall volume of possible imports in the long run and thus sustainable economic development. This is particularly true for Africa, Western Asia, and Southern Asia (including India). The main beneficiaries of global trade over the period have been China (US$600 billion of surplus) and Europe (US$150 billion).

The question that then arises is whether these imbalances are sustainable. Will they become heightened; particularly as the industrial power of China increases, and will governments around the world (like the United States) react to this in a brutal or a softer form? Another uncertainty is whether or not nonintegrated economies will eventually manage to join global trade exchanges and develop their economies at a rapid pace in the coming decades. These questions illustrate the major uncertainties going forward.

Capital Distribution: Toward Further Inequalities

While global trade helps us to understand dependencies in economic growth, it does not give a perspective on wealth distribution. Therefore, the landscape of capital is as important, if not more so, than that of trade and economic activity.

Global wealth is a result of the accumulation of savings from economic output. It can be of two sorts: real estate and financial assets (capital). It concerns the population (each household) and governments. There are thus four sources of wealth to consider: real estate (households, governments) and financial assets (households, governments).

Here we have analyzed the evolution of wealth since 2000 and its global distribution using five main sources of inputs: the global wealth distribution report (Shorrocks, *et al.*, 2015), a Bain & Company (2012) report on global assets, a study on global financial assets from Lund *et al.* (2013), a report by Barnes at Savills (2018) on worldwide real estate values, as well as a study on global debt detailed in the last part of this chapter. We have compiled and cross-checked the figures available to present this complex matter in the simplest way. The following analysis is pretty robust in terms of households' wealth but could possibly underestimate the actual real estate and financial wealth of governments as these figures are not easily disclosed (Littman, 2017). We have thus made estimations that were then cross-checked with other analyses (Bain & Company, 2012; Desjardins, 2017).

Global wealth has doubled in 15 years, increasing from US$143 trillion in 2000 to around US$297 trillion in 2015. These figures include both real estate assets and financial assets while debt liabilities have been subtracted. They accounted for US$185 trillion globally in 2015.

The wealth of households has more than doubled, from US$97 trillion to over US$218 trillion, representing 73 percent of total wealth in 2015. The wealth of governments has also increased, though much more modestly, from US$45 trillion to US$79 trillion. The main source of increase in wealth is real estate, which progressed from US$124 trillion to US$251 trillion over the period, and accounts for 85 percent of total wealth today. The wealth in financial assets rose only from US$19 trillion to US$46 trillion, crippled by rising debt liabilities (Figure 5.6).

The geographical analysis shows a clear divide between regions. Mature economies captured 56 percent of global wealth increase, with North America

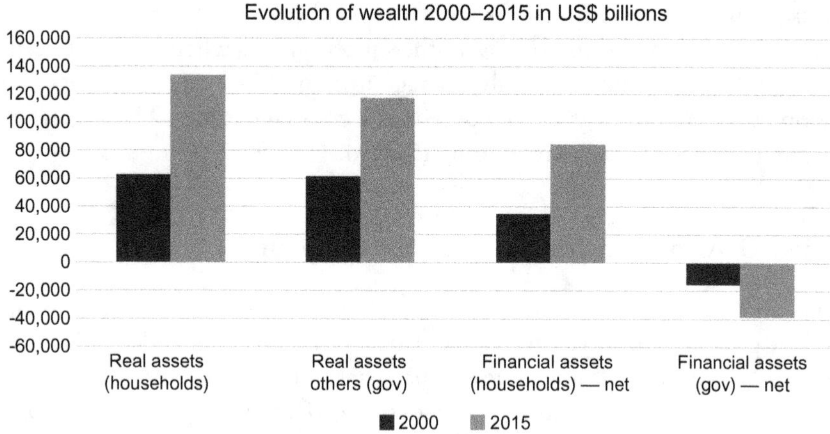

Figure 5.6 Evolution of wealth by type (Author's evaluation based on data from Bain & Company, 2012; Barnes, 2018; Desjardins, 2017; Littman, 2017; Lund *et al.*, 2013; Shorrocks *et al.*, 2015)

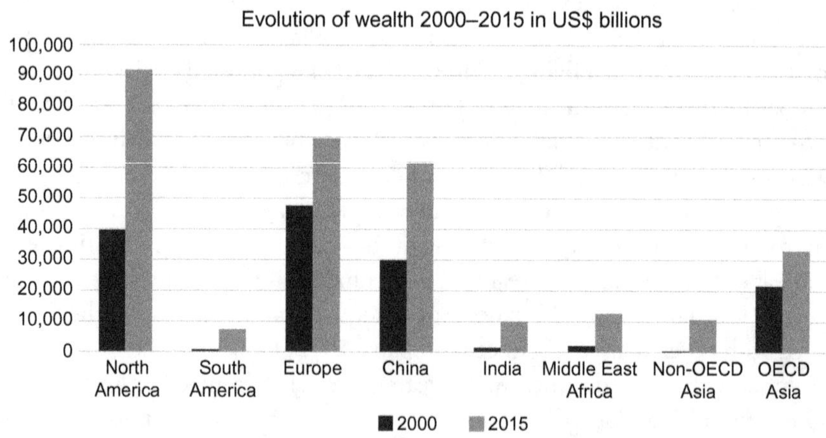

Figure 5.7 Evolution of wealth per region (Bain & Company, 2012; Barnes, 2018; Desjardins, 2017; Littman, 2017; Lund *et al.*, 2013; Shorrocks *et al.*, 2015)

alone accounting for 34 percent. China makes up 21 percent of the global wealth created, leaving other new economies with only 23 percent of global wealth. A further concentration of capital can be observed at a macro level. Wealth creation over the last 15 years has primarily benefited the rich. This is a factual conclusion that is often disregarded by many, which will cause dramatic consequences in the future, as the fracture lines across regions continue to grow (Figure 5.7).

Looking deeper into the details of wealth distribution per country, the analysis for 2015 shows the factor responsible for North America holding the greatest level of wealth distribution over this period is the significant rise in net financial assets, a unique situation globally. These financial assets are mainly in the hands of households and result from a financial deepening of the US economy, which is the largest in the world at 463 percent financial assets over GDP ratio, as per Lund *et al.* (2013). The financial deepening of an economy shows the level of financial services and exchanges for a given capital available, and the United States has the largest of the world. The nation is the bank of the world. Europe and China's have also seen a growth in wealth, which have mainly come from real estate valuation. Their volume of net financial assets has actually slightly declined over the years. Finally, and perhaps most strikingly, wealth creation has essentially benefited households in mature economies while they mostly benefited governments in new economies, with the exception of China, which has a nearly equal split. This is particularly true for South America, the Middle East, Africa, and India. While the world has gotten richer, it has not truly benefited most people (yet), and the actual wealth gap between mature economies and new economies has consequently worsened.

What does all of this suggest for the future?

One of the most provocative, yet unsurprising, outcomes of this analysis is that wealth creation has primarily favored mature economies, North America in particular. This is due to a natural financial deepening, which has enabled these economies to capture the dividends from increased economic output. Worldwide wealth per capita has increased, on average, from US$23,000/capita in 2000 to around US$40,000/capita in 2015. But this shows strong disparities across regions, as the 2015 variance (from mean to extreme) on wealth per capita is three times higher than that of 2000. What this regional study reinforces is the massive difference across mature and new economies that have increased in absolute value.

Obviously, there are also positive outcomes to this overall growth of wealth. Lakner and Milanovic (2013) have shown that poorer sections of population in new economies (particularly in Asia) have benefited more from this increase than middle-class populations in mature economies comparatively. Yet, compared to richer people, primarily located in mature economies, they have also received double the amount of lower benefits. If the global share of people living in extreme poverty is in decline, its rate is not even close to the pace at which already rich people accumulate wealth.

Piketty (2014) developed a theory on the natural concentration of capital in his book *Capital in the Twenty-First Century*. Piketty posits that concentration of wealth occurs when the rate of return on capital is higher than the rate of economic growth. His book puts this thesis in perspective by reviewing two centuries of national income reports in Europe and the United States. What Piketty also demonstrates is that at the beginning of the twentieth century, levels of capital concentration were much higher than today. He explains that the two world wars significantly transformed the landscape, leading to the belief that middle classes could elevate themselves through the ranks and build fortunes over one to two generations. His demonstration shows that the world, having previously enjoyed a sustained period of peace for several decades, is now getting progressively back to the initial situation it had known in the early 1900s. The previous observation of the last 15 years is another confirmation of Piketty's theory.

The actual spread of wealth distribution *within* a given economy also shows significant advancements in progress. Shorrocks *et al.* (2015) provide an extensive analysis of wealth distribution per category of the population and found that today 1 percent of the population owns 50 percent of global wealth and 8 percent own 85 percent. Thus capital is extremely concentrated across all economies (Figure 5.8).

Different countries show different patterns, with mature economies having a much larger concentration of wealthy people than new economies. The interesting factor is the growing share of Chinese population with wealth above US$10,000. One of the key achievements of the country in the last few decades has been to remove hundreds of millions of people from poverty, the results of which are demonstrated in this graph. As time passes, the question is whether more people from China and other new economies will eventually lift up their level of wealth. Reverting to Lakner and Milanovic, can this timid movement

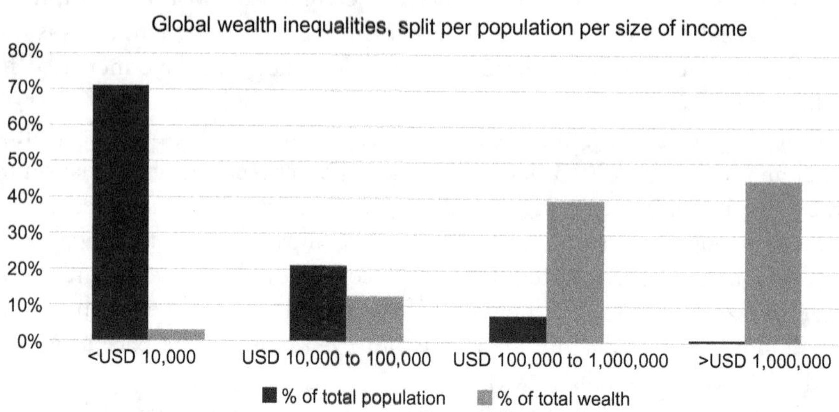

Figure 5.8 Wealth inequalities (Shorrocks *et al.*, 2015)

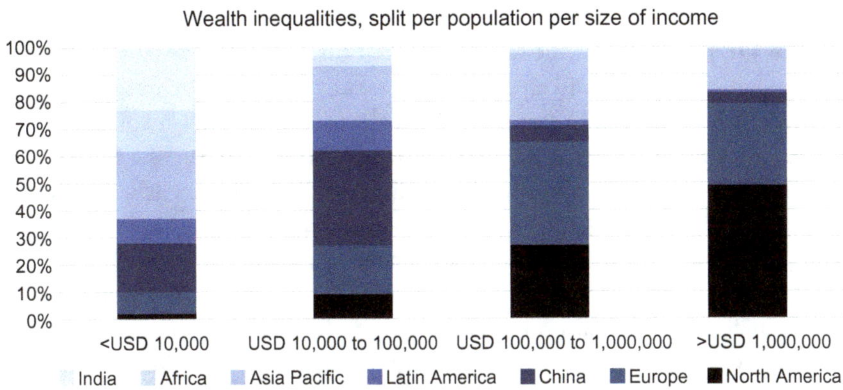

Figure 5.9 Wealth inequalities per region (Shorrocks *et al.*, 2015)

already engaged toward removing extreme poverty be dramatically accelerated? This would have significant consequences to the allocation of capital globally due to the size of population in new economies (Figure 5.9).

To summarize, global capital expansion has been concentrated in the last 15 years in mature economies, particularly the United States, thanks to its increased financial deepening. Globalization of exchanges has primarily benefited those who hold capital already, confirming Piketty's theory that rich people tend to get richer, relatively to others. This is also confirmed when looking at the evolution of inequalities within countries. The question, therefore, is whether this situation will continue de facto. With the rise of China as a new, yet powerful, economy, will the traditional paradigm of wealth concentration be upheld within mature economies? Will global institutions, which in some way enable this, continue as per their initial design? Will people globally accept this status quo? In new economies, wealth creation has notably been captured by governments. Will this be redistributed, and will the coming decades see a rise of living standards, or not? All these questions represent key uncertainties.

Financial Globalization Sustained Reality

It is often stated that financial globalization stopped after the 2008 crisis. It is true that global cross-border capital flows have significantly decreased over the last 10 years by more than two-thirds, from a high of US$12.4 trillion per year in 2007 to US$3.8 trillion per year (London and Lund, 2017; Lund *et al.*, 2017, 2018). As a result of this, global capital account imbalances have also decreased, making the overall financial system more stable.

Yet, if the volume of yearly flows has reduced, financial globalization has not retreated. On the contrary, the total volume of foreign capital assets (and liabilities) has continued to build up, even at a slower pace, and represents around 125 percent of global GDP today. This volume rose from US$30 trillion in 2000 to around US$107 trillion in 2015 (Lund *et al.*, 2013). The flows themselves represent US$3.8 trillion per year; double those of the early 2000s, or a similar level in share of GDP at around 4 percent. Financial globalization is ongoing, and interconnections have never been stronger.

Figure 5.10 shows the dominant position of mature economies' financial markets in foreign capital exchanges, though global financial centers such as Luxembourg, Switzerland, Singapore, Hong Kong, and so on, are excluded. We must note that two-thirds of foreign claims from European banks are within Europe itself (Lund *et al.*, 2017). Hence, the volume of foreign claims outside the borders of the region are much lower, likely closer to those of OECD Asia. The most interconnected region is North America, and this is consistent with everything we have seen thus far. Net flows are positive in Europe and OCED Asia, meaning that the regions export their capital. The situation is surprisingly different in North America, with a negative capital deficit of US$400 billion per year, an indication that the United States in particular is actually a destination of investment, even though it is also the largest provider of capital to the world. It shows the dynamism and the attractiveness of the American economy and is not necessarily an issue as long as the economy remains attractive, and investments are deemed profitable in relation to their safety. In addition, the level of yearly deficit in North America has declined in the past 15 years and is stabilizing. The United States is clearly leading the financial world, and this is possibly the most important tie and dependency that the country has with other regions, beyond goods trade and resource exchanges.

Foreign assets in North America represent 25 percent of total financial assets today, the highest level in the world. It shows that many economies in the world also benefit from the dynamism of the North American economy, and that the local population partially reaps some of the benefits from local growth, which are reinvested into financial assets in the United States, and abroad. In the long run, the volume of flows presents a potential risk for the economic activity (GDP) due to its volatility. In Europe and OECD Asia, the level of foreign assets is lower, at around 16 percent. For Europe specifically, it is probably significantly lower if we consider the volume of foreign assets coming from the Eurozone itself. Again, the United States holds a unique position in the globalized economy.

Going beyond the United States, China is a net supplier of capital to the world and has built some significant assets abroad in the last 15 years. The size of its net flows is, however, decreasing year on year, heading toward zero as demand in China picks up.

Outside of China, new economies have started to integrate into the global finance landscape, but they start from a very low base and many of these economies are net recipients of capital. The ratio of these capital investments over GDP is lower than for mature economies (in the range of 2 percent), however, they are subject to more volatility due to the uncertainties revolving around their economic output stability, which could play a non-negligible role in future. Economic and financial integration in the global system is not a given: size and stability matter. The levels of foreign assets and liabilities are generally much lower, in the range of 10 percent, except for South America, suggesting that these regions are more isolated from a financial standpoint. Yet, in the Middle East and Africa, the situation varies dramatically across countries. Sub-Saharan Africa particularly is known for its high share of foreign liabilities. Some countries are consequently very exposed to capital inflows and outflows and, for some of them, a financial crisis is never far away. This situation is likely to evolve in the coming decades. There is a notably high need for capital investments in infrastructures in most new economies, which, as previously discussed, will depend on the level of foreign private investments. The stability of these economies will play a critical role in enabling this to happen (Figure 5.10).

As discussed, the United States has a specific position in the financial landscape due to the financial deepening of its economy. Yet, who controls these flows? Who lends money to the world?

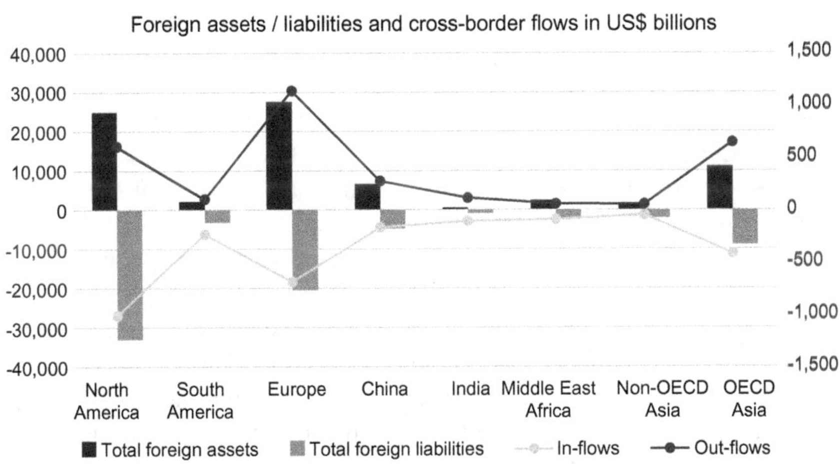

Figure 5.10 Foreign assets and liabilities (London and Lund, 2017; Lund *et al.*, 2013, 2017, 2018)

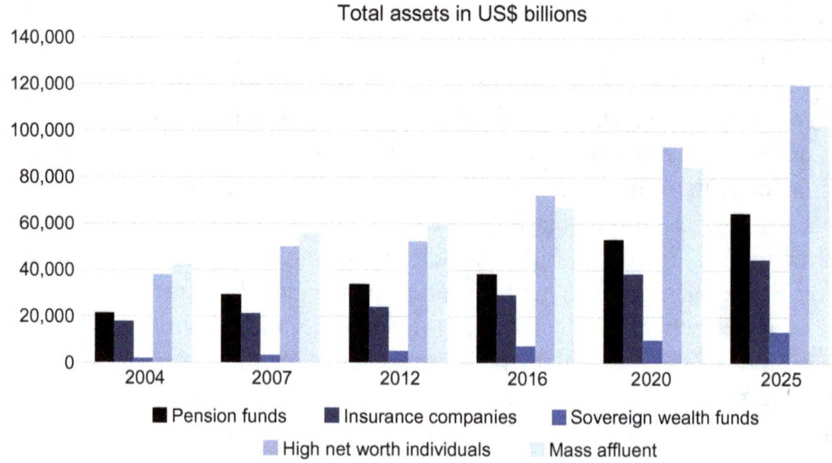

Figure 5.11 Total assets (London and Lund, 2017; Lund *et al.*, 2013, 2017, 2018)

All these financial assets can actually be privately owned or managed by institutions, such as pension funds or insurance companies. PricewaterhouseCoopers (2017) showed that pension funds and insurance companies represent one-third of total assets globally, while mass affluent and high net worth individuals represent two-thirds of the total (Figure 5.11).

A share of these assets is being managed by specialized firms. When this is the case, these assets are referred to as "under management." They represented around US$85 trillion in 2016, or close to 40 percent of total assets. This share has gone up in the last decade, despite the 2008 financial crisis, and PricewaterhouseCoopers (2017) believes it will continue to increase, though at a very slow pace. This makes a lot of sense in a world where capital is abundant and the race for higher returns and dividends is prominent. North America stands out as the region with the greatest volume of assets under management, a sign of greater financial deepening of the American economy (Fages *et al.*, 2018; Lund *et al.*, 2013; PricewaterhouseCoopers, 2017). Indeed, there are twice the number assets under management in North America than in Europe, two regions with similar GDP and — as seen above — relatively similar wealth (in Western Europe specifically). Pension funds play a significant role in those differences. While the use of pension funds is generalized in the United States, it is far from being the case in Europe, where pensions are largely controlled by governments in many countries. Other regions of the world have even lower levels of financial deepening (except South America, which ranges close to that of the United States). In the Asia Pacific, however, the level of financial deepening is generally low, yet developing with economic integration into global markets by countries from the region and the reforms on financial institutions (Fages *et al.*, 2018; Lund *et al.*, 2013; PricewaterhouseCoopers, 2017).

These assets under management are being handled by specific firms that specialize in optimizing returns. They look into different categories of investments: bonds (government and corporate) and equity form the bulk of those, at around two-thirds of the total if we consider Europe as a benchmark (European Fund and Asset management Association, 2018; Murphy *et al.*, 2018). Other types of investments include currencies, real estate, resources (commodities), and infrastructures. The top 400 asset managers manage up to US$66 trillion in 2018, or 75 percent of total assets under management (IPE Reference Hub, 2018). Current trends show an increased concentration of assets being managed by mega funds above US$5 trillion (MacArthur, 2018).

Finally, it is worth noting that the equity market has significantly transformed in the last decades. On the one hand, the number of public companies has dropped 50 percent in the last 20 years (Amine, 2018). On the other hand, private market assets have significantly increased, totaling more than US$5 trillion to date of assets under management (McKinsey & Company, 2018b), including US$2.3 trillion of private equity alone, the rest being invested in real estate, private debt, resources, or infrastructures. This is still a low number with regards to overall assets under management, or the total of public companies' market valuation, yet it is growing fast.

So, what can we conclude from all this?

First, financial globalization keeps expanding and has become a sustained reality of our time. In no way has it retreated. It is primarily a product of mature economies investing capital abroad and, despite a slowdown in recent years, new economies are getting more and more integrated into global financial (capital) exchanges. Most new economies (with the notable exception of China) are net recipients, with some regions seeing a significant share of their activity and assets funded from abroad. The levels are low, however. Within mature economies, North America stands out as a net recipient with US$400 billion of foreign (net) capital being injected into the country every year, and has 25 percent of foreign liabilities, the highest share in the world, while others have positive balances. The question of the sustainability of such capital flows is therefore apparent.

Let's also remember that the financial world has been operating with low interest rates for the last decade. The level of economic development of new economies can theoretically yield further wealth creation, notably as financial assets, which would further accelerate the economy (and lower capital costs). This is one of the key challenges and uncertainty of the coming decades. New economies have a greater need of foreign capital investments to achieve this development, notably through financing their infrastructure programs, and they are also very sensitive to global evolutions of interest rates and possible capital outflows in the case of global economic changes. One consequence of this is that the ability of global finance to accelerate new economies' integration into global exchanges will remain a key uncertainty going forward.

At the same time, the finance world sees a significant share of global finance assets available (40 percent) today being managed by specialized firms that tend to concentrate over time. This growth of assets under management is another indication of financial deepening of the economy. These firms have traditionally relied on bond and equity, notably from public companies and will play a growing role in the aforementioned challenge. In addition, for the last few years, a growing private market has emerged and, while the number of public companies has significantly decreased, a growing share of the equity market is managed privately with less public disclosures, leading to less overall transparency. These actors will also play a role in regulating global finance. How this will all develop remains uncertain.

Concern on Debts

Beyond investment in equity, the next (and oldest) investment is debt (or bonds and loans). There are countless documents that report on the big debt issue in the world today. Many economists point out that the world should have globally entered into a period of deleveraging because of the growingly significant volumes of debt repayments (interests). Yet, the reality is that the world, even since the 2008 crisis, has kept leveraging, increasing the financial deepening of the economy in almost all regions of the world. This was mainly done by governments to avoid a collapse of the economy after the global financial crisis of 2008. The massive recourse to debt has not helped reset demand and/or create inflation, making it very difficult for governments to actually deleverage, while the corporate sector naturally deleveraged in most economies (although less so in Europe than in other regions; Bank of America, 2018; Dalio, 2018; Dobbs *et al.*, 2015; Durden, 2017; Lund *et al.*, 2018; Petersen and Wiegelmann, 2014). Government debt is thus on many agendas today, in particular that of the International Monetary Fund (2018a).

Now, what is the reality of current debt levels?

Debt has progressed from US$99.7 trillion to US$185.7 trillion in 15 years across several types of debt forms and debtor types. Households represent around 27 percent of the debt, and both corporate and governments account for the rest, at similar levels. The debt from governments has increased faster than other debts in the last 15 years, gaining five points in the mix (Figure 5.12).

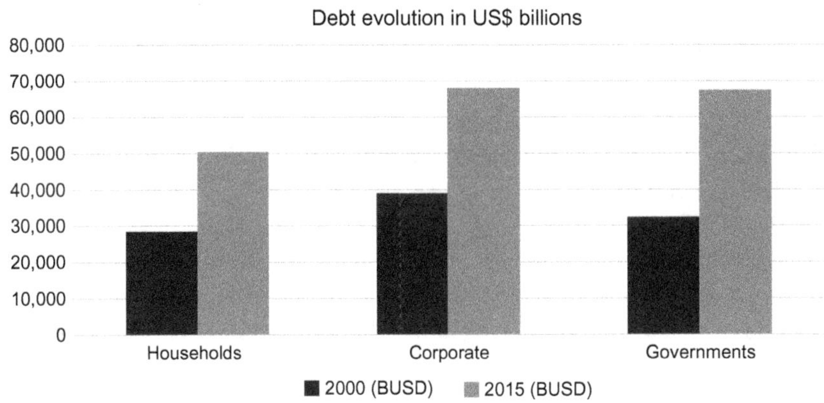

Figure 5.12 Debt evolution (Bank of America, 2018; Dalio, 2018; Dobbs *et al.*, 2015; Durden, 2017; International Monetary Fund, 2018b, 2018c; Lund *et al.*, 2018; Petersen and Wiegelmann, 2014)

This debt can take different forms. At a high level, debt can be broken up into bonds and loans and these two categories can be of household, corporate or government origin. Data has illustrated that government bonds and corporate loans have been the major sources of debt increase.

Most of the debt increase in total value comes from Europe and China, which, together, have represented around 60 percent of the increase with similar proportions, hence most concerns on debt today are revolving around these two regions. The debt level of Europe grew by 86 percent in 15 years, and 377 percent for China in the same period. Similarly, it also grew 91 percent in OECD Asia. Beyond the growth of debt, there is also concern in total levels of debt. The debt-to-GDP ratio helps size its impact and has shown that OECD Asia is the region with the highest level of debt-to-GDP ratio by far at more than 300 percent, while Europe ranges at 270 percent, North America at 230 percent, and China at 220 percent. Other countries range below 200 percent. The concern, therefore, is (and should be) particularly acute in OECD Asia, Europe, and China. Globally however, the debt-to-GDP ratio has remained constant over the last 15 years at a 215 percent average, and it has decreased in most economies of the world (including North America at −13 points). This is the exception when compared with OECD Asia (+110 points), China (+97 points), and Europe (+59 points), making these three regions prime areas of concern going forward (Figure 5.13).

One of the major sources of concern around debt is the volume of debt interest repayments, which could significantly alter growth by diverting necessary investments. This is typically what triggers a global deleveraging, and many economists predict that the world is on the verge of entering this new economic cycle, if it is not the case already (Dalio, 2018). Yet, interest rates have remained very low for the last 10 years, and the abundance of financial capital creates the condition for sustained low interest rates. In other words, capital is cheap. As a result of those macroeconomic conditions, the volume of debt interest has not yet reached a critical level.

But could this change?

There could be two main reasons triggering a significant increase of interest rates. First, a boost on demand triggering inflation could lead to a rise in interest rates. This is what has been happening in the United States in 2017–2019, following the implementation of the Trump administration's fiscal plan. At the same time however, inflation makes it easier to reimburse old debt. Alternatively, a local political and/or economic crisis could threaten investments and affect trade, potentially create currency issues, and eventually trigger a rise in interest costs. The latter is more likely to happen, as the boost on demand is unsustainable in the long run in mature economies. The short conclusion is that a political or economic event could eventually impact the current balance of debt repayments in OECD Asia, Europe, and China.

The key question, then, is who owns the debt, who could be impacted, and how? There is extremely limited information available on that question and we have only been able to compile a partial view of the landscape of debtors and creditors, with a focus on governments only (Broyer and Brunner, 2010; Eyermann, 2017; Kryger, 2009; McKinsey & Company, 2018a; OECD, 2017;

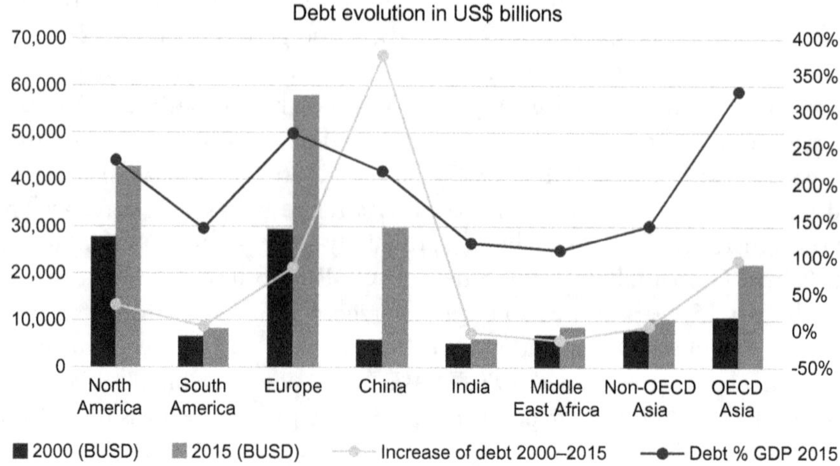

Figure 5.13 Debt evolution per region (Bank of America, 2018; Dalio, 2018; Dobbs *et al.*, 2015; Durden, 2017; International Monetary Fund, 2018b, 2018c; Lund *et al.*, 2018; Petersen and Wiegelmann, 2014)

Pettinger, 2017; Samuelson, 2018). The one conclusion of this partial view that we can draw out is that for all major debtors in the world (OECD Asia, Europe, China, North America), around two-thirds of the debt is possessed locally. What this means in practical terms is that a significant share of the financial assets of a population — or government when it happens across state-owned enterprises and public government — are tied to local debts. A default on total debt repayment would thus cancel the savings of a specific part of the population (or a state-owned enterprise), reducing the total volume of assets available within the region. This would have obvious catastrophic consequences on parts of the populations and local economic growth. However, it would not necessarily yield intricate financial consequences on other regions of the world, though it would result in financial trade disorders, with ripple effects on economies dependent on foreign capital (Figure 5.14).

The next order of business is to evaluate if there are enough assets to repay the debt and if country assets can guarantee the contracted debt. It is what we call the debt-to-asset ratio. It is actually more interesting to look at this factor than the debt-to-GDP ratio, as it gives a perspective on the volume of wealth that backs up debt. Figure 5.15 indicates the debt-to-asset ratio and its evolution from 2000 to 2015. The debt-to-asset ratio has actually declined in most economies in the world, including North America over the last 15 years. This means that the volume of assets has grown faster in those economies than the contracted debt, which again is mostly locally possessed. The situation is now considerably better across most economies in the world, particularly in new economies, than in 2000. However, many of these new economies keep very high level of debt

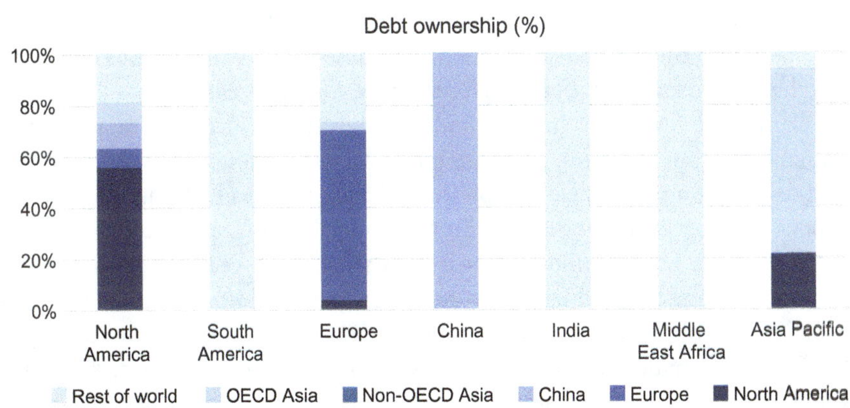

Figure 5.14 Debt ownership (Author's evaluation based on data from Broyer and Brunner, 2010; Eyermann, 2017; Kryger, 2009; McKinsey & Company, 2018a; OECD, 2017; Pettinger, 2017; Samuelson, 2018)

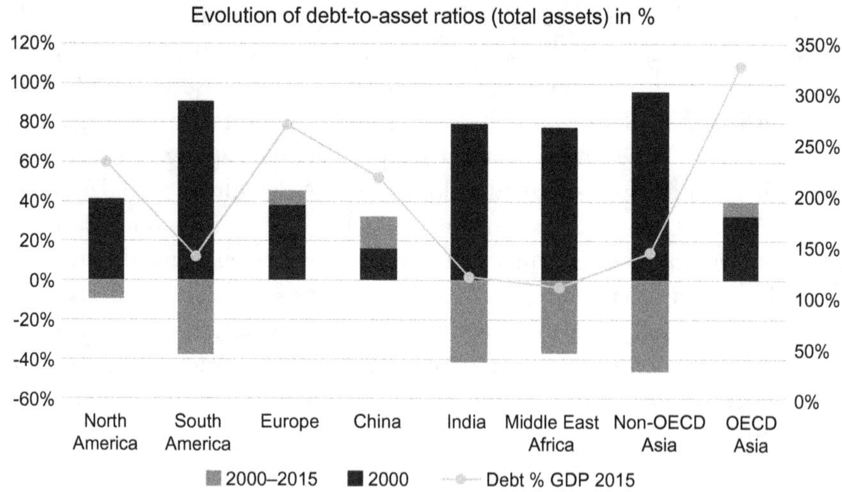

Figure 5.15 Debt-to-asset ratio (Broyer and Brunner, 2010; Eyermann, 2017; Kryger, 2009; McKinsey & Company, 2018a; OECD, 2017; Pettinger, 2017; Samuelson, 2018)

levels compared to their assets, at around 40–50 percent, particularly in South America, the Middle East, and North Africa (with significant disparities across countries), and non-OECD Asia. In addition, three exceptions stand out: Europe, OECD Asia, and, more importantly, China, which has doubled its debt-to-asset ratio. These economies still range below 40 percent, however.

The conclusion of this data questions whether there is a real problem of debt globally. Levels of debt have indeed reached significant amounts, increasing by more than 50 percent in 15 years. Yet, the debt-to-GDP ratio has remained stable globally, and the debt-to-asset ratio has declined. The world is thus comparatively less exposed to a debt crisis than it was 15 years ago — a rather counterintuitive outcome! In addition, the abundance of cheap capital yields sustainable low interest rates, preventing rising debt interest levels, and therefore forced deleveraging. Significant disparities, of course, prevail among regions, and the focus is on government debts in Europe and OECD Asia and corporate debt in China, which have significantly arisen in the last 15 years. A specific event (political, economic) could modify current conditions of trade, capital availability, the balance of currencies, and ultimately yields a localized rise in the cost of debt. This is the major risk when it comes to the debt going forward. As debt is essentially owned locally, the debt issue would primarily affect the local economy, leading to significant asset destruction (households and government financial assets being washed out). Ripple effects to other regions of the world would essentially revolve around trade, thus economic growth.

Key Interaction Points: The System Map

This chapter has been exploring key uncertainties that could affect the global economic landscape. It has found that the future of trade is one of the key uncertainties going forward. Then, the distribution of capital, which has seemed to follow a predetermined path toward more concentration, both across regions and within local economies themselves, could actually unfold in various ways. Then, the level of financial globalization highly depends on global politics, and could have significant impacts on wealth creation, trade, and capital costs. Finally, the level of debts in a number of regions also presents a future risk.

The geopolitical landscape, as well as the context around climate change, will have significant impacts on the future of the global economic landscape. The distribution of global capital will depend on the evolution of financial globalization and how debts will be handled. In return, this will weigh heavily on geopolitics, particularly on those plans to finance new economies' infrastructures (such as the Belt and Road Initiative), and what it means in terms of power projection. On the other hand, the future of trade (partially resulting from these investments) will also impact geopolitics of materials and resources, as well as innovation in these fields, hence global stances on the world scene (Figure 5.16).

Summary

Globalization of economic exchanges is a reality. Over the last 15 years, dependencies across regions have increased 50 percent. Global goods trade exchanges have increased three times in total value while world GDP doubled. These trade exchanges represent 15 percent of total GDP today, with Europe standing as the largest commercial partner of the world.

One of the key factors has been the increase in concentration of exchanges within regions. Europe has integrated further, and its intraregional economic exchanges represent two-thirds of its total trade. The American continent has further integrated, particularly between North America and Latin America. East and South-East Asian countries have also significantly increased their cross-dependencies, notably with China. Overall, these intraregional flows represent a sizeable share of global flows, with economic development primarily occurring within countries (at 85 percent of total GDP), followed by trade with neighboring countries, and finally across regions. Most other economies outside of these three blocs have remained largely nonintegrated within their region of origin (thereby not being able to form new economic blocs) and beyond within global economic exchanges. Resulting from this, these regions' ability to reap

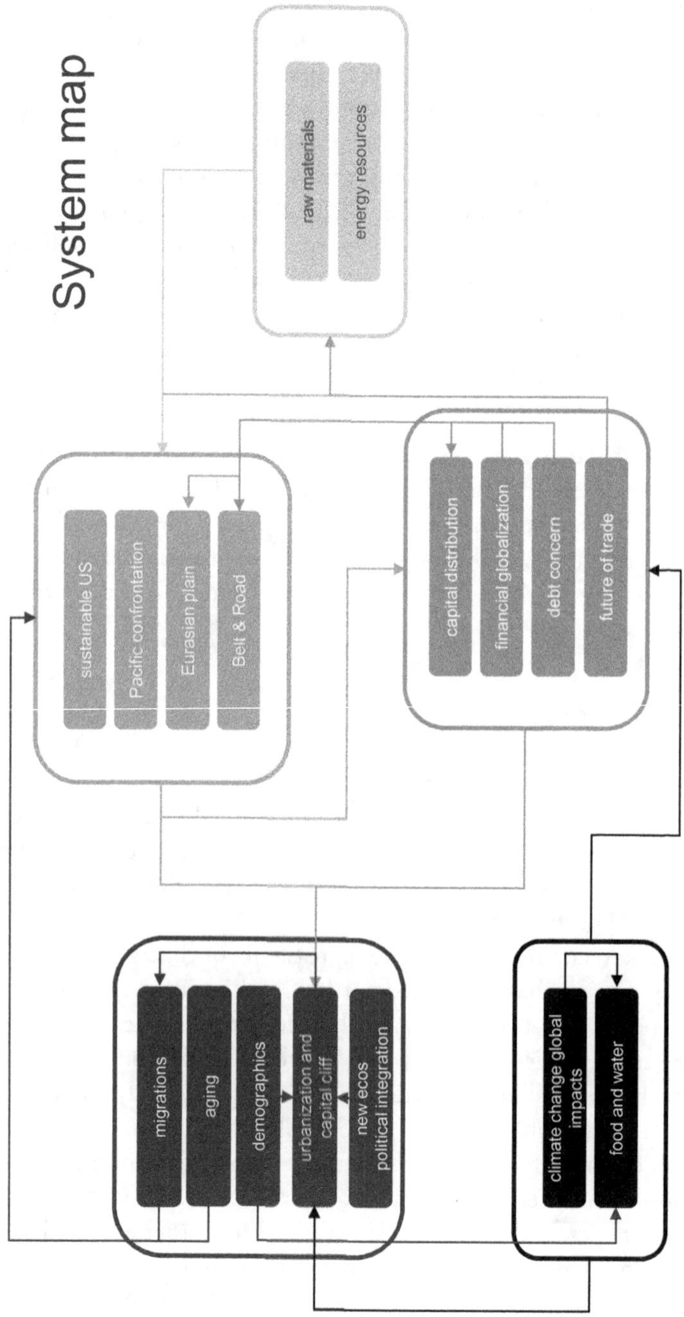

Figure 5.16 System map

benefits from globalization has remained extremely limited, increasing the development gap between them and others. This is one of the major challenges going forward, which could have critical implications on global relations.

At the same time, global wealth doubled in the last 15 years, but this result hides significant disparities. First, the largest increase of wealth (in total value) has come from mature economies, notably North America. The main reason for this is the large financial deepening of the North American economy. New economies have reaped much less benefits, with the exception of China, which managed to significantly improve its total wealth. Some would argue that the specific rules that China put in place enabled the country to attain these benefits, while most economies poorly integrated or without China's bargaining power were not able to do as much (Stiglitz, 2002). This also confirms the theory of capital concentration coined by Piketty (2014). What applies to global wealth distribution also applies within countries. Inequalities are extremely high and have not significantly improved in the last 15 years. Today 8 percent of the world population owns 85 percent of global wealth. Concurrently, wealth distribution has essentially favored households in mature economies, but it did mostly favor governments in most new economies (with the exception of China, to a certain extent). Again, this means that individuals did not reap much of the wealth generated in these last decades, though in new economies the financial situation of governments has improved. This also has long-term implications on demand in new economies and could threaten social stability.

Financial globalization is also a long-lasting trend of our time and, while it slowed down, it has not retreated. New economies are progressively being integrated into global financial exchanges. Most of these economies are net recipients, meaning capital is injected from abroad to develop their economy, though not nearly fast enough. Interestingly, North America is also the largest recipient of the world, a sign of the dynamism and attractiveness of its economy. The largest lender of the world is the United States, followed by Europe and China. Overall, global financial exchanges keep rising and the economy becomes more intricate. Once again, the rules of the game and pace of change are largely defined by those who own capital, namely OECD economies and China. In addition, a larger share of financial assets is being managed by global specialized firms, and they tend to concentrate over time, looking to improve return on assets. This is another indication of the progressive financial deepening of the economy. Not surprisingly, this activity is mostly developed in North America, though growing fast in Asia Pacific.

Finally, there has been a significant piling up of debt in the last decade, following the global financial crisis of 2008. Yet, the debt-to-GDP ratio has remained stable globally, while the debt-to-asset ratio has declined. Debt is less of an issue than it used to be, even though few regions such as Europe, OECD Asia, and China have seen an above average growth of debt. For most of these countries, however, debt is owned locally, limiting the risk of default. Yet, a sudden change in the cost of debt could trigger significant asset destruction.

The world economy has become increasingly more globalized. Trade of goods and financial exchanges have soared to the highest levels in history. Dependencies have emerged as a result of this, with the one between China and the United States the most concerning. The increasing financial deepening and economic development of several new economies have led to massive capital creation, hence low interests' rates. For a decade, this has been the new paradigm of the global economy. This, in itself, has been leading to a race toward creating returns on capital. Financial firms are becoming increasingly consolidated and private equity investments — deemed more profitable, though riskier — are on the rise. Yet, the level of investments in infrastructures in new economies, which forms the greatest challenge going forward, remains low and a key point of focus going forward. At the same time, and as a consequence of the above situation, debt levels have been soaring, notably in a few regions like Europe, OECD Asia, and China. The sustainability of these debt levels is not in question, but a sudden change in interest rates could trigger massive issues.

This situation invites us to reflect on possible futures. Will the economy maintain the rate of globalization, or will global exchanges retreat, as a result of interest rate increases or trade conflicts? How will people and countries react to the growing level of inequalities? How will the debt situation evolve if the economic paradigm of low interest rates continues? What role will financial firms play in making the world's economy more sustainable? These uncertainties will weigh heavily on the coming decades. While the populations of new economies keep expanding, and local economic development is an utmost priority, the ability of the global economy to support this transition will be crucial. The consequences of not meeting this challenge would have tremendous consequences on large populations and regions, and ripple effects on every economy around the world. Global institutions will most likely need to reform to cope with these upcoming challenges. Once again, who will take the lead? Both the United States (as the first financial place) and Europe (as the first commercial partner and one of the largest lenders) have large roles to play in this transition, together with China's rising status.

References

Amine, J. (2018). "How Private Equity Trends Are Changing Deal-Making," *Credit Suisse*, 1 June. Available from: https://www.credit-suisse.com/corporate/en/articles/

news-and-expertise/how-private-equity-trends-are-changing-deal-making-201806.html [Accessed: September 2019].

Bain & Company. (2012). *A World Awash in Money: Capital Trends Through 2020.* Available from: http://www2.bain.com/images/bain_report_a_world_awash_in_money.pdf [Accessed: September 2019].

Bank of America. (2018). *2019, The Year Ahead.* Available from: https://www.bofaml.com/content/boaml/en_us/home.html [Accessed: September 2019].

Barnes, Y. (2018). "8 Things to Know About Global Real Estate Value," *Savills*, July 2018. Available from: https://www.savills.com/impacts/economic-trends/8-things-you-need-to-know-about-the-value-of-global-real-estate.html [Accessed: September 2019].

Bernanke, B. (2005). "Remarks by Governor Ben S. Bernanke," *The Federal Reserve Board*, 10 March. Available from: https://www.federalreserve.gov/boarddocs/speeches/2005/200503102/ [Accessed: September 2019].

Broyer, S. and Brunner, C. (2010). *Qui détient les dettes publiques européennes?* Natixis. Available from: https://postjorion.files.wordpress.com/2010/04/qui-detient-les-dettes-publiques-europeennes.pdf [Accessed: September 2019].

Dalio, R. (2018). *Economic Principles: How the Economic Machine Works?* Available from: https://www.economicprinciples.org/ [Accessed: September 2019].

Desjardins, J. (2017). "All of the World's Money and Markets in One Vizualization," *Visual Capitalist*, 26 October. Available from: http://www.visualcapitalist.com/worlds-money-markets-one-visualization-2017/ [Accessed: September 2019].

Dobbs, R. Lund, S., Woetzel, J. and Mutafchieva, M. (2015). *Debt and (Not Much) Deleveraging.* McKinsey & Company. Available from: https://www.mckinsey.com/featured-insights/employment-and-growth/debt-and-not-much-deleveraging [Accessed: September 2019].

Durden, T. (2017). "Here Is the IMF's Global Financial Crash Scenario," *Zero Hedge*, 23 October. Available from: https://www.zerohedge.com/news/2017-10-22/here-imfs-global-financial-crash-scenario [Accessed: September 2019].

European Fund and Asset management Association. (2018). *Asset Management in Europe: An Overview of the Asset Management Industry.* Available from: https://www.efama.org/Publications/Statistics/Asset%20Management%20Report/EFAMA_Asset%20Management percent20Report percent202018 percent20voor percent20web.pdf [Accessed: September 2019].

Eyermann, C. (2017). "Who Owns the U.S. National Debt?" *MyGovCost*, 15 May. Available from: http://www.mygovcost.org/2017/05/15/who-owns-the-u-s-national-debt-2/ [Accessed: September 2019].

Fages, R., Beardsley, B., Donnadieu, H., Macé, B., Pardasani, N., Schmitz, L., Sheridan, B., Taglioni, G. and Xu, Q. (2018). *Global Asset Management 2018. The Digital Metamorphosis.* Boston Consulting Group. Available from: http://image-src.

bcg.com/Images/BCG-The-Digital-Metamorphosis-July-2018-R_tcm9-197509.pdf [Accessed: September 2019].

Frankopan, P. (2017). *The Silk Roads: A New History of the World.* New York: Vintage Books.

International Monetary Fund. (2018a). *World Economic Outlook 2017, April 2018.* Available from: https://www.imf.org/en/Publications/WEO/Issues/2018/03/20/world-economic-outlook-april-2018 [Accessed: September 2019].

International Monetary Fund. (2018b). *Global Finance Stability Report April 2018: A Bumpy Road Ahead.* Available from: https://www.imf.org/en/Publications/GFSR/Issues/2018/04/02/Global-Financial-Stability-Report-April-2018 [Accessed: September 2019].

International Monetary Fund. (2018c). *A Decade After the Global Financial Crisis: Are We Safer? October 2018.* Available from: https://www.imf.org/en/Publications/GFSR/Issues/2018/09/25/Global-Financial-Stability-Report-October-2018 [Accessed: September 2019].

IPE Reference Hub. (2018). *Top 400 Asset Managers 2018: €66trn at a Glance.* Available from: https://hub.ipe.com/top-400/top-400-asset-managers-2018-66trn-at-a-glance/10026664.article [Accessed: September 2019].

Kryger, T. (2009). *Australia's Foreign Debt Data and Trends.* Available from: https://www.aph.gov.au/About_Parliament/Parliamentary_Departments/Parliamentary_Library/pubs/rp/rp0809/09rp30 [Accessed: September 2019].

Lakner, C. and Milanovic, B. (2013). *Global Income Distribution. From the Fall of the Berlin Wall to the Great Recession.* The World Bank. Available from: http://documents.worldbank.org/curated/en/914431468162277879/pdf/WPS6719.pdf [Accessed: September 2019].

Littman, J. (2017). "Solving the Mystery of Government-Owned Real Estate," *Forbes*, 11 April. Available from: https://www.forbes.com/sites/bisnow/2017/04/11/solving-the-mystery-of-government-owned-real-estate/#29fb13092bd0 [Accessed: September 2019].

London, S. and Lund, S. (2018). *How Secure Is the Global Financial System a Decade After the Crisis?* McKinsey & Company. Available from: https://www.mckinsey.com/industries/financial-services/our-insights/how-secure-is-the-global-financial-system-a-decade-after-the-crisis [Accessed: September 2019].

Lund, S., Daruvala, T., Dobbs, R., Härle, P., Kwek, J. and Falcón, R. (2013). *Financial Globalization: Retreat or Reset?* McKinsey & Company. Available from: https://www.mckinsey.com/featured-insights/employment-and-growth/financial-globalization [Accessed: September 2019].

Lund, S., Mehta, A., Manyika, J. and Goldshtein, D. (2018). *A Decade After the Global Financial Crisis: What Has (and Hasn't) Changed?* McKinsey & Company, August 2018. Available from: https://www.mckinsey.com/industries/financial-services/our-insights/a-decade-after-the-global-financial-crisis-what-has-and-hasnt-changed [Accessed: September 2019].

Lund, S., Windhagen, E., Manyika, J., Härle, P., Woetzel, J. and Goldshtein, D. (2017). *The New Dynamics of Financial Globalization.* McKinsey & Company. Available from: https://www.mckinsey.com/industries/financial-services/our-insights/the-new-dynamics-of-financial-globalization [Accessed: September 2019].

MacArthur, H. (2018). "Bain & Company's Global Private Equity Report," *Bain & Company*, 26 February. Available from: https://www.bain.com/insights/global-private-equity-report-2018/ [Accessed: September 2019].

McKinsey & Company. (2018a). *Visualizing Global Debt.* Available from: https://www.mckinsey.com/business-functions/strategy-and-corporate-finance/our-insights/visualizing-global-debt?_sm_au_=iFV4VrTRsWG8Gj4r [Accessed: September 2019].

McKinsey & Company. (2018b). *Private Markets 2018: The Rise and Rise of Private Markets.* McKinsey Global Private Markets Review. Available from: https://www.mckinsey.com/industries/private-equity-and-principal-investors/our-insights/the-rise-and-rise-of-private-equity [Accessed: September 2019].

Murphy, A., Ponciano, J., Hansen, S. and Touryalai, H. (2018). "Global 2000: The World's Largest Public Companies," *Forbes*, 15 March. Available from: https://www.forbes.com/global2000/#712b22d1335d [Accessed: September 2019].

OECD. (2017). *Government at a Glance 2017.* Paris: OECD Publishing. Available from: https://www.oecd-ilibrary.org/governance/government-at-a-glance-2017_gov_glance-2017-en [Accessed: September 2019].

Petersen, H. and Wiegelmann A. (2014). "Financial Markets and the Global Debt Crisis: Toward a New Architecture for a More Reliable Financial Sector," *Norteamérica*, 9(1), 79–107.

Pettinger, T. (2017). "Japanese National Debt," *Economics Help*, 18 November. Available from: https://www.economicshelp.org/blog/1178/economics/japanese-national-debt/ [Accessed: September 2019].

Piketty, T. (2014). *Capital in the Twenty-First Century.* Massachusetts: Belknap Press.

PricewaterhouseCoopers. (2017). *Asset and Wealth Management Revolution: Embracing Exponential Change.* Available from: https://www.PwC.com/gx/en/asset-management/asset-management-insights/assets/awm-revolution-full-report-final.pdf [Accessed: September 2019].

Samuelson, R. (2018). "The $247 Trillion Global Debt Bomb," *The Washington Post*, 16 July. Available from: https://www.washingtonpost.com/opinions/the-247-trillion-global-debt-bomb/2018/07/15/64c5bbaa-86c2-11e8-8f6c-46cb43e3f306_story.html?utm_term=.2f72fc41670e [Accessed: September 2019].

Shell. (2018). *Sky Scenario.* Available from: https://www.shell.com/energy-and-innovation/the-energy-future/scenarios/shell-scenario-sky.html [Accessed: September 2019].

Shorrocks, A., Davies, J. and Lluberas, R. (2015). *Research Institute: Global Wealth Report 2019.* Credit Suisse. Available from: https://www.credit-suisse.com/corporate/en/research/research-institute/global-wealth-report.html [Accessed: September 2019].

Stiglitz, J. (2002). *Globalization and Its Discontents*. New York: W. W. Norton & Company.

UN Trade Statistics. (2018). *Analytical Tables*. Available from: https://unstats.un.org/unsd/trade/data/tables.asp#annualworld [Accessed: September 2019].

World Integrated Trade Solutions. (2018). *Export of Value Added by Country*. Available from: https://wits.worldbank.org/analyticaldata/evad-countrystats.aspx [Accessed: September 2019].

CHAPTER 6

Change 6 — Rise of a Digital Economy

As discussed in Chapter 5, globalization has been the main engine for economic growth for the last several decades. Global exchanges have soared. Despite a retreat in financial exchanges since the economic crisis in 2008–2009, global trade of goods kept increasing, at a level in line with global Gross Domestic Product (GDP) increases. The reality is that globalization has lost its role as an accelerator of growth, hence the general impression of partial de-globalization. The world is not de-globalizing, globalization keeps expanding, but at a slower pace. In addition, several regions remain poorly connected to global economic exchanges, and form a significant potential going forward. The rise of the digital economy also kicks in as the new paradigm for the decade to come. Will it serve global economic development? What are its implications on current relations and exchanges (Figure 6.1)?

Digitization's New Growth Booster

Manyika *et al.* (2016) estimate that the digital economy is set to become the new key contributor to global economic growth. They estimate that in the last 10 years, it has already contributed US$2.3 trillion to global GDP output, almost on par with global goods trade at US$2.7 trillion. A good indicator of this development is data flows, which have soared, increasing 45 times between 2005 and 2014, and are projected to increase another nine times by 2021. Another good indicator is the rise of e-commerce. Today, 12 percent of goods flow is already done using the Internet.

McKinsey & Company (2017) also explain that if half of the GDP growth of the last 50 years (3.5 percent compound annual growth rate [CAGR]) was due to the increase of the labor market (with the other half coming from productivity savings), the next 50 years will see a critical slowdown of the impact of labor on GDP growth due to an aging population. While the required level of GDP growth to achieve GDP/capita improvements ranges around 2.9 percent CAGR,

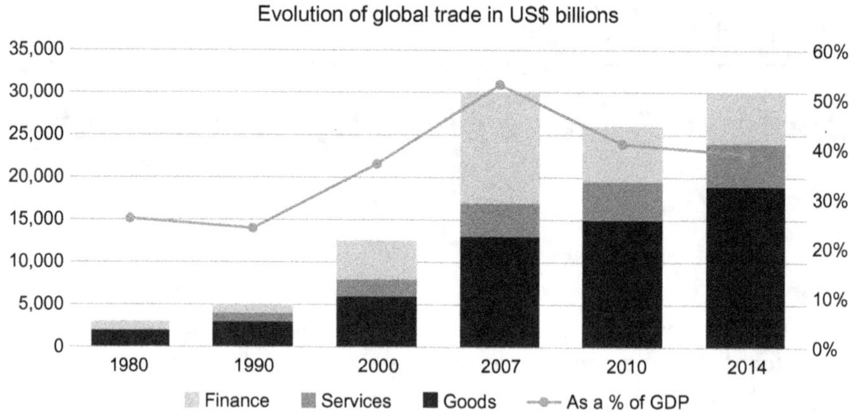

Figure 6.1 Evolution of global trade (Manyika *et al.*, 2016)

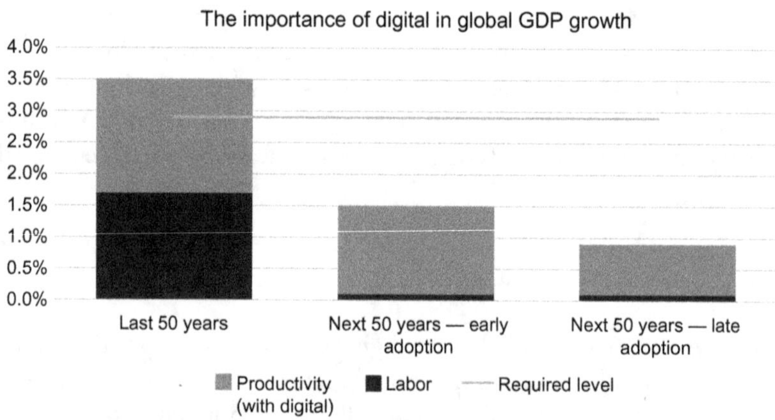

Figure 6.2 The importance of digital in global GDP growth (McKinsey & Company, 2017)

digitization could contribute between 0.8 percent and 1.4 percent. The rise of the digital economy would thus be a major driver of potential GDP growth in the coming decades, hence economic and social development (Figure 6.2).

Yet, increases in productivity and true benefits to the global economy have been hard to map thus far. The World Economic Forum (2016) has studied this issue and tried to map benefits per key sector of activity. It focused on industry value (in terms of profitability and value creation) and on societal value (including reduced costs or delivery times, improved jobs and well-being, and environmental benefits). Their report showed a potential benefit by 2025 of nearly US$20 trillion (including US$8.5 trillion for

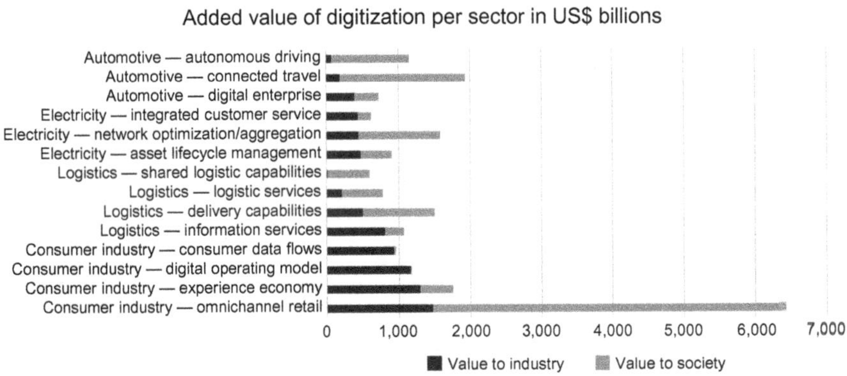

Figure 6.3 Added value of digitization per sector (McKinsey & Company, 2017)

industry value only). Half of these benefits would be concentrated in the consumer goods sector (Figure 6.3).

Proponents of the digital era claim that digitization is a new growth booster with significant benefits to be reaped worldwide as the digital economy develops. Time will tell to what extent these benefits materialize.

Digitization — A Great Equalizer?

There is a significant global divide when it comes to the penetration of digital in the economy. In 2016, 47 percent of the worldwide population had access to the Internet, with large differences across regions (DMCC, 2018). Levels remain low in Southern Asia and Africa, having slowly caught up in the last decade. Other new economies have increased faster, comparatively (Figure 6.4).

Another way to look at it is to see that, in 2014, 80 percent of data flows were still concentrated in the top 15 economies, with a limited increase in usage from other economies over a decade, estimated at less than 10 percent (Manyika *et al.*, 2016). Combining this factor with the increase of Internet penetration shows that connected economies are developing faster and reaping higher benefits than connecting economies, accentuating the divide.

Cloud traffic can also be a good proxy to check this assertion. Three regions stand out in terms of total traffic: North America, Europe, and Asia Pacific. In capita terms, however, North America is largely first, with nearly 10 times the global average of around 500 GB per year per capita, followed by Europe (at around two to three times the global average; Cisco, 2018). Other regions have slowly started to increase their usage.

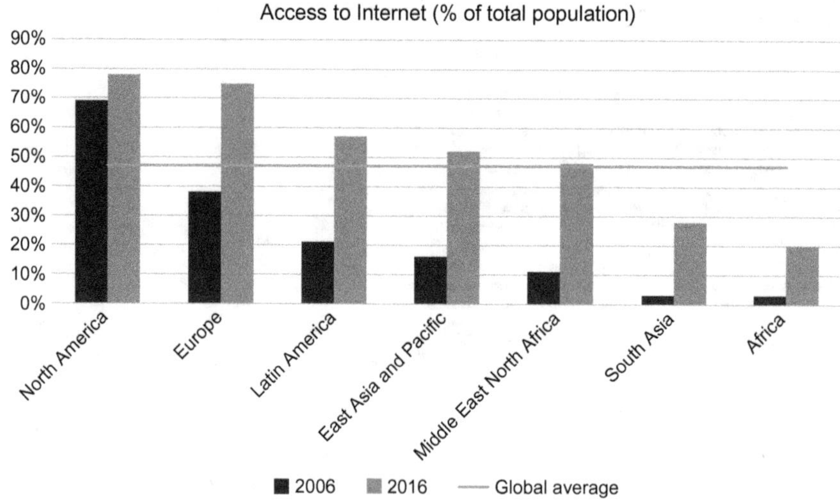

Figure 6.4 Access to Internet (DMCC, 2018)

Communication performance is also interesting to look into, since it is likely one of the many reasons that explains the global divide that has emerged in the digital economy (Cisco, 2018). It also significantly varies across regions. Download speeds are very similar across the Asia Pacific, North America, and Europe, with a significant gap in other economies including Southern Asia, the Middle East, and Africa, with a rate between four to five times lower. Much more than a gap, this is a clear line of fracture. The rise of the digital economy is thus primarily driven by (and benefiting) those economies who have embraced the transformation first.

Beyond this natural divide, in particular in Southern Asia, the Middle East, and Africa, the digital economy is predominantly yielding benefits where it locally operates. While interregional goods' trade flows exceed 50 percent of the total, only one-third of data transactions take place across regions. Most of these businesses, therefore, remain local. To a certain extent, the rise of the digital economy does primarily benefit already integrated economies that have developed a solid digital backbone (Manyika *et al.*, 2016).

Another way to examine trends is through observing the number of website visits. Most people in North America mainly connect to websites originating from that region. The same effect can be observed, though to a lesser extent, in Europe. This is compared to most new economies that still rely on content created in North America and Europe (Figure 6.5).

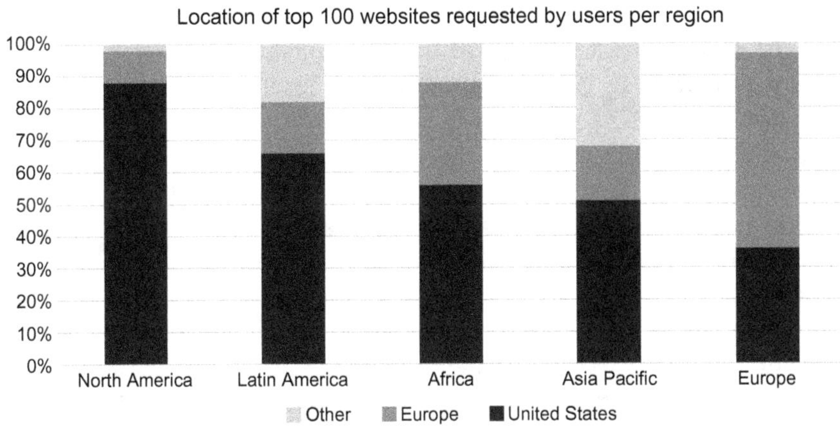

Figure 6.5 Location of top 100 websites (Manyika *et al.*, 2016)

This also shows that mature economies at the origin of the digital economy capture most of the benefits from cross-border data flows. North America and Europe represent almost 75 percent of the top 100 million websites visited.

There is a clear digital divide across key regions of the world, in particular with Southern Asia, the Middle East, and Africa, while most benefits from the digital transformation of the economy are reaped by leading economies today, with North America playing a leading role. This echoes the conclusions from Chapter 5 on wealth concentration. The key question that can be posed is whether the digitization of the economy will be an instrument of accelerated development in new economies, or simply another form of trade, which would primarily benefit mature economies.

Geopolitics of the Digital Economy

The Battle for Data

The digital economy primarily depends on the ability to store and compute data. The key question then is which country has the ability to store and compute the data and the answer shows that this ability is fairly concentrated. Today, 60 percent of the turnover generated by data centers is done in just 20 cities, and 90 percent of the global data storage capacity is held by American companies (Ambrosetti, 2018), which represent 50 percent of total investments in the field. Additionally, the development of new applications, notably Artificial Intelligence, calls for even greater computing power and data storage capabilities, leading to accelerated development of cloud-based hyperscale data centers. Cisco (2018) estimates the number of hyperscale data centers will increase by 50 percent in 2021 to reach around 600 (up from around 400 in 2018).

There are two ways to look at this concentration of capabilities. First, we can look at where data centers are actually located. The number of public data centers around the world reaches several thousand. There are, for instance, around 4,000 colocation data centers worldwide (Data Center Map, 2018). Yet, there are much fewer hyperscale data centers capable of providing these advanced storage and computation capabilities. There were around 400 of them worldwide in 2018 (Christian, 2018; Cisco, 2018; Sverdlik, 2017) (Figure 6.6). They represent around 40 percent of total data center servers (a figure expected to top 50 percent by 2021) and almost 90 percent of public cloud workloads. The two main regions are North America and the Asia Pacific. The latter accounts for 30 percent of the total installed base versus 48 percent for North America. China accounts for roughly one-third of the Asia Pacific numbers while Japan, Australia and, to a lesser extent, South Korea and Singapore form the rest. By 2021, the region is expected to surpass North America, mainly driven by growth in China. Forecasts should be taken with caution, though this one looks at very short-term perspectives and, given the tremendous activity in China, invites us to believe it is a very reasonable estimate. Other regions are far behind, including Europe, which is not expected to close this gap, and nothing indicates in current news (at the time of the writing) that it will change in the next few years. Though it has a similar population and GDP to North America, there would only be half the estimated number of hyperscale data centers in Europe in 2021. Other regions fall even further behind, with these numbers acting as another representation of the global divide (Ambrosetti, 2018; Christian, 2018; Cisco, 2018; Sverdlik, 2017).

The second way to look at this concentration of capabilities is to check where hyperscale operators are headquartered. We define hyperscale data operators as companies that provide infrastructure as a service (above one billion euros), software as a service (above two billion euros), Internet search or social networking services (above four billion euros), or e-commerce capabilities (above eight billion euros). Around 24 companies around the world meet these criteria today. Seven of these companies are headquartered outside of the United States, mostly in China (Cisco, 2018). This business is, therefore, dominated by both of these countries.

Two regions — the Asia Pacific and North America — are extensively harnessing and processing data to develop new applications and growth opportunities. While North America looks close to saturation, the Asia Pacific still has

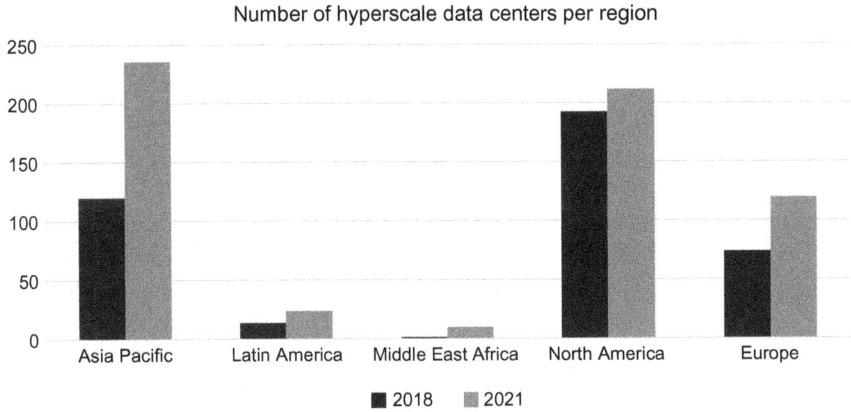

Figure 6.6 Number of hyperscale data centers (Ambrosetti, 2018; Christian, 2018; Cisco, 2018; Sverdlik, 2017)

a long way to go, as it has a population that is 10 times higher. China is playing a critical role as it has clearly stated its intent to become a leader in the field. With a population base above one billion, and limited data privacy rules, it clearly has the potential to develop cutting-edge technologies like Artificial Intelligence faster and with fewer restrictions (Gardels, 2018). From a geopolitical standpoint, China is dominating its own country while the rest of the world is dominated by American technologies, with a limited deployment outside of Europe thus far. All these peripheral regions, particularly South-Eastern Asia, will be a major playing field for competition between the two digital powerhouses in the coming years.

The Battle for Networks

The proper functioning of a global digital economy also requires secured data flows within and across borders. There are around 450 submarine cables around the world today, totaling 1.2 million kilometers of network. They have different capacities; the most modern ones can convey 1,000 GB per second. Most of the cross-border Internet traffic flows through these high-bandwidth networks (Ambrosetti, 2018; Starosielski, 2015).

The backbone of the Internet is now in the hands of private operators since its privatization in 1994 (Lee, 2014), however, this situation is evolving fast. While it is estimated that the network of submarine cables will grow 140 percent between 2017 and 2022, a reasonable assumption considering the increase in data flows, content providers (such as Amazon, Google, and other large organizations) are increasingly investing in network capacities. The capacity deployed by these companies has grown 14 times in the last decade and their level of investment now exceeds that of traditional operators (Ambrosetti, 2018). Concentration of the digital economy is also taking place in the networks sector.

A look at a submarine cables map (Christian, 2018; Lee, 2014) shows the inherent fragility of the digital network. North America is connected through a multitude of submarine cables with both Europe and Asia Pacific, leading to a large resistance to disconnection. On the other hand, however, Europe is primarily connected with North America, with the critical hub for connection between the two continents passing through the United Kingdom. Connections with the rest of the world pass through Egypt, the Red Sea, and the Arabian Sea, before connecting with the Asia Pacific through India (Mumbai and Chennai), Singapore, and Hong Kong. The resilience of this network to geopolitical incident is much lower than for North America, which directly connects with most regions of the world. China is mostly connected through Hong Kong with the rest of South-Eastern Asia, with Singapore playing the role of key distribution hub in the region. Today, Lee (2014) considers that while most of the American continent, Asia Pacific and Europe are estimated to have low exposure to disconnection, Africa, the Middle East, and Southern Asia are, on the contrary, considered highly vulnerable. This analysis can be further challenged in light of the above, by considering the high dependency of Europe to North America, Egypt, India, Singapore, and Hong Kong, as well as the maritime routes that submarine cables follow. Similarly, most of South America's connectivity goes through the US hubs. The rest of the world is obviously even more vulnerable, particularly countries with no access to the sea, hence dependent from regional terrestrial connections. This is the case for most of Africa, as well as Central Asia and some countries in South America. Therefore, networks play a critical role in terms of Internet resilience and, subsequently, the rise of a digital economy. Again, a critical divide can be observed between North America and the rest of the world with locations likes Egypt, Mumbai, Chennai, Singapore, or Hong Kong holding strategic stakes for most countries.

Beyond submarine cables, which form the bulk of international data flows, satellite telecommunications are also developing. The number of satellite launches has grown significantly between 2012 and 2019. There are around 5,000 satellites orbiting around the globe. Forecasts estimate that the number of satellite launches will grow four times within the next decade (Ambrosetti, 2018). Almost half of the total turnover from the satellite industry is related to telecommunications. These developments could significantly transform strategic dependencies induced by submarine cables. However, they would create new dependencies to those companies and countries with the corresponding know-how. It could be a way for Europe to reenter the game, or for Russia to play a role in the global development of the digital economy. Outside of these two, the United States, Japan, and China are the key players.

The Battle for Industry

Essential to the development of the digital economy are the semiconductors; "If data are the new oil, chips are the internal combustion engines that turn them into something useful" (*The Economist*, 2018). The semiconductor industry has key characteristics today. On the one hand, this US$400 billion industry (Ott, 2018) is truly global. A US member of the semiconductor industry association reported that, out of 16,000 suppliers — a staggering figure — 8,500 were from outside the country (*The Economist*, 2018). On the other hand, this is also a cutting-edge industry, relying on technologies developing extremely fast, following the Moore's law (in essence, computing capabilities increase exponentially while costs keep falling).

These industries work at the nanometer level, producing chips with nearly atomic precision. As a result, this is a very concentrated industry, with few key players operating globally. The industry is dominated by companies like Intel, Samsung, Taiwan Semiconductor, Qualcomm, Broadcom Inc., SK hynix, Micron Technology, Texas Instruments, Toshiba, or NXP. Most of these companies are from the United States, Japan, South Korea, or Taiwan, all traditional security and trade allies of the United States (Mims, 2013b; Walton, 2017). The US semiconductor industry represents 40 percent of the total sales of chips worldwide (Horwitz, 2018). Europe is largely absent from the list. There are few players in China, yet the share of the country in the industry remains low and limited to the bottom of the value chain so far (Mims, 2013a). Despite plans to catch up — including plans to reach autonomy in semiconductor production by 2030 — the country still relies heavily on imports. As a matter of fact, semiconductor imports exceed those of oil currently (Horwitz, 2018).

There is, therefore, a significant dependency from Europe and China to these countries and their advanced industry capabilities. Europe used to have a strong industry and represented over 15 percent of production in the 1990s, though this share has collapsed in recent decades (Productronica, 2018). This dependency then turns into a strategic issue. Recent examples of pressure from the United States to limit the development of China in this field are impressive. For instance, the US government banned Intel from selling to China in 2015. It also banned sales from ZTE in 2018, which nearly led to the bankruptcy of the large Chinese Telecom company. The conflict with Huawei in 2019 is a new development on a list that is getting longer every year.

On the flip side, China is the first importer of semiconductors and is critical to the development of the industry. Most large American companies are heavily dependent on the business they do in China, for example, in 2016, China imported over US$160 billion in semiconductors, more than 40 percent of the global market. In addition, all semiconductors are heavily dependent on rare earth materials for their performance (Albrecht, 2013; Lapedus, 2015) and China is the leading provider of such materials to the world, with over 80 percent of the global production and close to 40 percent of the world's identified resources, as discussed in Chapter 3. A strategic dependency emerges between the semiconductor industry and the industries using semiconductors (i.e., most modern industries, including the defense industry) and China for their needs and resources.

The semiconductor industry, which has been global for decades, has thus entered a competition for national security across borders and needs to reinvent itself. Semiconductor technology is in the hands of the United States and some of its close allies (South Korea, Taiwan, and Japan), with a significant barrier to entry for Chinese companies. At the same time, this industry is heavily dependent on Chinese imports and, more importantly, the rare earth materials that China supplies to them, which are critical for manufacturing these cutting-edge technologies. As the semiconductor industry is central to most modern and advanced technologies — including defense technologies — these strategic cross-dependencies weigh heavily on international relations, and the way they will develop will have a significant impact on the development of the digital economy.

The Battle for Competencies

The rise of the digital economy can only be ensured if critical competencies in Science, Technology, Engineering, and Mathematics (STEM) are available. The development of such competencies plays a critical role in the ability of a given country to develop its digital economy, if it does not want to rely on foreign technologies and services.

The number of STEM graduates per country and the relative share to the 20- to 39-year-old population can be retrieved from various sources (The Conference Board Canada, 2019; McCarthy, 2017; United Nations, 2017). China and India top the rankings with more graduates than all other countries in the world. As a percentage of their population, Russia, China, and Iran lead the pack with over 1 percent of the 20- to 39-year-old population enrolled in STEM college studies. Mature economies range around 0.7 percent comparatively. The staggering figure here is China, which both leads in terms of total figure and percentage, an indication of the commitment of the country to become a leader in the industry (Figure 6.7).

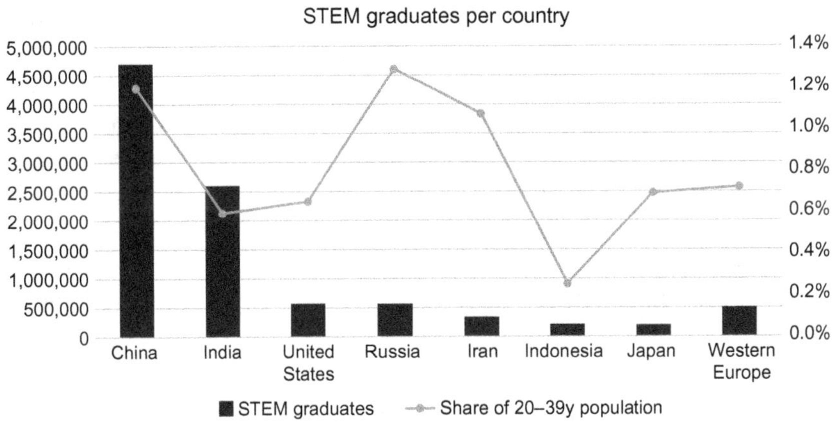

Figure 6.7 STEM graduates per country (The Conference Board Canada, 2019; McCarthy, 2017; United Nations, 2017)

This provision of college-level competencies, or lack of, will significantly contribute to the development of the digital economy in various countries. Many countries (notably those excluded from the above benchmark) are not prepared to face this transformation and will therefore depend on leading powerhouses, which will likely limit the benefits they will be able to reap from this transformation. This — again — will naturally accentuate the global divide previously mentioned.

There is thus a clear competition between China and the United States to dominate the digital economy. To date, the United States is the front runner, with larger capacities in terms of data computing and storage, and a more reliable cross-border network. But China is catching up fast, particularly on the data front, as well as increasing competencies and education. Beyond this, there is a strategic cross-dependency between the two giants on the semiconductor industry. While the technology is dominated by the United States and its close allies with strong barriers to entry, the entire industry depends on the Chinese market size and more importantly on its rare earth material mining industry. Outside of China and the United States, other economies are lagging, with more limited development capabilities and resilience, and remain to be "connected" to the opportunity, by one or the other giant powerhouse. The rise of the digital economy is, therefore, a major stake in geopolitics.

Looking forward, Schmidt and Cohen (2015) have shown that there is a significant probability that the Internet network, global and "flat" by design, will eventually become "balkanized" as a result of the competition described.

This balkanization could see the emergence of virtual multilateralism (states sharing similar interests building virtual borders), virtual statehoods (with minorities creating virtual states online), and the emergence of virtual conflicts, which could be aggravated by automated warfare. They also point out that different cultures will also lead to different Internet experiences. They consider that democracies could be weakened by the development of digital, at risk of more revolts and populism (through fake news especially), and powerful autocracies could use digitization to tighten their control over citizens. The future geopolitical landscape of the digital economy continues to unfold.

Trust in the Benefits from the Digital Economy

Going beyond these issues, several key questions relating to trust have arisen in recent years. Would a digital breakdown be possible?

Digital consumers are at the heart of the digital economy, and there is a growing concern on how much progress the digital economy brings to them. This is what is widely referred to as the digital trust issue. The topic of digital trust has been assessed holistically through an extensive survey and the compilation of results from several others by Chakravorti *et al.* (2018). They assessed four criteria: Attitudes (general feeling/trust about digital interactions); Behavior (user response to friction in digital environment); Environment (mechanisms existing for building trust); and Experience (users' experience with digital). The results showed that the level of experience (and digital environment) varies significantly between OECD (Organisation for Economic Co-operation and Development) countries and others, including China. However, the general attitude (or trust) is pretty much similar across all regions of the world, showing a much greater tolerance (behavior) and confidence from non-OCED economies — particularly China — in the promises of the digital economy. There are, therefore, different regional patterns to digital trust, and the situation varies significantly with the culture and the current state of Internet deployment. These behaviors are also extremely likely to evolve over time.

The Future of Jobs and Social Inequalities

The rise of the digital economy also means an increased share of automated activities, which will deeply impact the workforce. Several studies conclude that a significant proportion of current occupations could end up being automated, at least in part, with McKinsey & Company (2017) estimate that 60 percent of job types see 30 percent of their activity at risk. Their exhaustive analysis shows that significant displacements are likely to occur in most sectors, at least for a certain set of activities, such as collecting and processing data or performing physical activities in predictable (repetitive) environments. Their analysis shows that low-end services (food processing, warehousing, and retail, for instance) and manufacturing are critical areas where automation is likely to pervade (Figure 6.8).

From a labor perspective, the study shows that about 1.1 billion jobs could be lost due to automation. A literature review from the World Economic Forum (2016) invites us to remain cautious on figures, as different forecasts vary widely. Nevertheless, they quote figures in the range of those in McKinsey & Company's study, estimating around 50 percent of jobs being displaced. Their upper-end scenario reaches two billion jobs being displaced in the coming decades (Figure 6.9).

These studies also vary (and this is probably the most important) on the timeline for change. McKinsey & Company (2017) is likely one of the most conservative in its snapshot, projecting a transformation that could take decades to realize. They do, however, argue that the sooner the transition is done, the higher the productivity benefits.

No matter how wrong the available published forecasts are (and they could well be!), it is reasonable to assume that automation will displace a significant amount of jobs in a variety of sectors and the path toward new productive occupations is yet to be invented. Though there is global confidence, founded

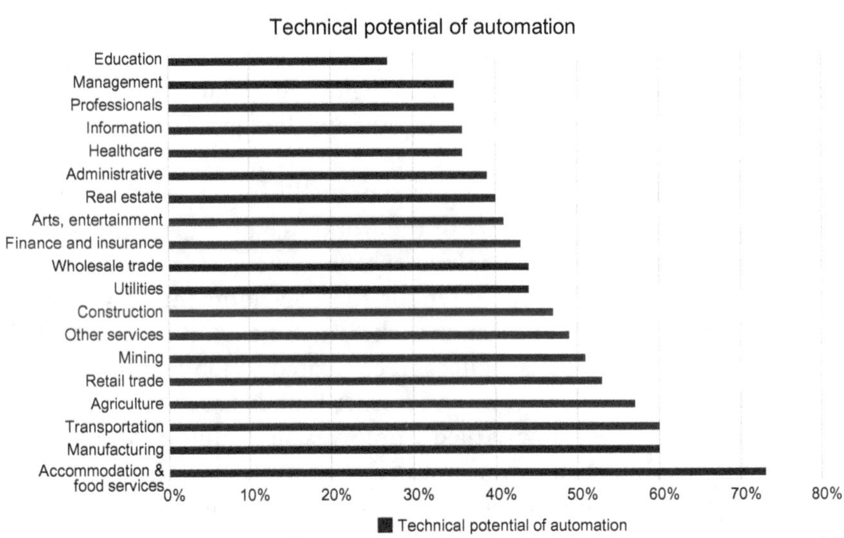

Figure 6.8 Technical potential of automation (McKinsey & Company, 2017)

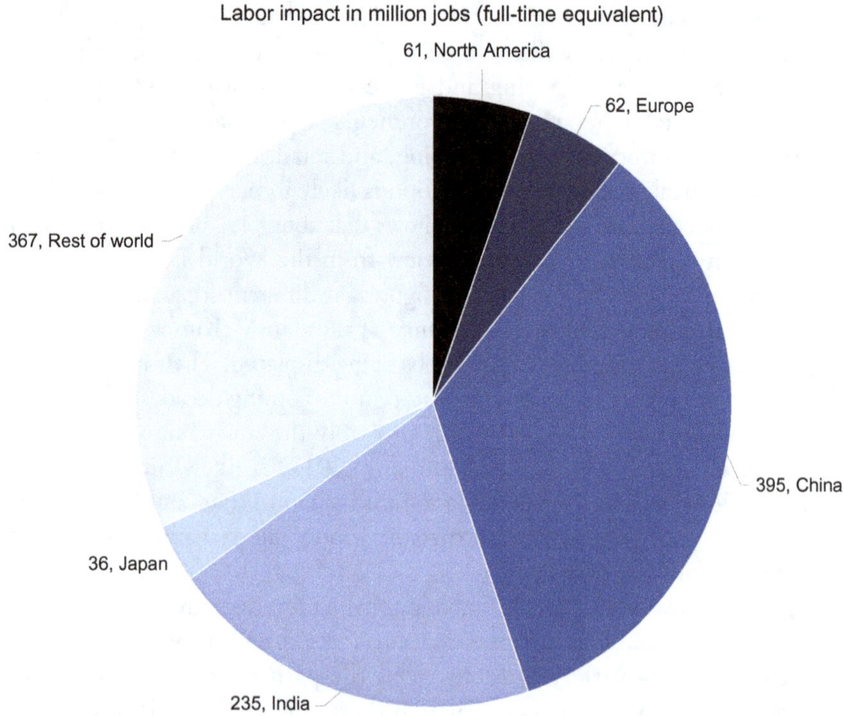

Figure 6.9 Labor impact in millions full-time equivalent (MFTE) (McKinsey & Company, 2017)

on current observations, that digital technologies will lead to new jobs that will compensate the losses, this is still an uncertainty (Bessen, 2016; Spears *et al.*, 2019).

Yet, the question of whether digitization will bring "wealth for all" can be posed. This relates to the ability of the workforce to either transition to a different (more digital) line of employment, or to integrate more digital into current work. The European Center for the Development of Vocational Training (CEDEFOP, 2016) finds that there will be 25–30 percent of the adult population with a digital skills gap compared to job requirements, an issue likely to increase in the coming years. It found that the people in this gap are part-time workers, low-skilled employees, and adult population over 40 years old. This skills gap could massively impact a growing part of the labor force, through employment opportunities and wages, modifying the current organizational structure of modern societies. There have been a lot of recent studies on the evolution of wage inequality across income groups

(Bernama, 2019; Muro *et al.*, 2017; Piketty, 2014; Rotman, 2014; Williams, 2017). Muro *et al.* (2017) notably demonstrates that there is a direct correlation between growth of employment and growth of wages. The study also found that jobs with medium digital skills are the most threatened today (lowest increase of employment, leading to lowest evolution of wages), leading to a polarization of employment between high digital skills jobs and low digital skills ones. A wage difference of up to three times exists between these types of jobs, leading to a strong polarization of wages and a subsequent rise of inequalities.

Ethics

Ethics is a wide subject that spans across information asymmetry and reliability, digital and human integration, and sustainability of the industry. Today, the lack of transparency on how data is handled leads to concerns around online profiling or discrimination. Two-thirds of Europeans believe that digital companies reap most of the benefits of digitization, in comparison to consumers (World Economic Forum, 2016). Virtual reputation is also a key concern as "nothing is forgotten" (Schmidt and Cohen, 2015).

Ethics, then, is also about information reliability and the rise of fake news is worrying. Martens *et al.* (2018) and Newman (2018) have both studied the digital transformation of the information economy and found a similar paradox. On the one hand, the use of social media as a source of news has significantly grown in recent years, but on the other hand, the trust in various news sources varies widely and is the lowest for social media at 20 percent. As a result of this, a rising number of people are exposed to fake news yet confused about it.

The next concern relates to digital and human integration in work and life. Firstly, the amount of time per day smartphones are being used has skyrocketed in the last five years by an average of 50 percent (Armstrong, 2018). Smartphone usage also pervaded most of people's daily activities. The question of digital addiction is a key emerging issue. Going further, the World Economic Forum (2016) points out the potential weakening of traditional human capabilities induced by digital advances (like mental computing, for instance) (Figure 6.10).

The final topic on ethics regards industry sustainability. The impact of the development of information and communication technology (ICT) on energy consumption (as well as rare materials mining), thus CO_2 emissions, has been notably largely debated, and is a key rising concern (Andrae and Edler, 2013; The Shift Project, 2018).

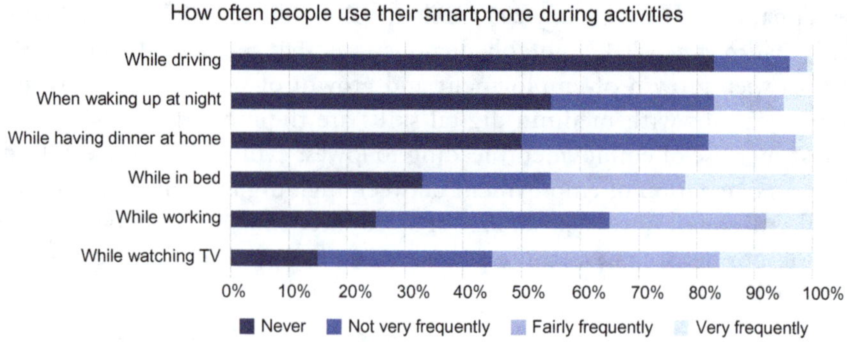

Figure 6.10 Smartphone usage patterns (Armstrong, 2018)

Security

Security is the last topic that impacts trust. For example, only 11 percent of the American people are confident that their data is well protected according to the World Economic Forum (2016). This impression is largely justified when looking at global figures of cybercrime. Ernst & Young (2018) provided the following statistics: 6.4 billion fake emails were sent every day in 2017, while 1.9 billion personal data records were compromised. The average cost of a data breach in business in 2017 reached US$3.62 million. The size of the issue is also getting bigger, with Morgan (2018) estimating that cybercrime damage could reach US$6 trillion by 2021 (a two-fold increase compared to 2015).

In a nutshell, the future of jobs and rising inequalities, ethics, and security could all impact the level of trust people place in the rising digital economy. Failing to address these demands could, at least in western democracies, impact its development. It could also shape it in ways that would eventually differ greatly from the initial promises of a global and open Internet.

Key Interaction Points: The System Map

This chapter has explored the potential impacts of the digital economy on the global landscape. It finds that the future of the digital economy remains uncertain as it still evolving. Firstly, the rise of the digital economy needs to prove its case for economic growth as well as overcoming major issues. Secondly, the rise of the digital economy could prove to be more of a dividing factor, aggravating trends that have already emerged as the world was globalizing. It could, for example, serve further political integration within new

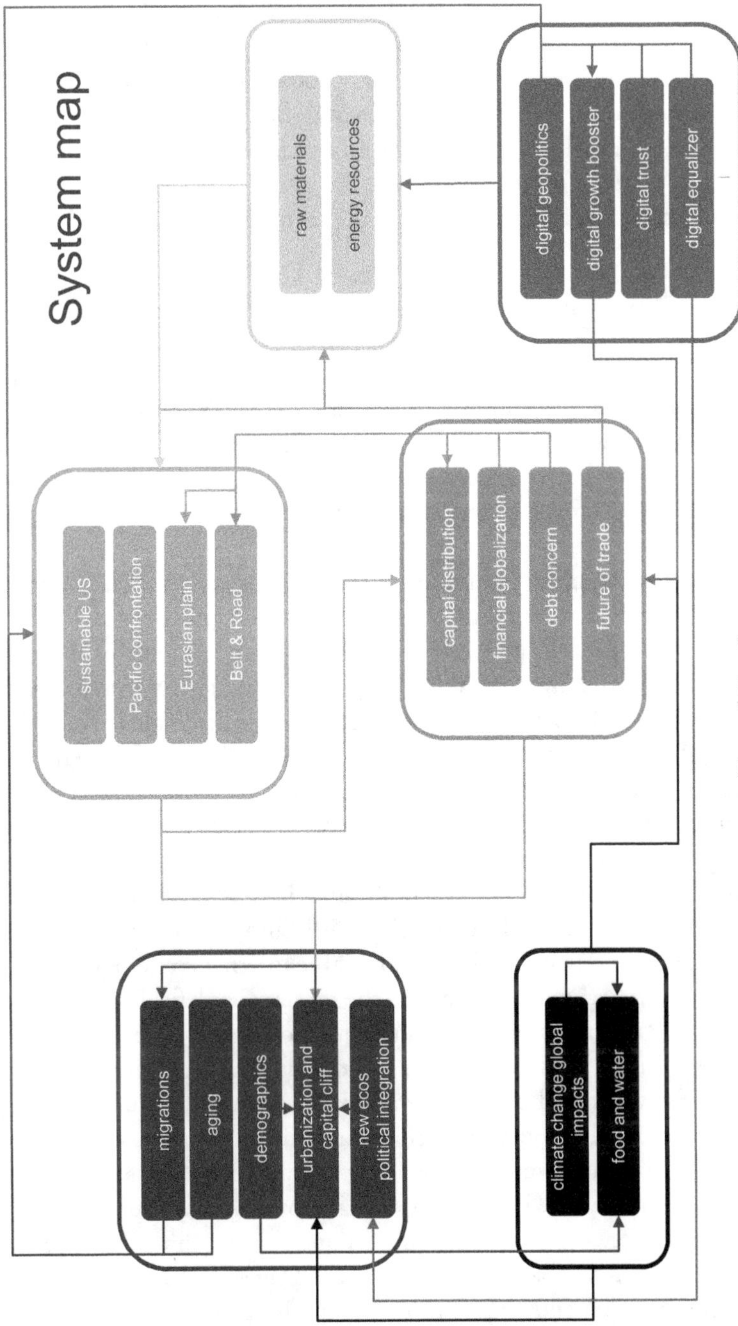

Figure 6.11 System map

economies or, on the contrary, weaken their development. Then, the digital economy still has to win the trust of consumers and significant questions remain to be answered. Failure to do so could lead to a digital slowdown, if not a breakdown. The digital economy also yields a new realm of geopolitical dependencies that could significantly impact global geopolitical stances from large powerhouses. Finally, digital technologies could enable new approaches to energy supply or the growing problem of resource scarcity by supporting a careful and thoughtful transition toward more sustainable models, or not (Figure 6.11).

Summary

The digitization of the economy has already provided significant benefits through a complete revolution on information and knowledge sharing. The rise of the digital economy has enabled access to more data at a faster rate and lower cost for a significant share of the world population, whether it is goods, information, or personal opportunities.

Alongside these benefits, digitization is also facing significant challenges that remain to be addressed, which could hamper its development going forward. Firstly, the actual impact on productivity and GDP growth remains to be fully demonstrated. Then, the rise of the digital economy could follow a similar pattern to globalization. It tends to accentuate the global economic divide between "connected" powerhouses and those still emerging. It also disrupts fragmented and complex networks of economic and human relations. It is also expected to displace a significant share of middle-class jobs. Secondly, foreign relations engage in the virtual space, transforming geopolitics. An exacerbation of the competition between the United States and China is already visible, as the two giants share strategic and conflicting cross-dependencies, with Europe thus far largely absent from this competition. Then, a balkanization of the Internet is also possible (if not probable), where new economies would be the primary battlefield. Finally, a large trust issue is emerging in mature economies, questioning the development of the digital economy. Rising social inequalities could be further aggravated with digitization, polarizing wages, and putting the middle class under pressure. Large ethical concerns also need to be addressed around information asymmetry and reliability, addiction, the potential weakening of traditional human capabilities, and industry sustainability. Lastly, the virtual world is a new playground for cybercrime, which is evolving in its complexity and remains difficult to prevent.

None of this is inevitable though. These challenges could, on the contrary, turn into significant benefits, in terms of productivity, living enrichment, and greater collaboration across the world. The way the Internet world will, together with governments, organize the digital economy of tomorrow, will have significant impacts on global economic development and geopolitics. Confrontation between digital powerhouses is, however, not likely to yield positive outcomes. A different voice needs to be heard. This is another major uncertainty.

References

Albrecht, B. (2013). "A Road Map to Technology Metals — Part 2: Rare Earths," *Kitco*, 13 September. Available from: https://www.kitco.com/ind/Albrecht/2013-09-05-A-Road-Map-To-Technology-Metals-Part-2-Rare-Earths.html [Accessed: November 2019].

Ambrosetti. (2018). *Geopolitics of Digital. New Borders, Growth and Security of the Country. Second Edition, November 2018*. Available from: https://www.ambrosetti.eu/en/research-and-presentations/geopolitica-del-digitale-nuovi-confini-crescita-e-sicurezza-del-paese/ [Accessed: November 2019].

Andrae, A. and Edler, T. (2013). "On Global Electricity Usage of Communication Technology: Trends to 2030," *Challenges* 2015, 6, 117–157. Available from: www.mdpi.com/2078-1547/6/1/117/pdf [Accessed: November 2019].

Armstrong, M. (2018). "Smartphone Addiction in the UK," *Statista*, 19 October. Available from: https://www.statista.com/chart/15838/smartphone-addiction-in-the-uk/ [Accessed: November 2019].

Bernama. (2019). "Digitalisation Threatens to Enlarge Wage Inequality: Research," *New Straits Times*, 17 November. Available from: https://www.nst.com.my/business/2017/11/304246/digitalisation-threatens-enlarge-wage-inequality-research [Accessed: November 2019].

Bessen, J. (2016). "Computers Don't Kill Jobs but Do Increase Inequality," *Harvard Business Review*, 24 March. Available from: https://hbr.org/2016/03/computers-dont-kill-jobs-but-do-increase-inequality [Accessed: November 2019].

Cedefop. (2016). "The Great Divide: Digitalisation and Digital Skill Gaps in the EU Workforce," *#ESJsurvey Insights, No 9*. Thessaloniki: European Centre for the Development of Vocational Training (Cedefop). Available from: http://www.cedefop.europa.eu/files/esj_insight_9_digital_skills_final.pdf [Accessed: November 2019].

Chakravorti, B., Bhalla, A., Chaturvedi, R. (2018). "The 4 Dimensions of Digital Trust, Charted Across 42 Countries," *Harvard Business Review*, 19 February. Available from: https://hbr.org/2018/02/the-4-dimensions-of-digital-trust-charted-across-42-countries [Accessed: November 2019].

Christian, P. (2018). "Where Are the World's Cloud Data Centers and Who Is Using Them?" *TeleGeography*, 10 April. Available from: https://blog.telegeography.com/where-are-the-worlds-cloud-data-centers-and-who-is-using-them [Accessed: November 2019].

Cisco. (2018). *Cisco Global Cloud Index: Forecast and Methodology, 2016–2021 White Paper*. Available from: https://www.cisco.com/c/en/us/solutions/collateral/service-provider/global-cloud-index-gci/white-paper-c11-738085.html [Accessed: November 2019].

The Conference Board Canada. (2019). *Graduates in Science, Math, Computer Science, and Engineering*. Available from: https://www.conferenceboard.ca/hcp/provincial/education/sciencegrads.aspx?AspxAutoDetectCookieSupport=1 [Accessed: November 2019].

Data Center Map. (2018). *Data Center Map*. Available from: https://www.datacentermap.com/ [Accessed: November 2019].

DMCC. (2018). "The Impact of Digitalisation," *The Future of Trade*. Available from: https://futureoftrade.com/the-impact-of-digitalisation [Accessed: November 2019].

The Economist. (2018). "The Semiconductor Industry and the Power of Globalization," *The Economist*, 1 December. Available from: https://www.economist.com/briefing/2018/12/01/the-semiconductor-industry-and-the-power-of-globalisation [Accessed: November 2019].

Ernst & Young. (2018). *Is Cybersecurity about More than Protection? EY Global Information Security Survey 2018-19*. Available from: https://assets.ey.com/content/dam/ey-sites/ey-com/en_gl/topics/advisory/GISS-2018-19-low-res.pdf [Accessed: November 2019].

Gardels, N. (2018). "The Geopolitics of Artificial Intelligence," *The Washington Post*, 28 September. Available from: https://www.washingtonpost.com/news/theworldpost/wp/2018/09/28/artificial-intelligence-3/?utm_term=.1f0ba4c39566 [Accessed: November 2019].

Horwitz, J. (2018). "Why the Semiconductor Is Suddenly at the Heart of US-China Tech Tensions," *Quartz*, 25 July. Available from: https://qz.com/1335801/us-china-tech-why-the-semiconductor-is-suddenly-at-the-heart-of-us-china-tensions/ [Accessed: November 2019].

Lapedus, M. (2015). "Searching For Rare Earths Again," *Semiconductor Engineering*, 19 February. Available from: https://semiengineering.com/searching-for-rare-earths-again/ [Accessed: November 2019].

Lee, T. (2014). "40 Maps That Explain the Internet," *Vox*, 2 June. Available from: https://www.vox.com/a/internet-maps [Accessed: November 2019].

Manyika, J., Lund, S., Bughin, J., Woetzel, J., Stamenov, K. and Dhingra, D. (2016). *Digital Globalization: The New Era of Global Flows*, McKinsey Global Institute, February 2016. Available from: https://www.mckinsey.com/business-functions/digital-mckinsey/our-insights/digital-globalization-the-new-era-of-global-flows [Accessed: November 2019].

Martens, B., Aguiar, L., Gomez-Herrera, E. and Mueller-Langer, F. (2018). "The Digital Transformation of News Media and the Rise of Disinformation and Fake News,"

JRC Technical Reports: JRC Digital Economy Working Paper 2018-02, European Commission, April 2018. Available from: https://ec.europa.eu/jrc/communities/sites/jrccties/files/dewp_201802_digital_transformation_of_news_media_and_the_rise_of_fake_news_final_180418.pdf [Accessed: November 2019].

McCarthy, N. (2017). "The Countries with the Most STEM Graduates [Infographic]," *Forbes*, 2 February. Available from: https://www.forbes.com/sites/niallmccarthy/2017/02/02/the-countries-with-the-most-stem-graduates-infographic/#2a6a3c0f268a [Accessed: November 2019].

McKinsey & Company. (2017). *A Future That Works: Automation, Employment and Productivity*. Available from: https://www.mckinsey.com/mgi/overview/2017-in-review/automation-and-the-future-of-work/a-future-that-works-automation-employment-and-productivity [Accessed: November 2019].

Mims, C. (2013a). "China Just Surpassed the US in Semiconductor Manufacturing — and the Trend Is Likely to Accelerate," *Quartz*, 9 April. Available from: https://qz.com/72542/china-just-surpassed-the-us-in-semiconductor-manufacturing-and-the-trend-is-likely-to-accelerate/ [Accessed: November 2019].

Mims, C. (2013b). "Just Four Companies Will Produce the Microchips on Which the Global Economy Depends," *Quartz*, 25 April. Available from: https://qz.com/78272/just-four-companies-will-produce-the-microchips-on-which-the-global-economy-depends/ [Accessed: November 2019].

Morgan, S. (2018). "Top 5 Cybersecurity Facts, Figures, Predictions, and Statistics for 2019 to 2021," *Cybercrime Magazine*, 29 March. Available from: https://cybersecurityventures.com/top-5-cybersecurity-facts-figures-predictions-and-statistics-for-2019-to-2021/ [Accessed: November 2019].

Muro, M., Liu, S., Whiton, J. and Kulkarni, S. (2017). *Digitization and the American Workforce*. Metropolitan Policy Program at Brookings. Available from: https://www.brookings.edu/wp-content/uploads/2017/11/mpp_2017nov15_digitalization_full_report.pdf#page=21 [Accessed: November 2019].

Newman, N. (2018). *Digital News Report 2018, Overview and Key Findings of the 2018 Report*. Available from: http://www.digitalnewsreport.org/survey/2018/overview-key-findings-2018/ [Accessed: November 2019].

Ott, S. (2018). "European Chip Industry Aims to Get Back on the Map," *Handelsblatt*, 30 April. Available from: https://www.handelsblatt.com/today/companies/semiconductors-european-chip-industry-aims-to-get-back-on-the-map/23582014.html?ticket=ST-930546-ICU0BQ5LPFdInseficp0-ap1 [Accessed: November 2019].

Piketty, T. (2014). *Capital in the Twenty-First Century*. Massachusetts: Belknap Press.

Productronica. (2018). *The Semiconductors Cluster: A Key Element in Electronics Manufacturing*. Available from: https://www.productronica.com/en/trade-fair/exhibition-sectors/semiconductor/ [Accessed: November 2019].

Rotman, D. (2014). "Technology and Inequality — The Disparity Between the Rich and Everyone Else Is Larger Than Ever in the United States and Increasing in Much of Europe, Why?" *Technology Review*, 21 October. Available from: https://www.technologyreview.com/s/531726/technology-and-inequality/ [Accessed: November 2019].

Schmidt, E. and Cohen, J. (2015). *The New Digital Age: Transforming Nations, Businesses, and Our Lives.* London: Vintage Books.

The Shift Project. (2018). *Rapport Intermédiaire Du Groupe De Travail Dirigé Par Hugues Ferreboeuf Pour Le Think. Tank the Shift Project—Mars 2018.* Available from: https://theshiftproject.org/wp-content/uploads/2018/05/2018-05-17_Rapport-interm%C3%A9diaire_Lean-ICT-Pour-une-sobri%C3%A9t%C3%A9-num%C3%A9rique.pdf [Accessed: November 2019].

Spears, M., Bolton, R. and Brown, D. (2019). "Rise of the Humans 1 & 2 & 3. The Integration of Digital and Human Labor," *KPMG*, 6 October. Available from: https://home.kpmg/xx/en/home/insights/2016/11/rise-of-the-humans.html [Accessed: November 2019].

Starosielski, N. (2015). "In Our Wi-Fi World, the Internet Still Depends on Undersea Cables," *The Conversation*, 3 November. Available from: https://theconversation.com/in-our-wi-fi-world-the-internet-still-depends-on-undersea-cables-49936 [Accessed: November 2019].

Sverdlik, Y. (2017). "Research: There are Now Close to 400 Hyper-Scale Data Centers in the World," *DataCenter Knowledge*, 22 December. Available from: https://www.datacenterknowledge.com/cloud/research-there-are-now-close-400-hyper-scale-data-centers-world [Accessed: November 2019].

United Nations. (2017). *World Population Prospects: The 2017 Revision.* Available from: https://www.un.org/development/desa/publications/world-population-prospects-the-2017-revision.html [Accessed: November 2019].

Walton, J. (2017). "The World's Top 10 Semiconductor Companies," *Investopedia*, 21 March. Available from: https://www.investopedia.com/articles/markets/012216/worlds-top-10-semiconductor-companies-tsmintc.asp [Accessed: November 2019].

Williams, J. (2017). "How Digital Technology Drives Inequality," *The Earthbound Report*, 11 October. Available from: https://makewealthhistory.org/2017/10/11/how-digital-technology-drives-inequality/ [Accessed: November 2019].

World Economic Forum. (2016). *World Economic Forum White Paper Digital Transformation of Industries: In collaboration with Accenture Societal Implications.* Available from: http://reports.weforum.org/digital-transformation/wp-content/blogs.dir/94/mp/files/pages/files/dti-societal-implications-white-paper.pdf [Accessed: November 2019].

CHAPTER 7

A View to the Future — Plausible Scenarios for a New Global Order

Why Scenarios Matter

This book has reviewed a number of paradigm changes that all could unfold in various ways in the decades to come.

One of the first key questions is centered on the future of the three billion people expected to reach cities by 2050. Will there be three billion people joining cities? Will those people access the middle class or not? These questions lead to significant uncertainties. Firstly, demographic projections show clear patterns of development in new economies. Then, aging global population is already a reality and should have very large impacts on the key concerned economies in the coming decades — namely in mature economies and China. A critical uncertainty is also the ability of new economies to absorb large contingents of the population within cities and meet the corresponding capital cliff in terms of infrastructures' investments. Finally, migration will be a definite trend of the times to come. Their level, however, remains a question.

The second key theme is that of geopolitical stances across regions, particularly large powerhouses. The first question here will be about the dominance of the United States going forward. Will the country keep its level of influence over world affairs, or could internal developments modify this situation in future? A second key question is how the inevitable confrontation in the Pacific will unfold between China and the United States. Then, the future of Europe and Russia is still developing and remains a key uncertainty. Finally, grand plans such as the Belt and Road Initiative have yet to prove successful or not. These questions will reshape global order in a variety of possible ways.

The third key theme is resources. Global economic activity is boosted by demographics and is likely to significantly impact raw materials and energy resources consumption. The geopolitics of these resources is already complex, and it will play a vital role in the future world order, as secured access will become a matter of national security, even more so than today. Dependencies are also likely to evolve, depending on innovation, possible scarcity of some materials, and risks to global supply chains.

Climate change is the next key unknown of the decades to come. Already, food and water scarcity are apparent in a number of regions, and likely to increase in the coming decades with rising population. Climate change is also likely to touch those regions primarily, but the extent to which it will materialize remains an unknown. Significant transformations of climate conditions could have catastrophic consequences on these regions and lead to a multitude of global impacts (such as economic crises, uncontrolled migration, or conflicts).

The future of the global economic context is also uncertain. For decades now, the world has globalized, accelerating trade across regions. This has led to a number of commercial imbalances that are likely to overshadow the future of trade exchanges. In addition, the world has seen a sharp rise of wealth creation, though its distribution has remained very unequal, leading to uncertainties on how this will evolve going forward. The world has, therefore, enjoyed a long period of low-cost access to capital, but it is unknown as to whether this situation will continue or not. Despite slowing down in the last decade following the crisis in 2008, financial globalization has soared reaching higher levels than ever, creating significant dependencies between mature and new economies. Finally, debt levels of several regions have significantly increased and, while not a current concern, in a period of low interest rates due to capital abundance, this situation could evolve going forward.

The last main paradigm change revolves around the rise of the digital economy. As productivity increases have dropped in recent decades, the digital economy is presented as a new growth booster for the world economy by many of its proponents. Yet, the case has yet to be proven. While digitization of the economy is accelerating globally, a number of challenges remain to be addressed, notably to what extent this new economy is able to heal global divides across regions and within countries, as well as the number of trust issues that could hamper its development. Finally, the rise of the digital economy is also creating a whole new paradigm of dependencies that will have an impact — where they have not already — on geopolitical stances.

This score of changes and their inherent uncertainty will play out and determine the Future of the Global Order. They are also related to one another and can accelerate or hinder critical evolutions. The system map, which has been progressively drawn out across the chapters, is an account of these dependencies. It shows that global political stances or economic relations do not exist in isolation. They are related and dependent on demographic and urbanization developments, as well as the evolving situation of resources and climate change.

So, what can we take away from all of this?

At this stage of the book, the complexity of changes and the uncertainty toward these changes can appear confusing. This complex account of facts and questions, dependent on one another, creates a multitude of possible pathways toward a future global order, which by nature is difficult, if not impossible, to predict.

This is where scenario planning comes into play. The whole purpose of scenario planning is to define plausible scenarios for how uncertainties will unfold and how the associated dependencies will play out. This is not an analytical exercise, rather a way to connect these uncertainties in plausible combinations. Many different scenarios could indeed unfold and it is impossible to be completely exhaustive. The intent of building scenarios is, rather, to illustrate what could be the most defining pathways our future world order will gear toward, in order to inform about possible developments.

Four Scenarios for the Future of the Global Order

The final part of this book details a set of four plausible scenarios, based on the analysis above, and will develop them as rich storylines. The purpose of this exercise is to provide a set of visions of the Future of the Global Order in 2050 that could be used to share understanding on the key uncertainties that propel our future in one direction or another. We believe this exercise to be useful to all those who want to further understand the key factors at play in shaping our common future. The following scenarios are all exclusive with one another, designed to draw attention to a number of possible developments and key questions at hand.

These four scenarios have been developed using the inductive method approach from the Oxford University Planning Approach (Ramirez and Wilkinson, 2016). Alternative methodologies such as deductive scenario planning are usually better suited for clarification of key specific issues, while inductive scenario building usually enables richer storylines to be developed. The complexity of the topic at hand naturally directed us toward an inductive approach.

The first scenario (multipolar) takes stock of the failure of the current multilateral framework, resulting in confrontation between key powerhouses, namely the United States and China. The world evolves toward a multipolar model, with China and the United States confronting across several regions of the world.

The second scenario (re-engineering), on the contrary, sees a complete renovation of multilateral institutions that balance out confronting powerhouses. From this, a deep transformation of international relations, a re-engineering of how the world operates begins.

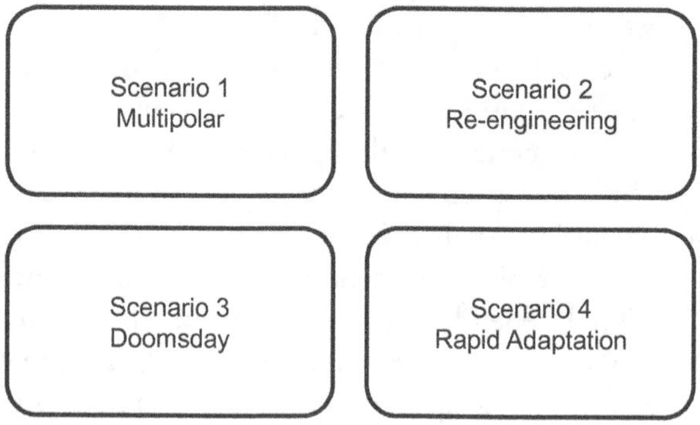

Figure 7.1 Four scenarios for the future world order

In the third scenario (doomsday), climate change kicks in. The materialization of profound transformation to the Earth's cycle leads to a global economic crisis, as well as local conflicts and humanitarian crises in many regions of the world. This scenario models a global collapse of the current system.

Finally, the last scenario (rapid adaptation) is that of a rapid and coordinated adaptation. In a world where climate change materializes progressively, robust and effective multilateral institutions are put together to deal with associated issues. These institutions, with countries from all over the world behind them, drive the necessary fast-paced adaptation response to these radical changes and invent a new model in response (Figure 7.1).

Each of these scenarios has been developed into rich storylines. Following a brief overview, each scenario provides a detailed perspective of each of the uncertainties described above. It then looks at specific development patterns per region before illustrating through the system map how critical uncertainties interconnect to drive the unfolding of each scenario. At the end of the analysis of these scenarios, a table summarizes the key findings and differences across the scenarios.

Scenario 1 — Multipolar

The multipolar world sees the rise of China as a dominant powerhouse, which confronts the United States. Europe has essentially failed to integrate and promote an alternative voice in the concert of nations. The region is essentially a large market, with a relatively wealthy population consuming products from abroad. Both the United States and China compete to thrive in this world. From a technology standpoint, they design different approaches, notably on the development of the digital economy and the energy transition. From a geopolitical standpoint, they strive to control and secure their access routes to economic growth potential, and resources of all kinds to feed their industrial footprint. The development of the Chinese military power is now in a position to confront the United States, particularly in the Pacific. The Belt and Road Initiative is a success, lifting up the international status of China in many regions of the world. The connection of China to European countries through this large network of infrastructure routes fuels economic growth significantly in the first half of the twenty-first century, particularly for these economies along the Silk Roads which have so far been poorly integrated. Yet, new economies react in a variety of way to this confrontation between the two dominant ruling forces. Some are able to reap significant benefits, reinforce their political integration, and fuel their development. For others, global competition exacerbates political instability and fuels corruption, yielding local conflict situations.

Demographics, social	**Limited openings in a competitive world** Population increases up to 10 billion people by 2050, notably in India and Africa. Aging of the world's population becomes more significant, leading to more issues with associated social systems in a number of regions. While already apparent in 2019 in mature economies from the West, the issue takes prominence in new economies, like China. Overall, economic development buys social peace. No government or regime is truly threatened or questioned. In this world of competition and confrontation, social opening remains limited in most countries. Strong and coercive regimes tend to reinforce this, while mature democracies tend to see rising nationalism with little attention to open and free information. Social divides remain and are exacerbated, notably with the rise of the digital economy. Political integration in new economies tends to vary depending on the situation. In countries facing social and political disorder, economic development remains limited, leading to more migrations toward mature economies, such as Europe and the United States.
Geopolitics	**Global competition in a multipolar world** The world is split between two areas of influence, with the United States and China as dominant ruling forces. Europe has not managed to build up further political integration, and essentially remains a free-trade zone. This results in

	Russia turning toward Asia to build strategic alliances, notably China. China is the rising force of this scenario. The country significantly increases its ties with new economies, particularly in Asia, but also in Africa and Latin America. Global institutions remain weak and become further diminished as China rallies new economies to denounce how these institutions have traditionally favored the United States. The country secures its access to critical resources and trade opportunities. The United States and China confront each other on many occasions. To a large extent, this competition becomes an ideological battle, with new economies forming the playground of this competition. Some benefit from this, attracting more financial capital and support than ever before. Others, however, suffer from it with endemic corruption, rising local conflicts or civil wars.
Resources	**Competition and new frontier exploration** Economic development continues as new economies reduce the economic gap with mature economies. The Belt and Road Initiative is a success, further fostering global Gross Domestic Product (GDP) growth. This yields intensified pressure on raw materials and energy resources, while creating further dependencies between exporters and importers, and an increased competition to access resources, notably by the two dominant forces — China and the United States. Both regions accelerate their development and participation in new economies, while influencing local politics in an attempt to compete for domination in these regions. This leads to increased corruption and political instability in many regions. Furthermore, as pressing needs for resources continue to intensify, significant capital is devoted to exploration for more resources in new frontiers, particularly at sea. The Pacific Ocean becomes a clear area of confrontation between the two powerhouses. Some innovation is also dedicated to developing new materials and increasing the rate of recycling, yet it remains limited in comparison to the budgets allocated to exploration. From an energy standpoint, two worlds emerge with different paradigms. The United States becomes the first exporter of oil and natural gas to the world, surpassing the Middle East, while China promotes an energy system founded on renewable energies. These two visions compete in a divided world.

Climate	**Climate change in some new economies** While access to food and water remains an issue in many new economies, climate change starts to materialize at a rather slow pace. It particularly impacts new economies around the Tropic of Cancer (Central America, Northern Africa, the Middle East, Central Asia, North of India, and a number of Eastern Asian countries). Adaptation increasingly becomes the norm, and some measures are taken, notably in mature economies, to cope with these changes. In new economies, measures are more limited, creating social crises here and there. As a consequence, migration is on the rise, but it is not extremely significant as yet. The United States adopts extremely restrictive legislations to prevent an upheaval. Europe is less coercive and, as a result, tends to be destabilized by increasing flows of migrants, which in turns increases populism across Europe and prevents further integration of the region.
Global economy	**Regional divide** The global economic environment remains positive in the decades leading to 2040, despite a small economic crisis in the mid-2020s, which is rapidly mitigated in the United States and China but leads Europe (alongside other OECD [Organisation for Economic Co-operation and Development] Asia economies) to significant deleveraging, yielding some social unrest and hampering the political integration of the region. Elsewhere, the economy keeps flourishing. The Belt and Road Initiative is a success, enabling China to increase its influence in many regions of the world, promoting an alternative model to that of the United States. While economic development continues, financial deepening of many economies accelerates, particularly in China. This results in a massive flux of capital that keeps costs of capital low and enables further capital investments, notably in new economies, boosting their growth. The rise of the digital economy also accelerates economic development, patronized by both the United States and China, further accentuating the regional leadership divide.
Digital and innovation	**Digital competitive space** Innovation is boosted by relatively low costs of capital. It is traditionally directed toward building technologies that could serve global leadership. This scenario is a one of intense

	investment in new capabilities to provide better infrastructures, secure resources (particularly in new frontiers like the deep sea), build up large military capacities, and accelerate the transition to a digital economy. In every sector, a fierce competition continues between Chinese and American technology leaders to gain supremacy and rally allies in new economies. The digital economy remains a very competitive space, which further aggravates the divide between regions under influence of the United States or China.

United States	**Leader of the "free" world** The United States is tied into a fierce competition with China for global leadership. Despite internal demographics that tend to push the United States toward a more inner focus, the government's elites all actively commit to a strong position on world affairs in order to maintain American leadership over China's ascent. The country promotes values of openness, free trade, and democracy to other countries, rallying its electorate to an ideological conflict with China, as it used to do during the 1950s with the Soviet Union. The country is, more than ever, the leader of the "free" world. Its ability to mobilize capital helps reap major benefits outside its borders, leading to a flourishing economy and unparalleled international position. The economy is flourishing, propelled by a huge rent from full energy independence and its status as first energy exporter to the world. The United States also enjoys significant access to raw materials and has privileged relations with many countries, particularly South America, which is rich in materials. Its military projection capabilities also help it to maintain status quo in a number of regions, confronting China for domination.
China	**New "harmony" leader** China is emerging as an alternative leader in this polarized world. Its economic power helps develop stronger ties with many new economies, particularly those from the Belt and Road Initiative. Its rising military power in the Pacific confronts that of the United States and leads to further political ascent in many of the surrounding countries. Its economy flourishes. China also leads the charge against global

	institutions, which it proclaims favor the United States. Many "non-aligned" countries are sensitive to its arguments and strengthen their relations with China, starting with Russia and several countries in South-Eastern Asia and Africa. The country promotes a different vision of the world, less reliant on opening and democracy, and more on organized harmony between people and the planet. Living standards progressively catch up with that of mature economies, yet they do not reach the levels of the United States, which have benefited from significant financial deepening for a long time, favoring private wealth growth. Aging also kicks in progressively and forces the country to reinvent its social protection system to cope with rising levels of the elderly population.
Europe	**Great stagnation** Europe faces an economic crisis in the mid-2020s that forces a deleveraging, leading to austerity measures and impoverishment for the population, alongside a rise of unemployment. Additionally, it suffers from large migrations from countries in Africa and the Middle East, which deeply destabilize its social cohesion. Significant social unrest emerges from these migrations, which create grounds for populism. Political attention is therefore directed to inner issues. As disconnect between Northern Europe and Southern Europe economies increases, the development of the Union is hampered. This results in global stagnation in the European economy and the European project. The region fails to integrate politically and remains essentially a "free trade" zone, with a multitude of small economies competing internationally against the two powerhouses. Politically, Europe remains tied to the United States and NATO survives, while Russia intensifies its collaboration with China. Economically, the region exchanges are more balanced. Europe remains significantly dependent on imports of resources and energy and is therefore very sensitive to price fluctuations and geopolitical evolutions outside of its borders. It does works efficiently at diversifying its mix, however. Traditionally very dependent on Russia for energy, it diversifies its supply with gas from the United States and renewable technologies from China.

Other mature economies	**Great stagnation** Mature economies from Asia are particularly impacted by population aging and stable to declining demographics, which limit societal transformation. In addition, the rise of Chinese leadership leads to significant difficulties in the balance of trade power with China, as well as with other economies in Asia. This leads to these economies stagnating, with a debt burden that keeps increasing although not to a point of significant deleveraging (as most of the debt is owned locally). Global influence and innovation capacities remain limited. Australia is a different case as it reaps massive benefits from the pressing needs of resources. The country remains a "global mine" of the twenty-first century and its economy flourishes.
New economies	**Disparate development** New economies develop at various paces depending on their ability to integrate politically and lay the proper foundations for development. Some of these economies, because they represent a stake in the global confrontation between China and the United States, or because they hold large reserves of resources, are able to attract significant capital to help develop their economy. This is particularly true of countries from the Belt and Road Initiative. The level of engagement of the two powerhouses can lead to political instability and fuel corruption in certain cases, thus hampering economic development. This is particularly sensitive in regions with massive amounts of resources available, be it energy or raw materials. The extent to which climate change materializes in various economies also hampers potential economic growth, further reinforcing political instability, humanitarian issues, and more migration abroad. While Central Asia and Russia naturally strengthen their ties with China, the future of other regions is less clear. Latin America, traditionally tied to the United States, develops further relations with China, notably on resource trade. Then, the Middle East and Africa and, more importantly, South-Eastern Asia become spaces of confrontation between the two giants.

The system map helps summarize how these aspects of the scenario interconnect. The key relationships that define the multipolar scenario are highlighted in Figure 7.2.

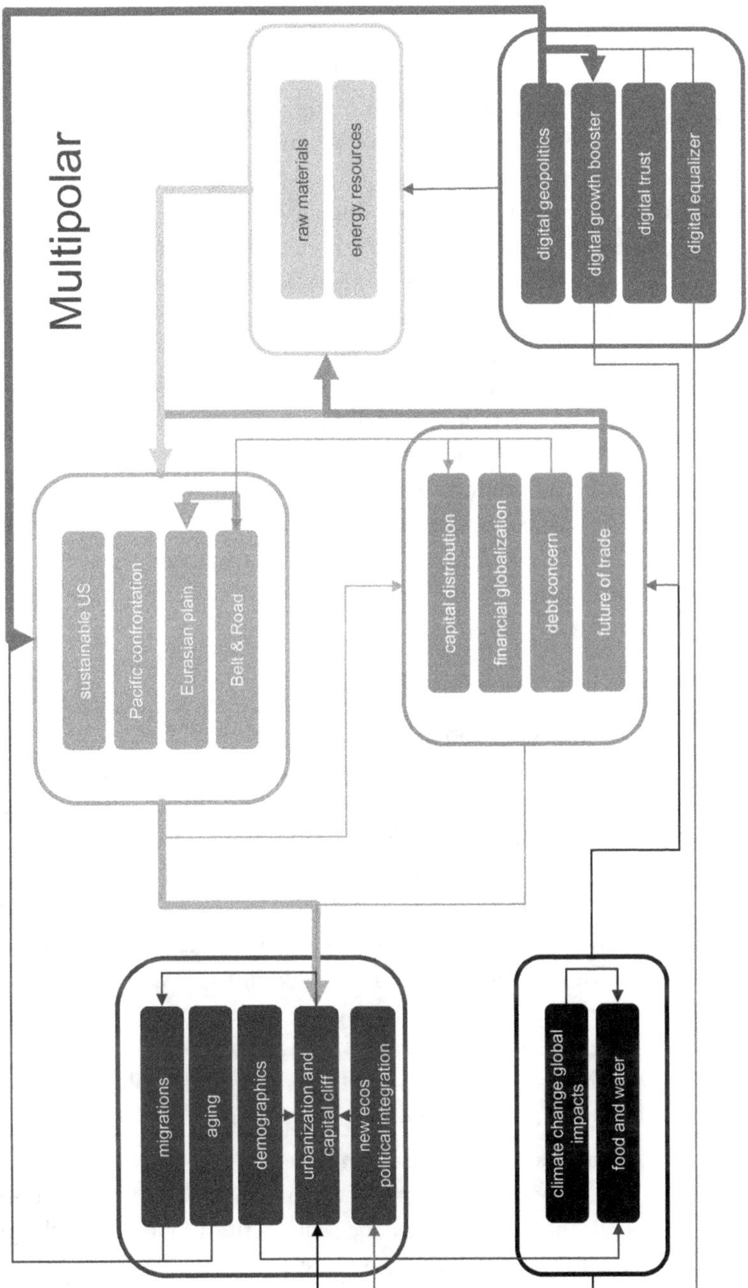

Figure 7.2 Multipolar scenario system map

Scenario 2 — Re-engineering

This scenario is characterized by revitalized multilateral institutions that take precedence in regards to global affairs. While China has been trying to rally new economies to a new framework of multilateral institutions, a reinvigorated European Union joins the effort and helps accelerate the development of a new set of institutions that are more representative. This framework is designed to cope with the challenges of global economic development, reduction of inequalities, and global issues including climate change and growing scarcity of resources. The Belt and Road Initiative is a success, and most new economies eventually stabilize and further integrate themselves in the global economy, while progressively accelerating living standards to parallel mature economies. The next generation plays a critical role in the "re-engineering" of world order. They are more politically active and socially participative, demanding greater opening and access to information. Political contexts and global institutions evolve accordingly. Climate change also begins to materialize, but it mainly impacts certain new economies in the first half of the twenty-first century, which are supported by global institutions in their efforts to adapt. Climate change mitigation is high on the agenda and critical steps are taken to move forward. The world is wiser, peaceful, and innovative.

Demographics, social	**New living model for next generation** Aging is a critical topic in the first half of the twenty-first century, mainly in mature economies and China, partially compensated by a rise in migration. This new paradigm leads to the emergence of new models of solidarity across generations. This follows a progressive opening in most countries, pushed by an always-on and connected new generation, which demands and obtains access to global information. The next generation is much more politically active and socially participative, willing to contribute to tackling global issues and demanding significant evolutions. Social inequalities tend to diminish over the period.
Geopolitics	**Renewed multilateralism** The key transformation of this time is that of multilateral institutions to cope with critical global challenges. China has managed to rally many new economies into

	criticizing the functioning of the existing framework in 2019, taking stock of the limited improvements to many global topics, such as climate change, inequalities, and overall development in new economies. Countries from the European Union have eventually joined this effort and force a transformation of the multilateral framework, setting the bases of a new philosophy of international relations, based on cooperation (rather than confrontation) to tackle specific global challenges. Yet, things move slowly. Competition remains the norm and this transformation is generally opposed by the US stance. The ability of the European Union to emerge as a global political force accelerates this transformation. By 2050, the new framework is eventually in place.
Resources	**Global supply chains security, efficiency, and materials innovation** As economic growth continues, driven by population growth in new economies and overall benefits from new digital technologies advancements, significant constraints on resources emerge. Regions such as Europe and China, both heavily dependent, strive to project capabilities in new economies rich in materials, develop new exploration techniques, notably at sea, and adopt more efficient approaches and alternative materials. Circularity emerges as a solution, yet it takes time to fully implement globally, despite the demand from the new generation. From an energy standpoint, the transition to renewable energies keeps flourishing in many regions of the world. The United States remains distant from these innovations, notably due to the large independence of the region.
Climate	**Progressive adaptation** Climate change begins to materialize, but at a slow pace. It mainly touches new economies around the Tropic of Cancer, where food and water scarcity are progressively aggravated. This results in a slight increase of migrations, despite significant efforts to adapt locally. In addition, renewed global institutions help reach and enforce multilateral agreements to help mitigate the associated issues of adaptation.

Global economy	**Open economy** The economic environment significantly benefits from increased cooperation in worldwide affairs. Global capital flows keep expanding, the financial deepening of the economy accelerates, and Europe catches up with the United States, unleashing new capital to be deployed. As a consequence of this, costs of capital remain low, enabling significant investments to happen. The efforts of renewed global institutions to alleviate global divides across countries allow capital to be properly funneled into new economies, and the Belt and Road Initiative is a world-acclaimed success. This enables new economies to catch up quicker on higher living standards. The rise of the digital economy also serves as a growth booster. With this opening comes greater social inclusion and initial issues of trust are resolved, leading to a sharp development of digital capabilities in virtually every aspects of the economy. Yet, in this "open trade" world, significant account imbalances continue to persist between large industrial powerhouses like China and service-oriented economies like the Western ones. Tensions erupt here and there, but they are resolved through multilateral agreements. In addition, the rise of digital services enables a smoothing of these imbalances, to a certain extent.
Digital and innovation	**Digital collaborative ecosystems** The digital economy remains fueled by innovations coming from the United States and China. Both countries thrive, particularly in everything related to consumer goods and services. The European Union partially catches up to both powerhouses and takes a leadership role in the development of digital solutions for the industrial sector, rebuilding leadership in a variety of critical sectors such as transportation, manufacturing, or energy. Europe also leads the charge toward a more inclusive digital economy, paying significant attention to education and the needs of the new workforce. This model eventually prevails, and the focus moves to developing collaborative ecosystems spanning across regions, both for new consumer interactions and new models of consumption (emerging circularity). This helps

	to resolve the global divide and creates a new paradigm for the next generation's living style. To a large extent, innovation is consumer-led.

United States	**Resources giant** The United States remains a dominant force of this world. Yet, the country resents the relative loss of global leadership from the rise of China and the emergence of a strong multilateral framework. Nevertheless, they stay engaged in this new multilateral world. The country also adopts a progressively inner focus, which leaves space for other powerhouses to emerge. This is mainly due to the increasing share of Americans with Latin American roots. Tensions arise in certain regions, notably South-Eastern Asia and the Pacific, yet they end up being resolved in a peaceful manner. The economy keeps growing, despite a certain level of deleveraging due to the progressive retreat of the dollar as the international currency of reference. Inherent social inequalities tend to diminish with the evolution of the political context and rising demands from the new generation.
China	**Industrial giant** China is thriving in this new world. It rallies many new economies and Europe to rebuild a new framework of multilateralism, and expands its international ascent as a result, while benefiting from the economic opportunities that emerge. The Belt and Road Initiative is a large success, and a key element in the rise of China's leadership. As the economy keeps flourishing, living standards progressively rise to meet those of other mature economies. This success also drives a further opening in Chinese society, which the government controls with close attention. Financial deepening of the economy also increases, lifting up the wealth of many Chinese citizens over these decades. Chinese industry also moves up the value chain and becomes a critical player in advanced technologies. It notably leads the emergence of a global digital economy that is more focused on services.

Europe	**Multilateral champion** A new wave of European leaders emerges and develops a new vision for the continent, turning the European Union into a greater political force. Integration accelerates, aligning fiscal, economic, military, and political systems. The European Union emerges as an important powerhouse on the international scene, with economic power comparable to the size of the United States and China. Another result of this is the strengthened relationship with Russia, which becomes a significant partner of Europe, and eventually joins the Union by 2050. As a consequence, Europe's economy is strengthened. The region manages to reform its work and social system, to create further stability and alignment across nations. Increased financial deepening of the economy also enables cheaper access to capital that further increases the capabilities of the region, allowing it to achieve a "beautiful" deleveraging (Dalio, 2018). This successful integration of various nations serves as a model for a greater multilateral framework that eventually prevails by 2050. It also enables the continent to secure access to resources of all kinds, while diversifying its mix. The development of new technologies, particularly the digitization of the industrial sector and an innovative approach to environmental protection, founded on circularity and clean energy, both accelerate economic development. Europe also leads the change in building a more inclusive digital economy, with a strong focus on social protection and privacy.
Other mature economies	**Great stagnation** The multilateral and open environment favors the economy of other mature economies that have traditionally been heavily dependent on global trade. The aging of the population takes its toll, however, piling up significant costs to society,

	while preserving certain conservatisms. This situation yields rather limited innovation and social structures that fail to develop in this new global context. Their global influence tends to diminish overall. Australia is a special case as its economy remains boosted by the pressing need for resources.
New economies	**Historical catchup** Most new economies are growing, boosted by a more global and interconnected economic network, alongside significant support from multilateral institutions. The Belt and Road Initiative is an internationally acclaimed success, which helps accelerate this trend. Population keeps expanding and reaching cities that develop at an accelerated pace. Capital inflows are on the rise, as well as GDP and trade. This new wealth enables governments to finance infrastructures and education, which help living standards to rise. The political and social environment tends to be more stable, as a result of this historical catchup. The rise of the digital economy also enables a new market for services to emerge, which enables further activity, and exports to rise. New economies leapfrog this potential to a great extent. Some countries, however, face increasing impacts from climate change. Food dependencies and water scarcity arise, but the new framework of multilateral institutions supports the necessary adaptation efforts of these regions.

The system map helps summarize how these aspects of the scenario interconnect. The key relationships that define the re-engineering scenario are highlighted in Figure 7.3.

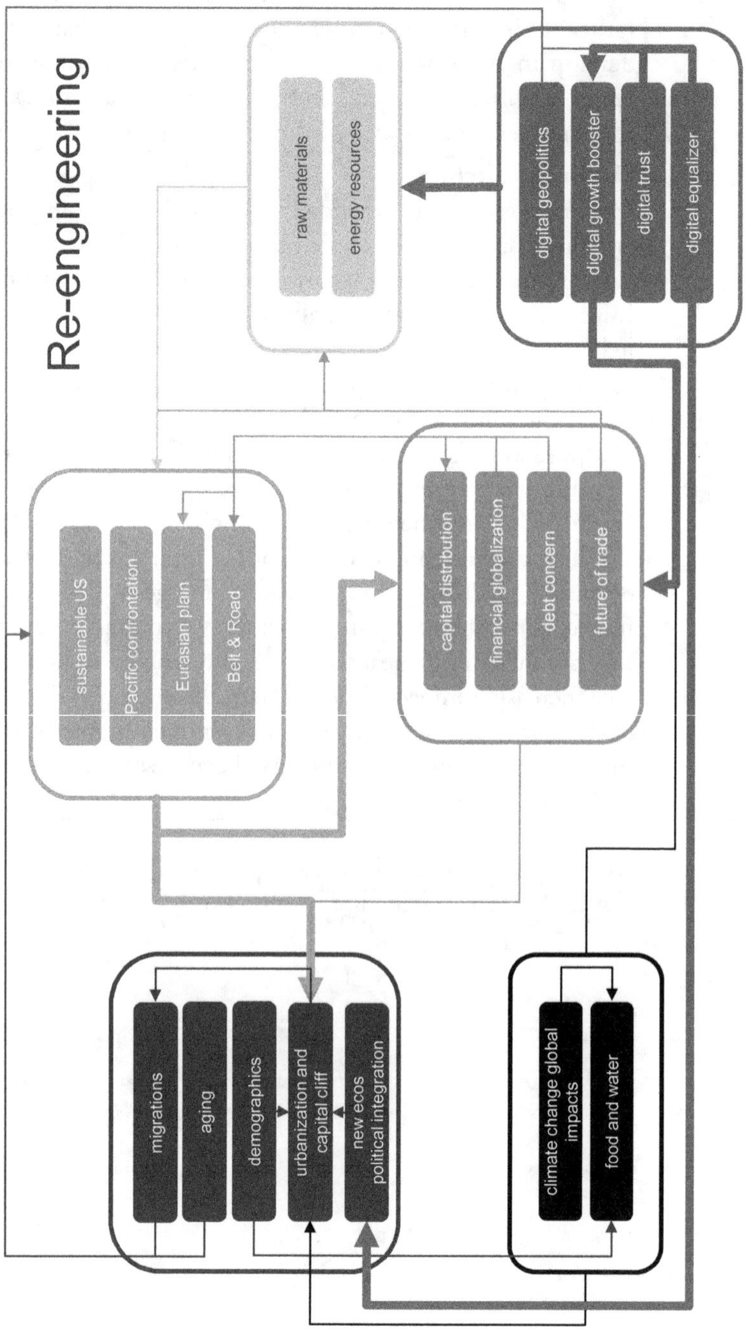

Figure 7.3 Re-engineering scenario system map

Scenario 3 — Doomsday

This scenario sees a significant acceleration of climate change impacts that materialize everywhere, though at different levels. Several new economies around the Tropic of Cancer (Central America, Northern Africa, the Middle East, Central Asia, North of India, and a number of Eastern Asian countries) are concerned by its effects. There, food and water scarcity aggravate dramatically, along with extreme weather events, leading to large humanitarian crises. In other regions, climate change also impacts economies by reshuffling entire industries, notably because of water drought and repeated extreme weather events. Climate change also leads to aggravated health issues and a rising number of diseases that spread around the world into pandemics. This acceleration leads to a global economic crisis, which the world faces with great difficulty. Capital outflows in new economies throw them into brutal recessions, while population keeps increasing and concentrating in cities. This triggers social unrest, local conflicts, and massive migration. Global supply chains are increasingly disrupted as many countries focus their resources and attention on their internal problems. Global trade declines and a large economic crisis unfolds. A significant financial crisis follows suit, leading to massive asset destruction and impoverishment of the people. This is a balkanized world, where every country is trying to face its own challenges.

Demographics, social	**Closing societies** Population increases by up to 10 billion people by 2050, notably in India and Africa. Aging of the world population also becomes more significant, pressing on social systems around the world. At the same time, global health issues become more pressing, aggravated by climate change. The global economic crisis and significant impacts of climate adaptation materialize in most regions of the world leading to massive social unrest, which governments tackle through coercive measures. Most economies, particularly new economies, see little to no opening, as security becomes paramount. Massive migrations from the most concerned new economies toward Europe and the United States also lead to significant destabilization and important repressive measures from mature economies, lowering the level of open information and overall democratic process. Social division tends to increase, particularly as prices soar everywhere as a result of the economic crisis. On the other hand, massive financial assets destruction from the crisis tends to tame the global divide overall.

Geopolitics	**World balkanization** The main driver of change in this scenario is climate change and its rapid materialization in many economies of the world. This leads to political instability in many new economies, fostering significant migrations toward mature economies. The United States manages to contain those brutally. Europe, on the other hand, fails to do so, and its economic and social contexts are significantly destabilized. As a result, Europe is weakened. In addition, climate change triggers a global economic crisis as many industries and countries around the world are affected by it. This leads to a brutal economic deleveraging, particularly in large indebted countries such as Europe, China, and Japan. This causes a large slowdown of consumption, thus growth. The world enters a deep economic recession. Massive asset destruction from the financial crisis that follows leads to significant impoverishment of many around the world, particularly in mature economies. China does not manage to rise as a global competitor and, while Europe descends into populism, the United States is the only country to remain afloat, preserving a "status quo," despite a significant economic crisis there as well. Most new economies are hit by the crisis and their progression stalls. The world of doomsday is balkanized and violent as most countries turn their focus inward and increase military powers to reap the resources and products they depend on from other economies. This is a world of local conflicts and reduced cooperation. Global institutions fade away.
Resources	**Global scarcity** In this world, scarcity of resources becomes the norm. The world's balkanization leads to disruptions on global supply chains and soaring prices on resources. Competition to access key resources from global reserve locations becomes paramount, leading to significant abuse of power, including the use of military force. Most dependent countries focus on reuse and lifetime extension, while enforcing stringent efficiency measures to limit their dependencies. There is limited innovation to mitigate these dependencies further because of lack of available capital.

Climate	**Global catastrophe** Climate change materializes beyond expectations. It happens primarily in many countries around the Tropic of Cancer (Central America, Northern Africa, the Middle East, Central Asia, North of India, and a number of Eastern Asian countries). There, water scarcity was already apparent in 2019, with rising issues on food availability with many of these countries highly dependent on food imports. As climate change materializes, extreme heatwaves, floods, and other natural disasters (tropical storms, tsunamis, etc.) kick in and aggravate the situation further. These regions become prey to regular catastrophes and, as a result, capital investments tend to outflow, leading the situation to become even worse for local populations. Governments are destabilized, and many conflicts emerge locally, creating further humanitarian crises. Consequently, migration rises sharply. Large industrial activities in mature economies are also deeply impacted by the frequency of extreme weather events, and experience growing water scarcity and heatwaves. The problem is indeed global, and wealthy mature economies are similarly destabilized. In addition, climate change also materializes through an increase in the number of diseases that spread across the globe, turning into recurrent pandemics that fuel a permanent economic crisis.
Global economy	**Global economic and financial crisis** Climate change triggers a massive economic crisis worldwide. Many new economies, traditional relays of growth, are hit hard by the first materializations of climate change. In addition, migration toward Europe and the United States leads to an economic slowdown. Mature economies are not unscathed by climate change and those with large industrial footprints are impacted. Overall, the economy slows down rapidly and the world enters a sustained recession period. This triggers a financial crisis fueled by rapid asset destruction. A brutal deleveraging then forces largely indebted economies (the United States, Europe, China,

	Japan) to adopt forceful measures of austerity, accelerating unemployment and recession. Some countries of Europe even default their debt. Capital flows are reduced and sometimes constrained, accelerating the decoupling of countries' economies and further projecting nations into economic crisis. Overall, this economic and financial crisis leads to significant impoverishment of the population, both in mature economies (asset destruction, unemployment, soaring prices) and in new economies (capital outflows).
Digital and innovation	**Balkanized internet** Overall, the economic crisis yields a further inward focus, leading to increased trade tensions, regulations, overall defiance in global exchanges, and less capital available globally. This, in turn, leads remaining available capital to move away from innovation, which consequently remains very limited in this crisis period. The rise of the digital economy is partly stalled, although it keeps developing at a slow pace in the United States and China.

United States	**Resilient economy** The United States, despite the global economic crisis, manages to maintain its dominant position in the economy. Large capital inflows increase as a consequence of the crisis, refueling the economy at a time of capital scarcity in most regions of the world. Despite the financial crisis and high-level exposure of the United States, its large market enables it to maintain a reasonable level of activity. Impoverishment and unemployment are on the rise, but social unrest is brutally contained. Security and stability are paramount. Some states in the United States are impacted by climate change, yet much less than many new economies. The country therefore dedicates significant budget on adapting to this situation. Massive migrations from the South also threaten the social stability in the country, but the government takes coercive measures to put an end to it. Additionally, its situation of energy independence and relative wealth of

	material resources helps the country to work through the crisis without too many significant material disruptions. On the international scene, despite some level of confrontation with China, notably in South-Eastern Asia, the United States remains the dominant military and political force as China fails to present a viable and competitive alternative. As such, the country keeps thriving, relative to others, and even regains a bit of its power over most new economies. Its posture as the ruling force of the world is strengthened.
China	**Further autocracy** Climate change impacts several regions of China, triggering migration toward less-impacted cities and subsequent social unrest, particularly for minorities. The country is also hardly hit by the global economic crisis, because of its high exposure to exports and its significant debt level. Growth slows down, triggering further protests and social instability in the country. The government manages to contain it brutally. As a consequence of this crisis, the rise of living standards is halted, meaning Chinese living standards do not eventually catch up to those of the United States. Its economic power remains significant, however, and the debt issue (notably that of state-owned enterprises) under control. Yet, this comes at the cost of significant asset (and wealth) destruction. As the situation in many new economies continues to deteriorate, China is taking steps toward developing its Belt and Road Initiative to gain further influence and secure its access to resources. Yet, the initiative is not a success as many of these countries remain mistrustful with the rising ascent of China, often preferring to keep their options open. This is with the exception of countries from the former Soviet Union, including Russia, with whom China is building extended partnerships.
Europe	**European disintegration** Europe is impacted by climate change, notably in the southern countries of the region, leading to significant

	transformations of the industrial footprint there, and fostering a further divide between those nations and those of the north. Massive migrations from the Middle East and Africa further destabilize these countries. From all of this Europe's population gradually loses faith in its institutions, leading populism to prevail. This is followed by a series of "exits" from the Union, with many large countries' defaulting on their debts, and the eventual collapse of the Union. This crisis means the end of Europe, significant impoverishment of its people, alongside increased violence. Russia consequently turns toward China, and the latter is increasing its domination over Eastern regions of Russia, notably with a significant migration in workers, which Russia has difficulties mitigating.
Other mature economies	**People impoverishment** Other mature economies from Asia are also hit by the economic crisis resulting from this dramatic climate evolution. The strong limitation on trade and the end of the reliance on global supply chains (particularly for materials and energy) yields recession in economies heavily exposed to international exports. Consequently, unemployment is on the rise and the imbalance in state budgets continues to rise, accelerated by population aging. Since the debt of governments is mostly owned locally, there is, however, no default over the period. Population impoverishment is a key pattern. Australia is again a specific case, with significant resources and the ability to keep supplying many countries from the west, particularly the United States. Its economy is therefore less impacted than others.

New economies	**Autarky and migrations** Most new economies (outside China) are hit by both the economic crisis and climate change. On the one hand, the economic crisis triggers massive capital outflows subsequently destabilizing most of these new economies, which have limited autonomous financial capabilities due to the rather low level of financial deepening. This accelerates the local crisis, with unemployment on the rise, in a context of increased population and demand. Inequalities are on the rise, and local authorities have huge difficulties to cope with rural migrations toward cities. This fosters social unrest that often leads to local conflicts. On the other hand, the effects of climate change materialize in several countries around the Tropic of Cancer. For those, the situation is aggravated, with water and food scarcity reaching unprecedented levels. In those countries, a large share of the population leaves the country. Migration jumps up, notably toward the United States and Europe. Climate change also aggravates the economic situation of these countries, as they are increasingly seen as speculative investments with high levels of risks, accelerating capital outflows even further. Overall, these economies return to a relative situation of autarky, and their living standards collapse.

The system map helps summarize how these aspects of the scenario interconnect. The key relationships that define the doomsday scenario are highlighted in Figure 7.4.

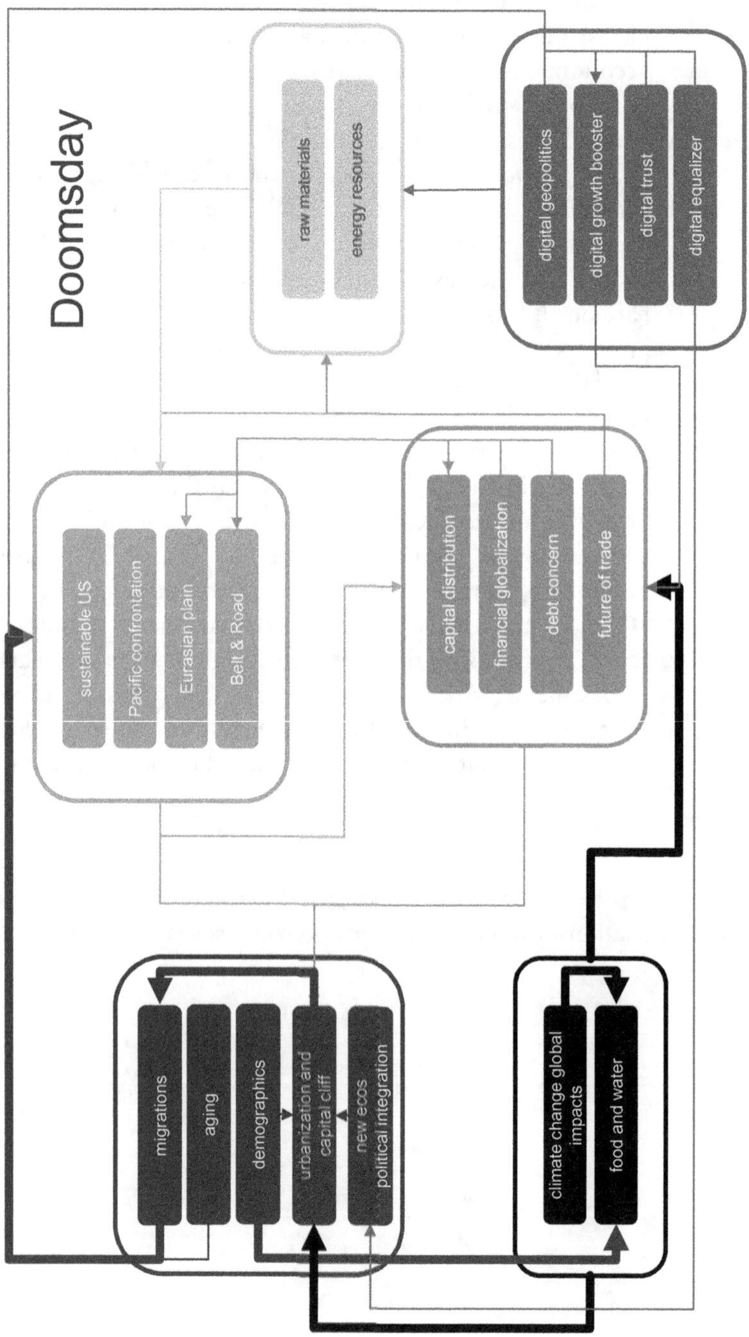

Figure 7.4 Doomsday scenario system map

Scenario 4 — Rapid Adaptation

The rapid adaptation scenario sees the emergence of global multilateral institutions with a unique capability to reach and enforce global multilateral agreements and legislation. As climate change materializes and significantly impacts most regions of the world, a new global agenda on climate change shapes up, developed and pushed by these renewed institutions, which now supersede national affairs. Significant capital reallocation is organized to support new economies that are in great need to adapt, while a focus on reducing the global divide around regions also takes center stage. The economic model progressively evolves to increasingly focus on efficiency and circularity as key measures of performance, where the impact on the planet takes precedence over any other considerations. Competition concedes to collaboration. The new "spaceship" economy (Boulding, 1966) is a fundamental shift from the principles that have prevailed over the last centuries. The world is wiser and starts becoming organized to survive in one of the greatest adaptation challenges in history.

Demographics, social	**World citizenship** The social environment is completely open as globalization accelerates, in light of critical climate change evolutions, in both mature and new economies. The world is less about competition and more about collaboration to tackle critical global issues. The new generation increasingly feels part of a larger community of people, a "species," and is resolutely committed to tackling climate change, environmental protection, and global poverty. Social inequalities tend to reduce over time.
Geopolitics	**Constrained multilateralism** This scenario sees the emergence of a solid and powerful multilateral framework. As climate change massively impacts all countries (some more than others), these renewed institutions become the cornerstone of a coordinated and common response, with significant capabilities to enforce agreements. The new world order is fully multilateral and, to a certain extent, global governance takes precedence over national affairs in light of the changes and challenges at stake. This is a world where cooperation is forced by external events.

Resources	**New circular economy** Rapid adaptation to change becomes the utmost priority. The critical impact from resource extraction and distribution needs to be tackled, particularly as population keeps expanding alongside consumption. Multilateral agreements are reached to quickly adapt to this new paradigm, fostering accelerated development on energy and materials efficiency, pollution mitigation, materials innovation and, more importantly, a new global approach to circularity. Global capital dramatically shifts from traditional polluting activities and fuels innovation in adjacent sectors. A large share of the industry gets partially stranded and renationalized.
Climate	**Fast, constrained adaptation** Climate change impacts all economies of the world. In new economies, impacts are particularly brutal, as they hit populations with limited ability to adapt, yielding large humanitarian crises. In mature economies, which are less impacted at first, entire industries are delocalized and transformed as heatwaves, extreme weather events and water scarcity grow in importance, fueling massive economic disorder. Multilateral institutions take significant steps to impose a new agenda for both mitigation and adaptation of various communities to this new environment, which largely supersedes national agendas. Resources (physical and financial) are combined to adapt in the most optimized way to what has become the world's agenda.
Global economy	**New economic model** Global economy is significantly impacted by climate change. Many assets around the world are destroyed by extreme weather impacts. Entire economies and industries are transformed by the rise of new climate patterns. Agriculture is particularly impacted and other industries are strongly affected by growing water scarcity. The global economic disorder rising from this fast pace transformation accelerates decision-making at the multilateral level, reinforcing global institutions. As a consequence, these institutions end up playing a critical role in helping reach global agreements, building joint funds for adaptation,

	and funneling capital effectively to these critical global issues. The world is increasingly governed by these institutions that supersede national affairs and have the authority to enforce decisions taken globally. The world evolves toward a "spaceship economy" (Boulding, 1966). A new economic model emerges where the impact on the planet takes precedence over traditional capitalistic measures and where efficiency and circularity become the new indicators of performance.
Digital and innovation	**Digital for climate** In this world of rapid adaptation, innovation is focused on solving critical issues like circularity, materials, and energy, in order to mitigate climate change, and adaptation solutions that emerge in agriculture, water, and so on. Innovation becomes problem-led and is funded by significant amounts of capital. The transition to a new economic model with an entirely new approach to consumption makes significant strides in the run up to 2050. Digital technologies are a powerful enabler and massive investments are dedicated to this field.

United States	**Green and inclusive** Some of the regions from the United States are severely impacted by climate change. Southern states are prey to rising temperatures that significantly impact the local economy, particularly agriculture. Eastern regions from the country are also more frequently affected by extreme weather events, while winters in the North become harsher. However, the impacts are comparatively lower than those of several new economies, particularly Mexico and the North of Latin America, affected by water drought. The country joins the global agenda on climate change and contributes actively to support new economies in despair both financially and with its projection capabilities. The United States also embraces a more circular economy and a fast pace transition to low-carbon energy, despite nearly obtaining energy independence from its vast reserves of fossil fuels. The next generation in the United States, connected and more globalized, embraces those changes and pushes the agenda forward at the federal and state levels. The economy of the United States continues to prosper despite climate change affecting economic growth significantly.

China	**Lighthouse of climate change** China dominates the "green" technology industry as the primary effects of climate change materialize. Consequently, the country is in a unique position to benefit from the rapid transition to a more sustainable economy. Additionally, China has long deployed new low-carbon technologies and it has been the laboratory of this transition. The country therefore becomes the new lighthouse of the world and thrives with rising international ascent and increased soft power. Economic growth continues and living standards reach those of mature economies. China is the new dominant force in a multilateral world actively transitioning to a more planet-friendly economic model. Yet, the development of stringent circularity measures tends to reduce its exports and unbalance its accounts, slowing down local growth. Some inequalities remain, particularly in the regions most impacted by climate change or water scarcity. Water pollution becomes a critical issue in China, which the government tackles with the appropriate sense of urgency. Social unrest emerges in some of these regions but both local and central authorities manage to contain it and maintain stability.
Europe	**Climate change activist** The region is taking active actions to reduce its environmental footprint. As new multilateral institutions have emerged, Europe has taken a leading role in developing coercive regulations. It also supports new economies most impacted with significant budgets and projection capabilities, thereby limiting the rise of migrations. Europe also acts as a role model and develops significant plans to achieve a net zero-carbon footprint shortly after 2050, before China. Its economy still relies heavily on key dependencies from China (energy technologies) and other countries such as Russia, Latin America, or the United States (materials), therefore it leads the change toward more circular models and advanced planet-compatible materials, actively investing in the field. Thanks to strengthened political integration, the region has also been able to efficiently reform its social and work structures to reduce unemployment and rebuild ground for economic growth. It has also developed

	a unique approach to social inclusiveness, regulating the first developments of the digital economy early on. As the next generation globally advocates for more of this, most countries progressively mimic its model.
Other mature economies	**Painful adaptation** Mature economies are impacted in various ways and they need to develop specific adaptations to their own issues. Significant resources need to be deployed to cope with these impacts. In addition, global trade tends to diminish with the increasing recourse to efficiency and circularity, hampering the economic potential of economies traditionally dependent on exports. Aging populations are also an issue and conservatism tends to dominate, limiting the necessary changes to be done to social and work structures. All of this leads to further stagnation and relative impoverishment of these populations. Their global influence on the international scene remains limited.
New economies	**Solidarity catchup** Some new economies (around the Tropic of Cancer) are among the primary ones impacted by climate change. Fortunately, new multilateral institutions emerge with an increased ability to reach global agreements and enforce them. This prompts rapid capital dispatch to mitigate humanitarian crises and enables them to adapt to these inevitable transformations. Other economies are also impacted, though to a lesser extent. These regions are well supported in their development as part of a broader plan to cope with climate evolutions. Most new economies are in a situation to grow economically, enabling living standards to equalize, despite remaining significantly lower than mature economies. The equalization of living standards and the reduction of the global divide now prevail over the fierce competition in the new model of a "spaceship" economy.

The system map helps summarize how these aspects of the scenario interconnect. The key relationships that define the rapid adaptation scenario are highlighted in Figure 7.5.

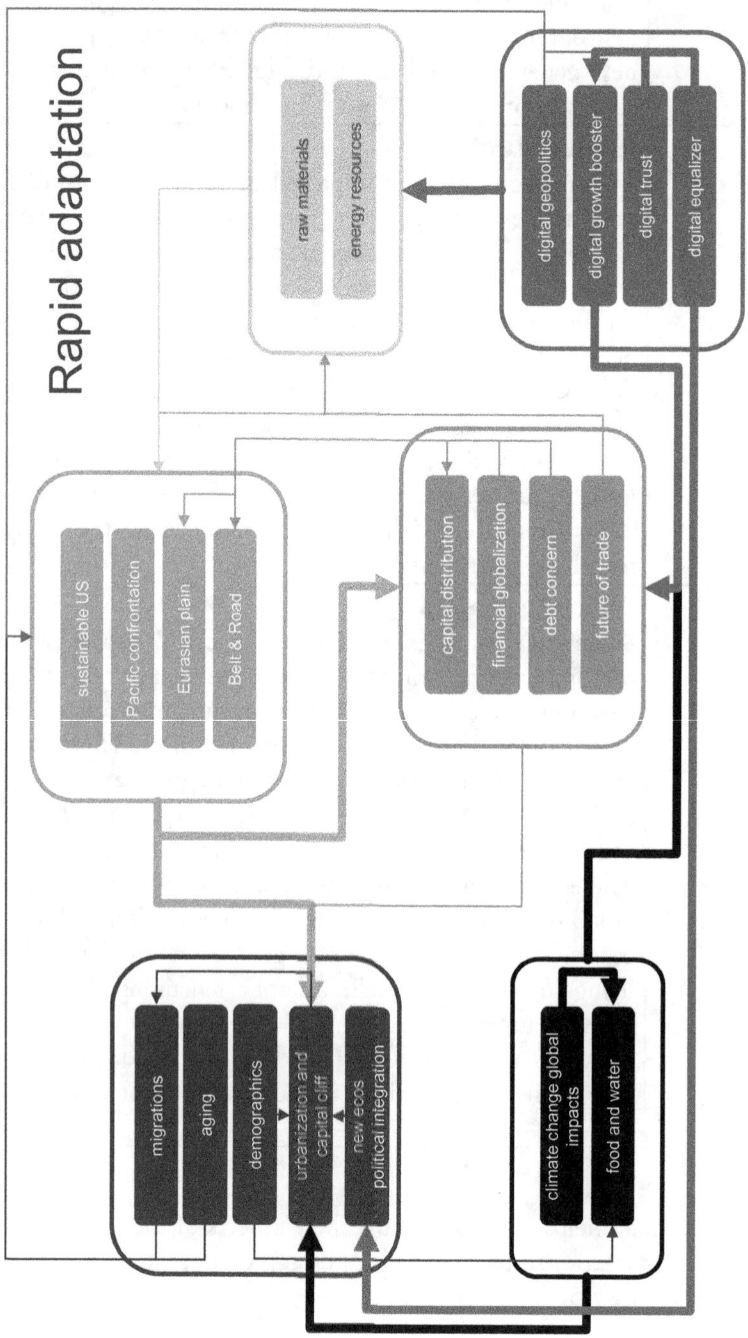

Figure 7.5 Rapid adaptation scenario system map

Scenarios Summary

These four scenario storylines are summarized in Figure 7.6. It provides an overview of the key differences between them. Each scenario represents a different combination of factors, meaning different futures are likely to unfold. They are mutually exclusive, with the objective being to assess critical uncertainties that could shape the world in one direction or another. We can, however, identify two critical patterns. On the one hand, the extent of cooperation across nations plays a critical role in defining the Future of the Global Order. Multilateral institutions could play a defining role, providing they are revitalized, pushing the future world order toward either the re-engineering or rapid adaptation world. On the other hand, large uncertainty remains around the true impact of climate change (and its associated effects, e.g., health) in the coming decades. An acceleration could yield significant transformations to relations across regions. What is important to understand is that this could also be true of other global issues like, for instance, the unfolding of a global financial crisis. Most published scenarios have detailed forecasts that traditionally assumed positive growth prospects, with only a few projecting what could happen in the event of a large, possibly permanent, crisis. What issues will arise and to what extent they will unfold is therefore a key question. Yet a more important question will be how nations around the world will respond to it: will they team up to solve these pressing issues, or not?

Finally, despite these modeled scenarios, everything could also be different because of factors or combinations not anticipated. Only time will tell.

An Unexpected Outcome: A Key Role for Europe in the Twenty-First Century?

The purpose of this book was to unveil key rationales that drive the agenda of nations and how they would be likely to evolve in the coming decades. As we are closing this book, what are the key messages to take away? What have we learned? What are the challenges that the world will face that could critically modify global order as we know it?

The first challenge is the significant gap in living standards between different populations on the planet. The world gets smaller every day, as economic and social exchanges have reached an all-time high and will continue to grow in the future. Information also travels at light speed across continents, bridging cultural gaps. An estimated 2.7 billion people will reach cities by 2050 to enter this globalized environment, with rural migrations forming a significant part of this large number of people, who will be looking to raise their living standards to those of more developed economies. This urban migration is likely to be the

A New Global Order	Scenario 1 — Multipolar	Scenario 2 — Re-engineering	Scenario 3 — Doomsday	Scenario 4 — Rapid Adaptation
Demographics, social	**Limited opening in a competitive world** Limited opening, social divide	**New living model for next generation** Politically active, socially participative, globally informed	**Closing societies** Significant social unrest, coercive measures from governments	**World citizenship** Open social ecosystem, collaboration to supersede competition
Geopolitics	**Global competition in a multipolar world** Two global leaders confrontation: United States and China	**Renewed multilateralism** Emergence of Europe, China and Europe alliance for renewed multilateral institutions, United States global leadership retreat	**World balkanization** Inward focus, conflicts over resources	**Constrained multilateralism** Renewed multilateral institutions to precede national affairs in a race to tackle climate change
Resources	**Competition and new frontiers exploration** Race for resources, and towards new frontiers	**Global supply chains security, efficiency and materials innovation** Open world of exchanges, efforts on efficiency and materials innovation, slow development of circularity	**Global scarcity** Disruption on global supply chains, focus on lifetime extension and localization	**New circular economy** Circularity the new critical industry and global priority
Climate	**Climate change in some new economies** Climate change in several new economies, migrations contained by mature economies	**Progressive adaptation** Climate change in several new economies, adaptation efforts supported by global institutions	**Global catastrophe** Massive impact: extreme weather events, industrial transformations, humanitarian crises, food and water scarcity	**Fast, constrained adaptation** Rapid adaptation through combination of physical and financial resources
Global economy	**Regional divide** Slow reduction of global trade, new economies development, Belt & Road Initative success, regional divide	**Open economy** Global trade and capital flows, new economies catch up	**Global economic and financial crisis** Economic recession, financial crisis, assets' destruction and people impoverishment	**New economic model** Spaceship economy, centered around efficiency and circularity
Digital and innovation	**Digital competitive space** Digital for leadership, increased social divide	**Digital collaborative ecosystems** Consumer-led innovation	**Balkanized internet** Digital economy stalled, limited innovation	**Digital for climate** Innovation entirely directed towards climate change
United States	**Leader of the "free" world** Flourishing economy, anchor of the "free" world	**Resources giant** Inward focus, global resources' exporter, flourishing economy	**Resilient economy** Social unrest and migrations contained, large resources independence, large capital inflows	**Green and inclusive** Active contributor to climate change, move away from reliance on large resources reserves
China	**New "harmony" leader** Flourishing economy, alternative model to the United States	**Industrial giant** Living standards catch up, societal opening, industrial and technological giant	**Further autocracy** Economic recession, social unrest, halted living standards improvements	**Lighthouse of climate change** Low-carbon technology leader, catching up living standards, strong international ascent
Europe	**Great stagnation** Europe as a "free" trade zone, limited economic and social developments	**Multilateral champion** Strengthened economy, strengthened ties with Russia, beautiful deleveraging, leader of economic and digital inclusiveness	**European disintegration** Regional divide with climate change, debt defaults, migrations, rise of populism, series of "exits"	**Climate change activist** Strengthened political role, circularity and innovation champion, socially inclusive
Mature economies	**Great stagnation** Aging economies, suffering from the rise of Chinese leadership Australia benefits from race for resources	**Great stagnation** Aging societies, prey to conservatism	**People impoverishment** Rising unemployment and austerity measures, debt burden and people impoverishment	**Painful adaptation** Adapting despite aging societies, prey to conservatism
New economies	**Disparate development** Various economic developments, political instability and climate change in some new economies	**Historical catch up** Political stability, successful urban migration, rising living standards	**Autarky and migrations** Economic recession, stalled development, political instability and social unrest	**Solidarity catch up** Supported by global institutions to adapt to climate change and reduce inequalities, catching up on other economies

Figure 7.6 Scenarios summary table

largest in history and subject to many challenges. Among them, a critical capital cliff in infrastructures — at 2.5 times current investment levels — in a context where capital is already unable to sustain current needs. Political integration and stability will be a fundamental enabler but, then again, there is high uncertainty on whether new economies, in light of their recent history and of the challenges they face, will be able to succeed. Such imbalances will continue to be accentuated. The population is aging and the share of people above 60 years old is expected to double, reaching 21.3 percent of the worldwide population by 2050, concentrated in mature economies and China. Will the elderly from mature economies retain the wealth of the world, thanks to the location of their birth, while many young populations from new economies live in hardship? Will the populations of new economies eventually close this living gap, or will we see massive inequality and migrations that will further impede world stability?

The second challenge lies with unresolved security issues globally. While the position of the United States appears on paper unchallengeable, the rise of China as a major economic, political, and military power of the twenty-first century threatens this balance. At the same time, the fate of Europe remains uncertain, as well as its relations with Russia, a giant with European cultural heritage. Finally, peripheral powers will join this new "Great Game," but they also face significant integration and security challenges and at the same time often represent the "prize" of competing interests.

A third challenge is the exhaustion of the planet's resources as the world population steers toward 10 billion people by 2050, four times what it was a century before. Many material reserves on which the current economy is built are already depleted, and scarcity could surge in the coming decades if alternative solutions are not found through new reserves or alternative materials. Several of these materials only have a couple of decades left of production at the current pace of extraction, in a context where production rises, and demand is expected to increase significantly (at 55 percent over 20 years).

Similarly, human activities continue to modify climate and its effects could be significant if nothing is changed in our way of consuming resources and energy, in particular. If carbon emissions are not halved within the next couple of decades (on a course to be fully zeroed), climate experts predict massive transformations of the Earth's cycle, with critical impacts to mankind. Maybe it is too late already. As a matter of fact, these uncertainties around the consequences of climate change (namely to which extent it will materialize, where and when) have led so far toward a sort of collective apathy, when it is not outright denial. One thing is certain though, and that is its inevitability. A new system of living will need to be invented based on the principles of a "spaceship economy" (Boulding, 1966). Nearly 10 billion people share one planet and that planet is too small for the world not to realize that it must save its resources to avoid dramatic depletions and climate transformations. Easier said than done! This is more than a transition, but a profound transformation on how the world has functioned in the last millennia — a complete change of paradigm is required. A circular use of materials and energy resources seems the only path toward minimizing the impact of world population living standards and make subsistence sustainable. Will this transition happen? Or will the world enter a dangerous period of scarcity, confrontation, or, possibly, self-destruction? How much time do we have left?

Another challenge is to create the conditions of a long-lasting stable and inclusive economy, which could enable global development across regions. The current system is critically imbalanced. Following a long period of low-cost access to capital, debt levels have soared (representing more than US$185 trillion in 2015). These spectacular levels are only maintained by cheap capital; if these conditions were to change, the system could collapse. A "beautiful" deleveraging is possible, but nothing indicates that it is happening at the time of writing. A major crisis could grow to prevent other challenges being met, while leading to global impoverishment and instability. At the very same time, capital has increased significantly in the last decades (US$297 trillion in 2015), yet it remains concentrated in the hands of a few (8 percent of the world population holds 85 percent of the wealth). In recent decades, mature economies have captured 56 percent of the wealth creation in the world, with the United States alone holding 34 percent. Again, will the world continue to perpetuate this trend or not? Is a significant crisis the only way to rebalance wealth across populations, as it played out in the twentieth century, after two world wars? Beyond inclusion, the allocation of capital will prove critical in the future decades. While new economies have pressing needs, the distribution of capital to these economies remains limited today, accelerating them into difficult financial situations. The key reason is that there has been little to no effort to "securitize" such investments in a context where safe returns remain the preference. This demonstrates a clear limit of the current financial system as it currently operates. Will this evolve with time?

The rise of the digital economy is the last challenge of the global economic landscape in the coming decades. While its proponents emphasize that its development will be able to provide the productivity levels required for a developing world globally, many point out its woes, and mistrust is on the rise. In theory, the digital economy could help accelerate access to higher living standards, global and transparent information (including education and opportunities) and enable the necessary technology developments (circularity notably) to adapt to the changing resources and climate. Yet, trust will be the key issue and it is uncertain whether it will be overcome. The future of work and social inequalities that could emerge is first in question, with projections ranging between one and two billion job losses and a rising social divide between those able to adapt and those unable to. Will there be a generation sacrificed in the switch to digital, with regions significantly impoverished? The ethical development of these technologies is also a concern, and ripple effects on democracies (and the spread of fake news), social contracts (privacy and liberty), or human development (addiction) could tear it down. Finally, security remains an issue, as the digital landscape has become a new space of confrontation between nations and for organized crime, which is not yet heavily regulated.

The extent to which the issues and challenges described in this book will unfold is uncertain, yet they will all develop over the course of coming decades. They are true paradigm changes and the world needs to prepare for them. The key question, then, is how humanity will respond to these. The evolution of the geopolitical landscape will prove essential in that regards. Will the world achieve the dream of a multilateral and collaborative mankind, which works together at enhancing its collective future? Or will it remain a space of confrontation and competition? The ability of countries around the world to cooperate on such matters will determine what future scenario will unfold, as Vladimir Putin says, "a new philosophy of international relations is needed" (2017). In essence, the world needs to set the foundations for a "Re-engineering" of the global order, while preparing for possible "Rapid adaptation." At the time of writing, multilateral institutions are weakened, and this situation has been exacerbated by the current United States administration. Two giants now confront each other: the United States, which has dominated for the last seven decades, and China. It seems that the world is entrenched into a "Multipolar" scenario and very little can be done to change this.

But is there really nothing that can be done? Should the world rely on a good conjunction of opportunities, or luck, for a better course to be drafted?

One thing is for sure, there cannot be multilateralism if the world is dominated by two giant powerhouses, only confrontation. Recent history has been particularly clear on that. Despite the creation of the United Nations, the domination of two superpowers (the United States and the Soviet Union) in the second half of the twentieth century has shown that collaboration is virtually impossible. The paradigm today has remained the same, particularly if we consider the current and growing confrontation between the United States and China. This is aggravated by the fact that China has vigorously criticized existing multilateral institutions as serving the interests of the United States (which is partially true as seen in Stiglitz, 2002), as well as criticizing the current nationalist stance of its rival. A concurrent approach to world affairs is emerging, with

China rallying (or attempting to rally) new economies, while the soft power of the United States is on a declining course. Again, confrontation appears to be inevitable.

How can the world reach the endgame of true collaboration across such a variety of interests? If there cannot be multilateralism with two powerhouses dominating world affairs, then the balance of power needs to evolve toward a different number of actors. Since the overwhelming domination of the United States is losing prominence in the world of today, the complete domination of one country or region is impossible. This means then that a third powerhouse needs to emerge and balance out international relations, but which one?

The only practical candidate in the coming decades is Europe, through a revitalized European Union project. A true multilateral approach to the concert of nations will never emerge if a third powerhouse does not appear on the international scene. Only the European Union has the capacity to achieve such a feat and has strong legitimacy to do so. First, it is, by design, a multilateral project, which initially aimed at ensuring peace and economic development on the continent after the wars of the twentieth century. In that regard, the project has been an overwhelming success, which creates legitimate ground for the European Union to voice its concerns and opinions on global issues. Additionally, the European Union is the largest commercial partner of the world, overtaking the United States and China. Again, by design, the continent deals with every nation of the world and depends on many as many depend on it, making it a powerful stabilization force, though this is not often acknowledged. Finally, some of the countries in Europe, notably France and Germany, have a powerful voice in the concert of nations, notably France through its permanent seat in the security council of the United Nations and its military force. Yet, politically, none of the countries in Europe can rival China or the United States. They are middle-size powers and need to collaborate to level up with these powerhouses.

What Europe really lacks is the perception of it as an integrated political force, with the world order lacking its power to push a global agenda and balance out vested interests in search of collective benefit. Yet, Europe is a political dwarf, and it has decided to remain one. But why? First, the European Union was developed in the context of the Cold War. Then, Germany was only reunited 30 years ago. For decades, the security of the European Union has been ensured by the United States. Many countries in the continent, starting with Germany and followed by all the countries of Eastern Europe, have relied on intimate relations with the United States to guarantee their security. How can a continent emerge as a political force while delegating its own security? Then, despite a common cultural heritage, the European Union has also lacked democratic legitimacy (despite a European parliament). Previous attempts to build a constitution for Europe have failed, and the European ambition has often stumbled over local politics. Each country from the Union has maintained vested interests but often placed more importance on its own interests over the collective good. Finally, and maybe as a consequence, the European Union project has remained inward looking, turning into a regional collaboration platform across middle-size nations, instead of building and promoting a common ambition for the world.

The situation today is however changed. Global issues have arisen, and the scenarios outlined above show that a bright future for the continent is only possible provided it emerges as a political force. A global project, outward looking and ambitious, is now vital need for the continent. In short, the good of Europe now depends on its political integration, and that political integration would be a positive balancing force in renewed international relations. What would such an ambition look like?

This ambition could build on most of the global pressing challenges described above. As the first commercial partner of the Middle East and Africa, a stronger Europe would facilitate a peaceful transition in these regions and their economic development. The Middle East and Africa will be at the heart of all opportunities (and possibly challenges) to 2050 and beyond. The emergence of a strong European Union would also, quite paradoxically, smooth tensions with Russia, because of the lesser dependence on NATO and the US foreign policy, possibly helping to bring Russia back into the European fold, which it culturally belongs to. Such an alliance, because of Russia's wealth in several resources, could significantly transform the global context of international relations and dependencies, providing a new global platform for the commercialization of the country's vast reserves, resulting in a unique event in history and a tectonic shift in geostrategic relations.

Additionally, a stronger European Union could effectively embrace the Belt and Road Initiative and help develop it at an accelerated pace, actualizing this mutual interest between China, Russia, and the European Union, and a source of economic growth, and peace, for all of Central Asia and the Middle East. Its political weight and commercial footprint could also enable a more coercive (and political) plan on climate change mitigation. From an economic standpoint, the commercial and financial weight of a renewed European Union would certainly help stabilize future global economic and financial exchanges, while fostering the necessary reforms of the World Trade Organization and other global financial institutions. A true industrial plan for the European Union, particularly in digital technologies, would certainly enable a conciliation of the current confrontation between China and the United States, while developing a more inclusive approach to the future economic system.

It appears that such a development could serve as a base for renewed multilateral institutions, more focused on the pressing global needs identified earlier in this book. Further integration is therefore compulsory. But is it possible to achieve such ambition with 27 member states? My personal belief is that any significant progress can only be triggered if the two powerhouses of the continent, France and Germany, unite their views and political power, through a more profound integration. This European "engine" would then have the legitimacy to surpass discontent and disagreements within the Union itself, and accelerate reform. The political context has so far prevented two leaders to emerge and build, in good faith, this enthusiastic agenda.

As improbable as it may seem at first sight, the future of the world order could largely rely on the European Union project, particularly the capability of its two powerhouses to accelerate reform. The United Kingdom could — and should — have played a role in this project. Yet, the country has been the first victim of the rise of populism in a "Multipolar" world. This outcome might, however, represent a chance for the European Union project, if France and Germany are capable of taking the lessons of this collective failure.

One could deny that such an agenda is possible to be met in the coming decades, and that the idea of a peaceful multilateral world or the emergence of Europe as a strong political force will remain a long-term dream. Yet, there is also reason for hope.

The global community, under the leadership of the United Nations, has begun to coalesce around key global issues to actively work at taking steps in the right direction. The United Nations has proven that, when problems beyond the reach of individual nations arise, they are able to regroup and build collective intelligence. Also, most political leaders in key European countries have kept advocating for a stronger organization to emerge. Despite setbacks, the European Union has been a formidable success thus far, inspired by various leaders in the 1950s and 1960s, in a much more complex political context. The only issue is that all this progress is not happening fast enough, as the world order remains a prisoner of its history, entrenched in quarrels from the past. One final hope to leave with is that these necessary transformations occur before the negative realities catch up with us.

References

Boulding, K. (1966). *The Economics of the Coming Spaceship Earth.* Retrieved at University of Barcelona. Available from: http://www.ub.edu/prometheus21/articulos/obsprometheus/BOULDING.pdf [Accessed: June 2019].

Dalio/Economics. (2018). *Economic Principles. How the Economic Machine Works?* Available from: https://www.economicprinciples.org/

Putin, V. (2017). *In the Putin Interviews,* Oliver Stone. Available from: https://www.imdb.com/title/tt6840134/

Ramirez, R. and Wilkinson, A. (2016). *Strategic Reframing. The Oxford Scenario Planning Approach.* Oxford: Oxford University Press. Available from: https://www.amazon.com/Strategic-Reframing-Scenario-Planning-Approach/dp/0198745699

Stiglitz, J. (2002). *Globalization and Its Discontents.* Available from: https://www.amazon.com/Globalization-Its-Discontents-Norton-Paperback/dp/0393324397

Index